" A gripping, unforgettable family odyssey through the terror of war and its aftermath. Definitely a page turner . . . A different view of both the victors and the vanquished. One woman's spellbinding adventure in keeping her family intact."
- Douglas Muir
author of TIDES OF WAR

"A vivid account of a German musician's Odyssey from war-ravaged Danzig in early 1945 towards a new life in the Americas. Reads like romantic fiction, yet has the genuine ring of historical truth."
- Dr. Henry Meyer
History Dept., U.C. Irvine

"*Eva's War* is a powerfully impressive tale of women and war . . . and Eva Krutein's gifted eye repeatedly engages the reader with the kind of surprising detail that chills the reader with its realistic vividness. This book is compelling and very human, an engrossing saga of the **sorrows of survival.**"
- Patricia Geary
author of "Living in Ether"

"*Eva's War* gives us not only a spellbinding account of the horrors and hardships of war, but also a portrait of a brave and compassionate lady who balances with ease and grace the three careers of wife, mother, and professional musician. Her courage and dedication are an inspiration to us all."
- Dr. Malcolm Hamilton
Professor of Music, U.S.C.

"A marvelously moving and often humorous real-life story. . . sad revelations, painful memories, excruciating experiences are tempered by compassion, love and a powerful, contagious optimism. Music permeates this tale."
- Alfred-Maurice de Zayas, J.D., Ph.D.
Senior Legal Officer, The United Nations
Geneva, Switzerland

"This is a gripping memoir of a courageous woman's escape from Danzig on the Polish corridor at the end of World War II. ... an absorbing story of a heroic young couple's shocking and growing awareness of the evil of totalitarianism, including the murderous death camps and war machines running amok. It's also a testament to the virtues of peace."

— Judah Landes, Ph.D., Clinical Psychologist,
Director, SHORELINE INSTITUTE, Mountain View, CA

EVA'S WAR

A True Story of Survival

Eva Krutein

Printed in the United States of America
First Printing, 1990
ISBN: 0-938513-08-7(paperback)
ISBN: 0-938513-09-5(hardcover)
Library of Congress Catalog #89-81193

AMADOR PUBLISHERS
P.O. Box 12335
Albuquerque, NM 87195

To my children:

Lilo
Ursula
Renate
Wernher
Irmgard

Publisher's Preface
Adela Amador

"This book is a war cry against the glorification of wars," Eva tells us. Book publishers, as well as toy makers and history writers, bear some responsibility for that poisonous glorification. Amador Publishers proudly offers to the world this important antidote.

Our planet has enjoyed the deceitful tranquility of more than four decades of "Mutual Assured Destruction," accompanied by total war budgets, disinformation and secrecy. Lies and secrecy are war thinking and war behavior. It is important to note that Hitler did not keep his secrets from the Allies – he kept them from the German people. And here, our secret satellite launches and our security-clearance-only laboratory facilities are not designed to keep "our nation's enemies" in the dark. The secrets and the lies are for the sovereign people. We drive by our local cannonball factories and one says to the other, "I don't know what they're doing in there. I only know it's kept secret from me, and I'm almost certain that I wish they WEREN'T doing it!"

We have not had peace in these recent decades. The stream of refugees from wars all over the world seems endless – from Vietnam, Guatemala, Mozambique, El Salvador, Palestine, Ethiopia, Afghanistan, Sudan – the list goes on. Uprooted and disowned, the ordeals of all these people remain largely unknown to the world. Most of them are women and children, whose ballad has hardly ever been sung. EVA'S WAR sings that song, telling how one woman and her family survived.

We met Eva and Manfred through an international organization dedicated to world peace and understanding. SERVAS (esperanto for "service") enables international travelers to be housed in private homes, where persons become acquainted face to face.

We humans are ONE, one threatened species, to be sure, but ONE, and only enriched by the differences in language and culture and experience, as long as that underlying oneness is held firmly. We gladly offer this book to the world, inviting all our fellow humans to discover and enjoy that solidarity, and to nurture it.

vii

Foreword

by Alfred-Maurice de Zayas, J.D., Ph.D.

Danzig, birthplace of the philosopher Arthur Schopenhauer, is known to most of us as Gdansk, birthplace of Solidarnosc. This famous Hanseatic city, proud Baltic port at the mouth of the River Vistula, is also the birthplace of the author of this marvelously moving and often humorous real-life story. It is thus appropriate that she should begin and end her tale in this historic town over which the monumental tragedy of the Second World War broke out.

Sad revelations, painful memories, excruciating experiences are tempered by compassion, love and a powerful, contagious optimism. Music permeates this tale of stubborn resistance against injustice and despair.

There are many good reasons for reading this memoir. Firstly, even if it is not fiction as such, it reads like it. Real-life characters captivate the imagination and make us identify with the action. Here is the subject matter of a great movie like *Gone with the Wind:* a hell of a woman caught in the maelstrom of war and defeat, confronted with destruction, hunger, loss of her parents and friends, separation from her husband. An indomitable love of life and of her family makes her prevail.

Another reason for reading this book is the novelty of the subject matter. American readers, even those seriously interested in history, know little or nothing about the flight and expulsion of 14 million Germans from their homelands in the former German provinces of East Prussia, Pomerania, Silesia, from Danzig, from the Czechoslovak Sudetenland, from Hungary, Romania and Yugoslavia. Over two million German civilians did not survive this brutal displacement, victims as they were, of politics and of politicians.

Professional historians who do know about the expulsion of the Germans have largely brushed it off as retribution for the Holocaust. Yet, we all know that two wrongs do not make a right. The East Prussian farmer or Silesian industrial worker and their families were men and women like we are; they themselves suffered greatly under the Hitler tyranny, lost their friends and relatives in that mad war. And then, when the Third Reich collapsed and the Wehrmacht surrendered unconditionally, they were subjected to a most cruel collective sanction, evicted from their homes, despoiled of all their property, physically abused and forcibly deported to what was left of Germany in the West. The 700-year-old German provinces East of the new "provisional" frontiers at the Oder and Neisse Rivers, with cities as famous as Breslau, Stettin and Königsberg, were occupied by Russians and Poles; the German Sudetenland with cities as German as Eger and Karlsbad, were swept clean of the native population to make room for Czech settlers. The Danube Swabians and other ethnic Germans who had done so much to cultivate the land and develop the areas now known as Yugoslavia and Romania were either expelled, placed in concentration camps, deported to slave labour, or even liquidated.

These were undoubtedly crimes against humanity which have gone not only unpunished but also unpublicized. Needless to say, neither the author nor I would presume to compare crimes or want to establish a balance sheet of injustices committed by or against Germans. The issue here, of course, is one of morality, because innocent persons were taken as scapegoats, just because they were Jews or because they were Germans.

The late American Ambassador Robert Murphy, the political advisor of Generals Eisenhower and Clay, was a participant at the Potsdam Conference (17 July to 2 August 1945) where the decision on the "orderly and humane transfer" of the Eastern Germans was adopted (article 13 of the Potsdam Protocol). He focused on the moral question in a telegram to the State Department dated 12 October 1945:

"Knowledge that they are the victims of a harsh political decision carried out with the utmost ruthlessness and disregard for the humanities does not cushion the effect. The mind reverts to other mass deportations which horrified the world and brought upon the Nazis the odium which they so deserved. Those mass deportations engineered by the Nazis provided part of the moral basis on which we waged war and which gave strength to our cause.
"Now the situation is reversed. We find ourselves in the invidious position of being partners in this German enterprise and as partners inevitably sharing the responsibility. The United States does not control directly the Eastern Zone of Germany through which these helpless and bereft people march after eviction from their homes. The direct responsibility lies with the Provisional Polish Government and to a lesser extent with the Czech Government ... As helpless as the United States may be to arrest a cruel and inhuman process which is continuing, it would seem that our Government could and should make its attitude as expressed at Potsdam unmistakably clear. It

*would be most unfortunate were the record to indicate that
we are participants in methods we have often condemned in
other countries."*

Unfortunately, very little was done by the Anglo-American Allies to arrest the disaster, and the record does show that our insensitivity about mass expulsions and our abandonment of the principles of the Atlantic Charter made this post-war catastrophe possible.

Forty-five years after the Second World War is not too early to reassess certain aspects of it. The Allied decision to amputate over one fourth of Germany's pre-war territory (let us remember that Germany had a territory smaller than the State of Texas and that what is left is smaller than California, and that is taking both the Federal Republic of Germany and the German Democratic Republic into account), and the decision to expel its population, deserve such reassessment.

What did it mean in human terms to spoliate and expel fourteen million human beings? This book is important because it helps us to visualize the statistic. We can perceive existentially this statistic by imagining the half-starved mother and child, the raped woman, the broken old man with vacant eyes and bundles holding his last belongings -- not just once, but millions of times over. It is this picture of human misery, the sum total of individual tragedies that should have been considered by the Allies in Yalta and Potsdam when the decisions were taken. Indeed, if the Allies fought against the Nazi enemy because of his inhuman methods, could they then adopt some of those same methods in retribution? Who was it then, who succeeded in imposing his methods on the other? Whose outlook triumphed? These are disturbing questions. And they should be answered.

And how were the Germans expelled? The late Victor Gollancz, a noted British publisher and author, a Jewish philanthropist and recognized moral authority in his time, put it plainly:

*"If the consciences of men ever again become sensitive, these
expulsions will be remembered to the undying shame of all
who committed or connived at them ... The Germans were
expelled, not just with an absence of over-nice consideration,
but with the very maximum of brutality (Golancz, OUR
THREATENED VALUES, 1946, p. 96).*

The German expellees, their children and grandchildren realize the impossibility of returning to Königsberg, Breslau or Danzig in order to settle and live there. They also realize that the new generations of Poles growing up in East Prussia and Silesia, the new generations of

Czechs who now populate the Sudetenland, also have a right to their new homelands. No one would ever propose a reverse expulsion of Poles and Czechs out of the German territories which the governments of Poland and Czechoslovakia annexed at the end of the war. On the other hand, it would be unreasonable to expect the German expellees simply to forget and write off what happened to them. They remember and they will continue to remember. There is hardly an expellee who did not lose a mother or a sister in the course of the expulsion. In this sense, although the expellees have established new homes in the West -- and many, including the author, emigrated to the United States, became American citizens and now have their children and grandchildren here -- they would appreciate a measure of recognition for their not insignificant sacrifice. The more idealistic among them also hope that their experience may serve as an example, so that other peoples may be spared the tragedy of being uprooted from the homeland. But, in order for the experience of the German expellees to serve as a case study and warning against future population expulsions, the facts will have to become more generally known. There is a need for more scholarly studies of the subject matter. But there is also a need for accounts like these that show real people -- not stereotypes -- with real feelings, in good times and bad. Eva's story was worth writing. It is also worth reading a second time. Perhaps it should be made into a mini-series for television, because her personal story is representative for the experiences of millions of German refugees and expellees. Indeed, there are thousands upon thousands of such reports in the Federal Archives of the Federal Republic of Germany at Koblenz. Moreover, there is much to be learned from the example of victims who knew how to make the best of things, how not to give up, how to begin again and continue this great adventure, the challenge of life.

The subject matter of this book is of general importance and throws its shadow far beyond the German experience, since mass exoduses are a phenomenon of the twentieth century. If we are committed to human rights in the world, we shall cease asking about the nationality of the victims, about the colour of the refugees. We shall hear their story, and we shall try to understand them, for all victims of injustice deserve our compassion and respect.

Dr. Alfred de Zayas
Senior legal officer with the United Nations in
Geneva, author of *Nemesis at Potsdam: The
Expulsion of the Germans from the East*

Prologue

The historic port of Danzig, now called Gdansk, is located on the southern shore of the Baltic Sea, where the Vistula discharges its waters in a fan-shaped delta into the halfmoon of the Bay of Gdansk. A crescent of sandy dunes and dense forests stretch toward the water, as if claiming their share of the Baltic. Cream-colored sea shells and translucent amber in varied shapes dot the white beaches. Blackbirds and nightingales fill the cool, fragrant pine forests with their songs.

In the late Middle Ages, the German merchants of Danzig converted their wealth into splendid architecture. They built houses with ornate entrance terraces and gilded gables and cathedrals of immense proportions, which towered over the residences like guardians of treasuries. Danzig became known as the Venice of the North. Meticulously preserved, the Old Town filled spectators with awe and inspired artists to create countless paintings, etchings, novels and poems about Danzig's glory.

During the thousand years of its checkerboard history, Danzig was a bridge between Slavism and Germanism. Among its famous sons are the astronomer Hevelius, the physicist Fahrenheit, the philosopher Schopenhauer and now the Polish hero Lech Walesa, who won the Nobel Peace Prize in 1983. The city alternately paid tribute to Polish and German rulers.

Gyddanyzc	In 997 St. Adalbert of Prague baptized the slavic inhabitants and set out from there to convert the pagan Prussians.
Danzig	1308. The Teutonic Knights seized the city and built their castle in it.
Gdansk and Danzig	1454. The city returned to Poland, but received local autonomy from the King. During the sixteenth and seventeenth centuries the city rose to world importance as a member and principal port of the Hanseatic League.
Danzig	1793. Returned to Germany.
Free City of Danzig	1807. Napoleon conquered Danzig and declared it a Free City.
Danzig	1814. Returned to Germany.
Free City of Danzig	1920. Autonomous under the sovereignty of the League of Nations.
Danzig	1939. Hitler annexed the city to Germany, simultaneously attacking Poland, starting World War II.
Gdansk	1945. Returned to Poland.

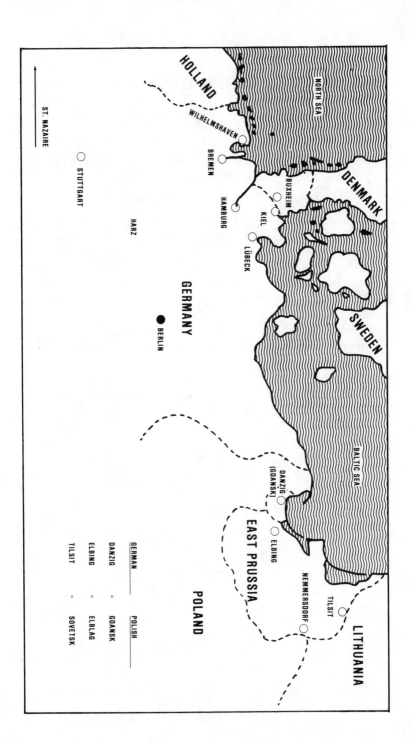

Glossary

Abend	evening
auf Wiedersehen	good-bye
danke	thank you
gut, guten	good
halt	halt
ja, jawoll	yes
kaputt	broken
Leberwurst	liver sausage
Licht	light
Maestro	master
Meister	master
Morgen	morning
Mark	German currency
pan (Polish)	Sir, Mr.
Pfennig	Penny
Quatsch	baloney
Reichsmark	former German currency
Scherkohl	cabbage
Schnaps	German liquor
Tag	day
verdammt	damned
Zloty	Polish currency

STORM CLOUDS OVER DANZIG

Danzig, January 1945

As heavy gray clouds gathered over the medieval towers and cathedrals of Danzig I relentlessly paced the length of my living room, my thoughts and emotions in a whirl: should I stay or flee? Face the Russian hordes or go into the unknown with my child, leaving everything behind? Just turned twenty, and facing the possibility of death, I had to answer the question: where was the greater chance of survival for myself, my 14-month-old daughter Lili and my parents?

My eyes focused on the white grand piano. Music had always calmed me. Stepping to the keyboard I began playing a somber Bach fugue, hoping Bach's orderly music would help me make the decision that would shape the rest of my life. Suddenly, my fingers faltered on the keys. I got up and closed the lid of the piano. What should I do?

Irritated, I went into the entrance hall and in the long mirror saw my tense face -- pleasant, not beautiful, and today sorrowful. Staring into my eyes with their disorderly mixture of green and brown, I remembered my husband's voice teasing me, "Your eyes always show your inner chaos."

I'd laughed at Manfred. "Do you mean I'm all mixed up?"

"No, but you have so many incompatible interests," he said, pulling me to him, kissing me. "I think that's why I love you so much, Little Bear." He stroked my mop of brown hair.

How much I missed him! He was so far away now, like most of the men, far away from their wives and scattered all over Europe. How handsome he had looked in his Navy uniform the day he'd left, a lieutenant in the German Navy! How long it had been! Now, the days of dancing and laughing were over. I hadn't seen him for a year. If I fled -- how would he find me?

Suddenly, the telephone rang in the entrance hall. I quickly picked it up. "Hello?"

"This is Helmut Kalmbach," the faint voice said. Although I knew Helmut was calling from the Navy barracks only ten kilometers from my house, the connection was so bad I had to press the earpiece hard against my ear to understand him.

Helmut was Manfred's long-time friend from college and the Navy -- I felt as close to him as if he were my brother. I wondered if he had news about his wife, Irene, and their baby in the country outside Danzig.

His message came in fragments. "Last night, Irene called from the country -- she and the baby left -- for the West -- today I got a permit for a mother and child on the oceanliner DEUTSCHLAND -- you can use it -- Eva, you must leave Danzig immediately!"

"But where is the DEUTSCHLAND?" I yelled back.

The phone crackled.

".... on the ship DEUTSCHLAND ...."

Oh my God, he couldn't hear me. "The DEUTSCHLAND.... where is it?"

".... the Russians have ...."

"What?"

Only the crackling noise and then silence.

Confused and alarmed, I wondered what Helmut had tried to say about the Russians. Had the SS tapped the phone? Or the Gestapo? Each of those damned Party organizations usually tried to outdo the other.

The doorbell rang. On the front step was a very tall army lieutenant in a crumpled field-gray uniform, his black hair disheveled, his unsmiling mouth lost in a ragged black beard. As he pushed his dark-rimmed glasses up higher, I realized he was my girlfriend, Erika's, husband, Dr. Fritz Moldenhauer. I threw open the door. "Fritz! Where did you come from? Come in!"

In spite of his rumpled condition he stepped in with his customary dignity. "I come straight from the Russian front and have orders to go to Berlin." He put down his small suitcase. "I understand there's a train to Berlin tonight. May I wash up and spend the afternoon here?"

"What a question! Stay as long as you can. We haven't seen each other for a year." And we hadn't argued for a year either. Quarreling had become part of our friendship. I showed him the bathroom -- complete with sunken tub, bidet and sun lamp -- and went to the kitchen for coffee and cake.

After his bath Fritz looked poised and lofty again.

"That's how I remember you," I kidded.

"I hardly remember myself." The bitterness in his voice was most certainly due to his hardships at the Eastern front.

I led him into my living room, a world of playful daintiness with Louis XIV style furniture, richly ornate Dresden figures and paintings of royal chamber musicians in powdered wigs, playing ancient instruments. Although Fritz had seen my rococo room quite often, he stood there, startled. "This is unreal -- after coming out of hell -- I'd forgotten civilization --" His face had lost its arrogant mask and I suspected he was still haunted by the cruelties of the fierce war in the East. He had seen first hand the burnings, famine, and dismembered bodies that I had seen only on the newsreels.

"Sit down," I urged my friend. "Have some good fresh coffee and Bienenstich." These were slices of "bee sting," a sweet, Eastern German, honey-golden cake. I saw him breathe in the aroma of coffee and pastry. He eagerly took a slice of the cake. "You live here like in peacetime," he said between bites. "Where does all this food come from?"

"Poland, Hungary, Rumania. Whatever country the German troops have conquered." In a flash, I saw the defeated people of other countries working and providing food for the Germans, for me and my family.

Calmly Fritz reached for another piece of Bienenstich. "Have you heard from Manfred?" he asked.

Ten times a day people asked me the same thing. "He-- he's in St. Nazaire, on the French Atlantic coast. They're encircled by the Americans. I haven't had a letter for six months. He directs the repair of submarines."

Fritz nodded, chewing his cake with obvious delight. Eager to hear about his wife, my chum for years, I asked, "Tell me, how's Erika? How's the baby?"

He adjusted his glasses, which he always did when he had an uneasy thought. "They are still in the country. I'm afraid it's about as safe there as a shoal before high tide."

I quickly got up to pour him more coffee. "Do you think the Russians will get any closer?"

He adjusted his glasses, then looked at me directly. "Yes."

"And if they come in, do you think it will be ... bad?"

His lips curved in a bitter smile. "Do *you* think there'll be any sanity left when drunken Mongols overrun the city? Remember Nemmersdorf!"

The name of the village, 250 kilometers east of Danzig, had shocked the nation four months ago when the German forces recaptured Nemmersdorf from the Russians. Every woman and girl had been raped. Then, the entire population of seventy-four had been murdered. The nation's outcry had whipped up the German soldiers' last energies as they tried to beat back the Red Army and prevent a repetition of Nemmersdorf.

"Can't the German troops stop the Russians?" I asked.

"Our battered troops against those hordes? The army is beaten, Eva. Tired, exhausted and without weapons."

"But we hear only victory news from the East."

Fritz hit the table with his fist. "You're blind as a mole! Don't believe that crap! You'd better get out of Danzig while you can!" He pushed back his hair. "And that is why I really came here. To tell you just that."

"You're an incorrigible pessimist," I said.

"And you are an optimist to the point of feeblemindedness," he retorted.

He is a pessimist, I thought. Should I believe his warning? "No matter what the Russians have done in Nemmersdorf," I said, "that was months ago and far away. It won't happen here in Danzig, it won't!"

His voice was almost inaudible, "I know Danzig has had no air raids during all these years. And you people believe your wonderful city will be spared."

"Danzig is a treasure of art and beauty," I insisted. "It couldn't possibly be destroyed."

Fritz slammed his cup down on the table. "The Russians don't give a damn about Danzig's beauty. And bombs have already fallen on the most precious art monuments -- as you know. In Dresden. In Cologne. In Berlin. Don't be a fool, Eva."

"So, fleeing is the only solution?"

He looked at me, annoyed. "What are you waiting for? Believe me, if you're caught by the Russians, you'll find out how the people in Nemmersdorf felt."

"Thank you," I said after a while. "Thank you for warning me."

After Fritz left to catch his evening train to Berlin, I walked back and forth in my rococo sanctuary. Suddenly, I stopped. The angry cries of women and children, so loud they penetrated the double thickness of the storm windows, came up from the street two floors below.

St.Katharine's Gothic brick cathedral, magnificent and powerful, stood tranquilly in the drifting snow -- a symbol of steadfastness and eternity. But below, at the cathedral's feet, were hundreds of women in heavy winter clothes and woolen turbans, with their children trying to squeeze into an already overcrowded brick school building. Oh God, refugees. Fleeing from the Russians. I ran to the entrance hall, pulled my coat on and hurried down the stairs.

Turning up my coat collar against the whistling wind, I rushed to the crowd which pushed and shoved in despair. I focused on a young woman and her crying baby, then approached them. "Would you like to stay in my apartment? I have space for you."

In surprise, the woman turned her pale face to me and nodded. She touched the arm of the man next to her. He had only one arm, his empty sleeve stuck in his coat pocket. They both looked to be my own age. I led them upstairs and into my bedroom.

"Oh," the refugee woman said, "how warm and bright!"

Danish-modern birch furniture, white airy lace curtains, two single beds (the usual sleeping arrangement for a couple) and a crib -- heaven for people who had fled through Europe in the snow.

I brought fresh diapers. As the woman unwrapped her baby boy I was shocked to see the dried and caked feces in the old diaper, the baby's raw, inflamed bottom. "My God, when did you last change him?" I asked.

"Three days ago."

"Oh my God. Where have you come from?"

The husband, sitting on the bed, still in his overcoat, answered in a low voice. "We got the last train from Elbing. There were thousands of people, pushing and beating each other to get on the train. Sitting on top of the cars and hanging between them." He stopped, then continued. "In the crowd I lost my grip on the suitcase. It contained all the baby things. We were lucky just to hold on to the baby."

Frantically, I pushed my fright back, converting my anxiety to activity. I prepared a bath for the baby, brought powder and ointment for his sores, served hot chicken soup and ham sandwiches and then left my guests alone. They'd probably soon fall into their beds.

Hesitantly, I walked to my living room. Was this what was waiting for me? Or would our soldiers bring the Russians to a standstill? As so often in a crisis, I turned to Dorothea, my parents' housekeeper and my close friend. I left my own apartment and walked, as though following my umbilical cord, the few steps down the hall to my parents' flat where I went for my meals every day.

Short and slim, her blond hair braided and pinned up into a bun, the housekeeper stood at the kitchen stove, stirring soup. "Dinner won't be ready for a while, Frau Eva."

I told her about the refugees and my agitated conversation with Fritz.

She looked up from her cooking. "Frau Eva, you should leave. The Russians are only 150 kilometers from here."

"How do you know?"

"I heard it on the radio," she replied, staring into her cooking pot. I was thoroughly alarmed. Had Dorothea been listening to the enemy station? A dangerous venture, high treason.

"When did you hear it?"

She put down the ladle. "If you don't leave soon it might be too late." She raised her eyes to mine. "Remember Nemmersdorf."

"Will you come with me?"

She shook her head. "I have no child. I'll never get permission to leave."

"How can I leave? I have no permit. And what about my parents?"

She shrugged. "They are too old to get a permit. You know, only women with children count."

I heard the door open, heard my parents come into the apartment.

BREAKING AWAY

My parents sat down at the dinner table. Surprisingly, they never looked tired after a full day's work in their factory for electric appliances.

At 62, my father was bald. His full-moon face radiated satisfaction from the work he cherished. I loved him dearly. "Where's Lili?" he asked. His first thoughts always concerned his granddaughter.

"At Aunt Margret's," I replied. "She'll be back any minute."

He reached for the plate of open-face sandwiches, the usual evening food. The scent of egg and onions lingered over the table.

"Ah, the tea is good after a long day," my mother said with a sigh. She was the chief designer and director of the factory's lamp-shade department. At 61, she was slightly overweight, but her wrinkle-free face, framed by natural black hair, denied her age. Her huge chocolate-brown eyes registered everything within 180 degrees at once. She was said to hear the grass grow. I'd always felt rebellious in her presence.

At this moment, Dorothea led Lili in. "*Guten Abend,*" the housekeeper said for Lili. "I'm back from Aunt Margret."

The child looked like a baby doll with a huge red bow in her silver-blond hair. Still unsteady on her little legs, she fell down on her hands and knees and began to crawl towards me. I sat her on my lap and kissed her.

"Let's go hear the news," my mother said. "It's five to seven."

Taking his granddaughter from me, my father carried her into their living room. We sat down on leather-covered armchairs. He switched on the radio. Marching music blared forth as a prelude to the eternally victorious news. The *Meissen* clock struck seven with a sonorous C-sharp tone as the radio's musical interlude ended.

"This is the Greater German Radio Network with the evening news. On the Western front, our divisions repelled a heavy attack of Anglo-American troops and pushed the enemy back. They had heavy losses."

"But *our* losses were zero," my mother quickly interjected.

"On the Eastern front, Communist troops attacked our positions in continuous waves and suffered heavy losses. German troops moved toward new fortified positions farther to the West."

"Meaning our troops are fleeing." Mother grimaced at me. To her, as to most Germans, Nazism and war were an act of God, like earthquakes. They couldn't be stopped.

"The Führer, in a speech last night, expressed his confidence in the German armed forces. The long-awaited new weapons will soon be implemented. He assured the population of our imminent final victory."

As the announcer droned away, I listened with only half an ear.

"In the Pacific, American bombers attacked Iwo Jima, an island south of Japan. The Americans suffered extremely high losses of men and material."

"Mass killing all over the earth," my mother said. "What will happen to us all?"

"Panic monger," my father said lightly, not even looking up from his granddaughter, who sat on his lap and had taken hold of his nose.

"But the Russians are only 200 kilometers away," she said, anxiety chilling her voice.

"They'll stop them there," father's voice boomed. He, too, believed Danzig was sacrosanct.

"Who'll stop them?" my mother asked angrily. "We're reduced to drafting children to do our fighting. I can already see Danzig destroyed."

This was the moment to announce my decision. "I must leave, father! I'll take Lili and go to the West!"

My father took Lili's hand from his nose and looked at me with a fearful expression. "You want to take my Lili from me?"

"But, father," I managed to ask, "what of Nemmersdorf?"

My father, still seated, Lili on his knees, obviously was in control again. "The West isn't necessarily safer. There are the bomb attacks."

"But the British and the Americans are humane. They aren't beasts like the Russians."

"You don't have a permit for leaving town, do you?" He sat like a rock.

"Why don't you help me?" I blurted out in despair. "You've helped so many Jews and Poles, why not me now?"

The rock didn't move. "As long as there's no official permission for a mass evacuation you'll just risk your life and Lili's."

"Please, listen," my mother said, getting up from the sofa. "I've heard that the district commanders give official permission to leave at the last moment. The moment may come soon ...."

"How about you and father? Would you come with me?"

Slowly my mother shook her head. "We're too old." She smiled, sadly. "And we have to stay here to protect our property."

Silence.

"I think I'll take Lili to bed," I said, removing her from my father's lap. Holding Lili tightly in my arms, I walked the few steps over to my apartment. The bedroom was dark and quiet, the refugees all asleep. Since the fugitives' baby occupied Lili's crib, I tucked her into the large streamlined wicker baby carriage, kissed her good night and wheeled her next to the grand piano. The couch would be my bed, so I lay down and switched off the small table light.

As always before I fell asleep Manfred's image rushed in from the Atlantic like a fresh breeze. I heard his stormy steps, his artistic whistling, his laughter. I saw his handsome face smiling at me, his blue eyes radiating confidence and lightheartedness. I heard his tender voice, "My Little Bear." Longingly, I sighed. He'd been away too long. Married for two years, we had only lived together for two months. Now he was with his other love -- his ships. Ships, my eternal rivals.

Suddenly I heard a sound. I strained my ears. Again, a very faint knock. I tried the light switch. Nothing. The electricity was off for the night to conserve energy. Nervously, I got up in the dark and went to the apartment door. "Who's there?" I asked softly, not wanting to waken the refugees.

"It's me, Fritz."

Why wasn't he on the train to Berlin? I opened the door. An icy wind entered from the landing, making me shiver in my nightgown. "My God, what happened? Come in, quick! It's freezing."

He stumbled forward into the dark entrance hall and I closed the door behind him. "There was no train," he said gloomily. "The Russians have encircled the town and pushed on to the Baltic. All roads to the West are blocked."

"Oh no."

"May I sleep here for the night? Tomorrow I'll try to find a ship in the harbor."

"Of course." I found a candle and matches. Danzig was encircled! Why had I hesitated so long? Now it was too late.

"There's a refugee family in my bedroom," I said. "I'm sleeping on the couch in the living room. You'll have to sleep on the floor." I pulled a child's mattress from the closet. It was a foot shorter than he was. I managed a smile. "It's a little short, I'm sorry."

He didn't smile. "Anything will do." Wordlessly he carried the mattress into the living room, squeezed it between the piano and baby carriage, took off his uniform cap and belt and lay down.

I held the candle high over his fully clothed body. "You need a blanket. I have one in the closet."

"Come on! Keep your blanket. I have my uniform on, that's enough."

I didn't argue with him. I simply took the blanket from the closet and put it over the lieutenant, who complained in vain. Blowing out the candle I placed it on a chair now serving as my night stand and crawled back onto my couch. "What did it look like? The railway station, I mean," I asked into the darkness.

"Awful." His voice sounded horrified. "Stranded refugees. Lying on the platform half frozen. Babies crying with hunger. No trains anymore. See to it you get out of here first thing in the morning."

"How?"

"By ship," came the answer from the dark. "It's the only way open. Don't wait one more day!"

The *Deutschland*! Helmut Kalmbach had offered me a place on it and then the phone connection had been cut.

And as if the word "ship" contained magic, it touched in me a fountain of energy, bubbling over with frantic thoughts. I suddenly saw it before me: get on a ship and sail away into the

Baltic! With wide open eyes, I listened to Fritz's snoring. He must have learned at the front to sleep under any circumstances. And I was awake because the fever of adventure had kindled this fire in me.

Suddenly I heard a noise at the door again, someone putting a key into the lock. I sat up on the couch, staring into the dark.

The intruder opened the door and came in with a flashlight. I froze.

"Frau Eva?" Dorothea's voice asked. Of course, Dorothea had a key to my apartment. "What's the matter?" I asked.

Dorothea came forward, holding the flashlight out in front of her. As the light fell on Fritz she asked in surprise, "Who's that?"

"Fritz. There are no more trains. He asked to spend the night."

"Hmph." She added with bitterness, "Who knows who we'll have to sleep with in the future." Nemmersdorf and the rapes. But it didn't frighten me anymore. My decision had been made. My thoughts were on the future.

Dorothea switched off the flashlight and sat down on my couch. "Listen, I came to tell you the Russians are fighting only fifty kilometers outside of Danzig. The German resistance is breaking down."

I was amazed to find myself no longer terrified. Wondering about her knowledge I asked: "How did you find out in the middle of the night? There's no electricity, no radio."

"I have a small battery radio."

In the darkness my eyes widened. Battery radios weren't available even in my father's factory! Dorothea must have connections I'd better close my eyes to. What one didn't know couldn't harm one -- the slogan of the time.

"I came to warn you," Dorothea whispered. "You must leave. At dawn take Lili to the harbor and get on this ship." She switched on the flashlight and lit up a slip of paper. It read:

PERMIT FOR BOARDING THE SHIP PREUSSEN

ONE MOTHER AND ONE CHILD

DANZIG, JANUARY 30, 1945.

Eyes and mouth wide open, I realized I had been given a helping hand on my new way to the future. And I promised myself never to ask about the origin of my permit.

"I don't know how to thank you," I whispered to my friend.

"Put enough diapers and clothes for Lili into her buggy and leave early in the morning," she commanded. "Now go back to sleep."

As she left I was overwhelmed by my feelings of gratitude and the excitement of going into the unknown. But much more so, I felt I had at last cut my umbilical cord. I'll run! I'll run to the West. Manfred, I'll find you! Somewhere in the West we'll find each other again.

My struggle for survival had begun.

EXODUS

Dawn rose over Danzig as my father and I hurried through the icy morning, ignoring the exquisite beauty of the medieval fortresses and Gothic cathedrals. In a black Persian-lamb coat and stylish fur hat, legs in high boots and hands in wool-lined kid gloves, I pushed the baby carriage over the cobblestones. Deeply buried under the eiderdown quilt, Lili slept undisturbed; the burning cold couldn't reach her.

We had to force our way through hundreds of people who were pushing baby buggies, their precious belongings in suitcases and rucksacks.

"I hope Lili sleeps until you're on the ship," my father shouted over the east wind that howled through the narrow streets. He carried the one suitcase I had allowed myself.

I pressed my lips together and nodded. Move on! was the thought that propelled me through the streets down to the inner harbor. Move on, the Russians are coming! They're only fifty kilometers away from Danzig. Forget what you left behind, your home, your music, your mother, and soon your father. Oh God, would we make it to the ship?

From side streets, more and more bundled-up women with children and a few older men hastened in the same direction. They all wore high boots, long winter coats and thick-knit mittens. Most had slung woolen shawls over their heads. Many children, dragged along by frantic mothers, were crying.

"Mommy, I want to go home!" a child screamed.

"Hurry! We have to catch the ship!" the mother shouted back. She carried two suitcases and could not hold the small boy's hand.

"Put one on my buggy," I called to her. Relieved, she placed one on Lili's carriage and grabbed her unhappy boy's hand.

The wind whipped my face as my father shouted at me: "Do you have your permit handy?" For a moment, our eyes met, his face reddened, his eyes watering. I nodded, pulling the paper from my coat pocket.

PERMIT FOR BOARDING THE SHIP PREUSSEN
ONE MOTHER AND ONE CHILD.

"It's here," I yelled back. Carefully I slid the permit back into my coat pocket.

Suddenly, I heard a muffled sound like a pianissimo beat on a kettle drum. Then another and another in irregular rhythm and from far away. Artillery fire!

Many women panicked. "They're shooting!" Pandemonium broke out. Everyone pushed forward, crashing into each other's load of bags and children. A woman stepped on my foot, another one bumped into me from behind, pushing the other woman's suitcase from the buggy and me against it. I clutched the handle tighter as the pressure increased from all sides.

"Stay closer to me!" my father shouted. But I had little choice in the terrified crowd. Propelled by fear, the mob surged to the end of the street. I couldn't see my father anymore. Move on! The Russians are coming! Oh God, where was father?

The building that for centuries had blocked the end of the street, marked also the end of the town. An arched vault, like a short tunnel, led to the other side of the house and to the quay. The crowd squeezed through the narrow passageway. Elbows, bundles, baby carriages bumped and banged as we fought to get through the opening.

Lili started shifting under her cover and cried a little. Caught in the crowd, I could do nothing.

A moment later we spilled out onto the quay and suddenly came to a halt. The quay, called Long Shore, was a narrow sidewalk, running along a row of ancient burgher houses, all facing the river. The stone-paved sidewalk overhung the river so that the crowd of mothers and children looked down on the tops of fishing boats and ferries. This morning, a heavy fog hung over the water and partially over the Long Shore, as if to conceal the exodus of Danzig's women and children. The notorious smell of oily mold and dead fish saturated the air.

I looked around hoping to see my father but saw only strange faces twisted with desperation and panic. Children cried, "Mommy! Mommy!" and mothers shouted the names of their children. In the foggy air, the cries sounded strangely muted.

Everyone tried to crowd into the various ferries that served as shuttles to the large ships in the outer harbor; once filled, the ferries got under way. With no one there to supervise, the people milled like terrified cattle in a slaughterhouse pen. Oh God, would there be enough shuttles?

"Eva!" My father's voice called. I jerked around and saw him. Only a few steps from me, but separated by the pushing people, his full-moon face stood out over the maddening crowd like a setting moon. He held up my suitcase, pushed through to me and managed to put it into my outstretched hand.

An instant later, the crowd thronged forward toward the gangway of a boat. Along with the others I stumbled down the gangway, pushing the buggy, the suitcase on top of it, my handbag hanging on my arm.

Suddenly, my handbag slid and fell onto the gangway. I saw feet trample it. I tried to pick it up. But before I could reach it some foot shoved it into the river. "My handbag!" I cried, but no one listened to me. With the shock of comprehension I stared down at the water. My ID, my money, my food-ration coupons, the few family pictures -- they all sank with my purse into the icy water of the river.

The crowd swept me onto the ferry. I and the buggy were wedged between women, children and the bulkhead of the ferry boat's deck house. Suddenly, I realized I hadn't been able to say good-bye to my father. Where was he? In the thick fog the shore and those left behind were invisible. A soft throbbing under my feet and the muffled sound of the engine told me the boat had left the quay. No one said a word, even the children kept quiet.

All of a sudden, I heard my father's voice from the shore. "Eva! Eva!" He who seldom showed his emotions was now breaking down. "Eva! Eva! Eva!" His desperate cries penetrated the fog. I yearned to go back to him, into the shelter of his arms, to promise him never to leave again. "Eva! Eva!" His cries tore at me, pulling at me over the cold gray void that separated us.

But there was no way back. The ferry steadily widened the gulf between us. Helplessly, I heard his voice until I couldn't bear it anymore. Crouching close to the deck, as if to hide from the outcry, I covered my ears with my hands, but the muted cries followed me still: "Eva! Eva!"

Trying to conquer the pain in my heart, I gritted my teeth. How can I live with his cries? I thought in desperation. I'll hear them forever. God, how can I bear this? I want to forget this -- I want to forget this! My ears began ringing and black stars danced before my eyes. Fortunately, the bulkhead of the deck house prevented me from falling back, so I gently slid toward a woman next to me, while everything went black in me.

After a moment I regained my consciousness and found myself sitting on my suitcase. I couldn't see more than people's legs and backs, but I could hear the stamping rhythm of the ferry engine and smell its oil and the salty breeze from the river.

A matronly face bent over me. "Are you sick?"

"Just weak from a sleepless night," I answered. "Thank you for your help."

Looking into the baby carriage I saw Lili awake. Caressing the small round face I saw Manfred's features, reduced to doll size. The same deep-blue eyes, the line of high forehead flowing gracefully into a straight, perfect nose -- how fortunate for Lili to inherit his good looks. With her built-in pacifier she resembled him too: thumb in her mouth, index finger arched over her nose -- she looked like Manfred's baby pictures. Obviously, she also had inherited her father's deep-sleep pattern. Just as he was able to sleep through air raids, his daughter was slumbering through the flight from the Russians.

Lili's small fist was red from the cold air. I pulled the upper blanket a little higher to cover the child's fist. "Keep warm, my love," I murmured. Immediately, Brahms' lullaby came to mind. My fingers gently moved as if playing the piano arrangement.

The music enlivened me. I got up from my suitcase. "Thank you again for taking care of me," I said to the friendly matron.

The fog made it hard to tell how far we had come from the Long Shore. I looked back, thinking something painful had happened in the fog, but my mind recalled nothing.

"We'll soon be at the outer harbor," my neighbor remarked. "We're already on the Vistula river."

"Did we pass the Old Citadel?"

"Yes."

A strange euphoria spread over my body, making me quiver with the love of adventure.

Suddenly, the pitch of the engine lowered and its rhythm slowed, we were approaching another quay. The ferry bumped against the wharf, once, twice, until the sailors moored it. The outer harbor.

As I stepped from the short gangway, I found myself on a pier. Huge ships lined up on one side, a gallery of tall cranes on the other. The cranes' slender bodies looked like giraffes bending over, ready to grab at the people below. I took in the smell of tar and seaweed, which I loved.

Like ants at the feet of metal giants our flock of fugitives plodded from one ship to the next, finding and boarding our assigned vessels. I slipped my hand into my coat pocket: thank God, the permit was there.

After passing several large ships I read the name PREUSSEN on a small homely freighter, gray from smoke-stack to water line. The only relief from the grayness was a white lifesaver on the bridge. The PREUSSEN didn't exactly look like a luxury yacht, but it certainly could take me and Lili away from the Russians. With its name, Prussia, it would take a big chunk of Prussia's population along.

I saw several sailors in front of the gangway shuffling the women and children in disciplined lines, checking everyone's permit and counting heads. In single file with the others, pushing the baby carriage, I walked up the gangway. On top, an ensign collected the permits and let the passengers step onto the ship's deck. We had made it!

For a moment, through a break in the mist, I caught sight of Danzig's skyline far away. *Sankt Katharinen*'s peaked-onion top protruded from the fog layer, which spread like a pall over the city. "Farewell," I whispered. "Farewell, Danzig...."

ON BOARD THE PREUSSEN

The crowd swarmed onto the PREUSSEN's deck, shoving me around the gray superstructure, until we came to a halt before a yawning hole. A wooden ladder led down into the darkness. Spontaneously, the priestesses' dirge of the opera *Aida* began to ring in my head. So this was how it felt to descend to the tomb. Sailors helped us below deck. Gray, everything was gray, the color of misery. A strong smell of tar penetrated the air, which I loved.

"Pew! What a stench!" a brunette complained to me.

"How strange," I said to her, changing the subject. "The ship is dead. No engine noise, no vibrations."

"It will come alive soon," she answered.

At last we arrived in a large loading room. It had been converted to a makeshift dormitory with a dozen bunks on each side and no other furniture. A solitary ceiling light barely illuminated the Spartan setting.

"We must be below the water level here," I said to the brunette, who occupied one of the upper bunks. "We are mermaids now."

I picked the lower bunk, placing the baby carriage next to it. The uncovered mattress sagged in the middle as if the ship's entire crew had used it. Unperturbed, I changed Lili's diaper -- a simple task compared to the problem of what to do with soiled diapers here. At last, I took a food package from the suitcase, unwrapped it, rolled the dirty diaper into the brown paper and threw it under my bunk. A bit self-conscious, I looked at my neighbors' bunks. The woman on the upper berth, bending down to the one below her, asked: "I'm sure I'll get seasick. How about you?"

"I'm scared stiff," replied the other. She lay on her bunk as if paralyzed.

Neither one seemed to care what I had done with the dirty diapers, so I shrugged it off. The ancient rule "Do not trouble your head about others!" apparently was followed here, too.

The room temperature gradually rose, making me uncomfortable in my many layers of clothing. In order to carry as many clothes as possible, I had put on two dresses, two slips, and two sweaters this morning. Now I felt like a stuffed doll. Taking off as much as I could I breathed a sigh of relief. As I sat on my bunk, holding Lili, my spirits became more cheerful. Finally, I was on the ship which would carry us to security. I had a place to sleep and I could easily see everyone entering the room -- young mothers and their children, a few older people.

Suddenly, a curly-headed blonde from the other side of the dorm came over to me, calling, "There's our famous pianist."

I recognized her immediately. "Neither famous nor with a piano. How wonderful to see you here, Ruth!"

She pointed to Lili. "Yours?" I nodded. "Cute. She can play with my twins," Ruth said. She called to two curly-headed girls. "Five years old," Ruth explained. The twins shook hands with me and curtsied. Ruth instructed her children to hold Lili's hands and walk her up and down between the bunks. Lili wiggled with joy.

Ruth sat down on my bunk, and we plunged into conversation about the whereabouts of our husbands. "Do you realize," she finally asked, "that we are right in the middle of an adventure? Going into the unknown."

"I hope we'll go abroad."

"To Denmark?"

"Maybe Sweden?" Sweden -- just across the Baltic Sea....

As if to confirm our euphoria, a group on the other side started singing: "*Muss i denn, muss i denn zum Städtele hinaus...* Must I now, must I now leave my hometown," an old folk song. The general spirit was gay, if only by way of hysteria. The children played hide-and-seek between the bunks, while Lili still waddled between Ruth's twins.

In the middle of the tumult a tall young sailor appeared, his round, brimless cap with the label *Kriegsmarine* straight above his clean boyish face. He carried a gray bucket. Everyone looked at him, ready for whatever surprise. Even the children stood still. He put the bucket in the middle of the room and said, "All toilets are clogged and out of order. You have to use this bucket. We'll replace it from time to time." He left in a hurry as if to escape protest and uproar.

But there was no uproar. Discipline and subordination to authority had been reinforced in us from childhood on. Just the same, everyone looked horrified at the bucket. Reality had destroyed euphoria. The singing didn't resume.

When I awoke next morning, I saw that my co-passengers had learned how to use the bucket, and I followed their example. We all had one thing in common, the century-old Spartanic upbringing that strictly forced us to accept even the unacceptable. Minute after minute I waited for the engine noise and vibration which would indicate the ship's imminent departure. But the ship didn't move. The air became stickier, litter accumulated on the floor. I yearned to be home.

On the second day, the passengers began to grow restless. "Mommy, I want to play outside!....You stay where you are!....I want a candy!....I want another!....Why isn't the ship leaving?....Did the Russians enter Danzig?" An atmosphere of fear began to prevail.

Just then, a sailor came in to replace the overflowing bucket. Determined, I approached him. "When are we leaving?"

He stopped his unpleasant job, assumed the position of attention and looked straight into my eyes. "I don't know, madam."

"What's the reason for *not* leaving?"

His eyes avoided mine. "I can't say."

"Are all the other ships waiting too?"

"No, madam, they're all gone."

In the silence I heard a little girl tinkling into the empty bucket.

"Is anything wrong with the engine?" I asked.

The sailor still didn't look at me but nodded his head. "I think so, ma'am. But they're working on it. The weather is so bad in the Baltic, we can't risk sailing." He retreated with the full bucket.

I stood as if paralyzed. The hull seemed to close in on me. I felt like an insect in a spider's cobweb. Anger rose in me.

"We're prisoners here," I heard a woman shout.

This ship was dead. Dead in the water with no place to go. My anger exploded. Resolutely, I packed my things.

"What are you going to do?" the brunette asked.

"I'm going home!" I shouted. "This is worse than the Russians! I can't stand it anymore!"

"You're crazy!" Ruth called from her bunk. "Don't you know what the Russians have done in Nemmersdorf?"

I didn't respond. Going home or not -- at least I was going to do something. First of all, leave this impotent ship!

"She's a spoiled child," someone said.

I ignored it, put Lili into her carriage and went upstairs for help. Two sailors helped me without asking me questions.

On the outer deck, a cold gale blew into my face as if to punish me. I breathed in the pure icy air and felt enormously relieved. On the gangway down, I stopped in amazement at the scene on the pier. It had changed completely. Only two days ago, mainly local refugees had formed lines in front of the gangways. Now, a strange landscape, buried in snow, lay before me. All the ships were gone except the PREUSSEN. The pier had become a chaotic place with shouting women, crying children, abandoned horse-carts and bicycles. Most women wore babushkas -- peasants from the Eastern parts of Europe. They carried their belongings wrapped in large handkerchiefs or sacks. It looked as though they had trekked in their horse-carts for weeks. Finally they had reached Danzig's harbor, but without permits for a ship they were doomed to wait in the cold for a possible return of the vessels. Germany's Dunkirk, only magnified beyond measure.

Two women in thick long winter coats sat on their bundles, one of them with her face buried in her hands, the other one nervously bit her fingernails. She stopped biting and asked me: "Is there room for us on the ship?" She had a strong accent.

"I don't know," I replied. "You've got to ask the sailors ..."

"They said we'd have to wait. Until another ship comes back."

"Where are you from?"

"Lithuania."

"How did you get here?"

The woman pointed with her thumb to a horse-cart.

"What's going to happen to the horses?" I asked.

The woman shrugged. "They'll starve. We have no guns to shoot them."

I saw a small girl sitting on a bundle, holding a small mutt on her lap. Nearby, a woman was tying a goat to a horse-cart. A young boy hugged the animal and cried. I felt like hugging these children.

At this moment, more people tried to press into the area. The baby carriage and I were pushed aside. That's when I saw the navy-blue uniform. The insignia on the left arm -- a golden eagle and three triangles, was the sign of the E.D.s, engineering duty officers -- Manfred's division! I knew their group was small and all of them were involved with each other. I'd never met this man, but he would certainly know Manfred. He seemed nervous, constantly checking his wrist watch.

Feeling as if I were sleep walking, but with automatic precision, I approached him. "*Guten Tag*."

He saluted me, hand-to-forehead, his thin face serious and tense.

"I'm Manfred Krutein's wife," I said.

His eyes lit up in recognition of the name. He bowed lightly. "Kurt Vanderheim. What a pleasure to meet you, Madame." His formality seemed awkward in this situation.

A flash shot through me: Helmut's phone call -- the DEUTSCHLAND.... "I know you're stationed on the DEUTSCHLAND", I said. "Please, take me there."

Vanderheim smiled politely. "I'm sorry, Madame, I can't take you there. The ship's berthed far away from here."

"But you're going there, aren't you?"

"Yes." He obviously hated my questions.

I said firmly: "I'll go with you."

"Impossible." His formality was gone.

"How will *you* get there?"

His face froze in a mask. Obviously, he answered only out of politeness for the wife of his fraternity brother. "A boat is picking me up any moment."

The wind pulled at us and the refugees shouted around us in East Prussian dialect and Lithuanian.

Suddenly, a small motorboat approached the quay, stopping close to where we stood. Promptly, Vanderheim walked up to the landing spot. Determined, I followed him. He stepped onto the rope ladder hanging down from the quay while two sailors helped him into the boat.

I made a quick decision. "Stop!" I called down to them. "Here. Help me down. First, the baby carriage."

I had spoken with authority and the sailors, used to obeying, followed my orders automatically. Maybe they thought I was the wife of the officer they picked up. "Please hurry, Madame," one of the sailors said, "We're running late." They took the buggy and the suitcase and helped me down. Vanderheim said nothing. The moment I jumped into the boat, it left.

As we stood in the icy breeze, coat collars turned up, it began to snow a little. I pulled up the carriage's canopy to protect Lili. While the sailors' yellow foul-weather gear hung stiffly from their shoulders, the wind ruffled the ribbons on their caps. Whenever they gave each other short commands, frosty vapor came from their mouths. Grateful for the fresh air after the long confinement on the PREUSSEN, I inhaled deeply the aroma of salt and sea and listened to the irregular rhythm as the river's choppy waves slapped against the boat.

Unperturbed by the elements, my reluctant savior quietly gritted his teeth so that the sailors couldn't hear him. "It won't help you, Madame. The DEUTSCHLAND is guarded. No one without a special permit can get on. There are two controls." I said nothing, hiding my excitement about this ride into the forbidden.

Cutting quickly along the Vistula River we passed by mine sweepers and tug boats, all loaded with women and children standing on deck in the freezing cold. We had almost arrived at the mouth of the Vistula as our boat steered toward a huge oceanliner berthed by the left bank. It looked slender and elegant, even from far away. I could read the white letters on the bow of its long black hull: DEUTSCHLAND. The two smoke-stacks, flanked on both sides with masts and loading beams, which looked like giant stakes, impaled the sky like threats. Manfred, I thought, I'll get your little daughter on this ship at any cost!

As our boat approached the oceanliner, its black, rivet-studded steel cliff seemed to rise higher and higher, finally becoming a frightening black monster. Straining my neck while looking up at its white painted rim, I felt like a tiny bug trying to intrude into this iron colossus.

The boat stopped right in front of the DEUTSCHLAND, berthed at the wharf. The tiny boat rocked heavily as the two sailors lifted the baby carriage, then helped me up to the quay. The place seemed completely deserted. A restricted area?

As if in protest over my intrusion the mild snowfall became a sudden storm. It roared and whistled, and within seconds everything was covered with fresh snow. My unintentional rescuer rushed toward the gangway which slanted sharply upwards. He made no effort to adjust to my slower pace as I doggedly tried to keep up with him.

As we drew near the gangway, a group of four naval officers and two young women, each hand-in-hand with two toddlers, approached from the other side. We reached the gangway simultaneously.

A very young petty officer down on the quay asked for permits. All except me passed them to him. Bracing against the snow storm, which almost tore the papers from his hands, he checked them.

My heart pounded heavily. The moment I saw him counting the permits, I forced my luck. I jerked my foot and screamed. I saw everyone looking at me, including the checking petty officer. "I sprained my foot," I cried.

Through the howling gale the petty officer shouted up to his colleague on deck, "They're all from the same party." Then he hurried to me to support me. I faked a limp, and I prayed. Just a few steps up the ladder and Lili and I would be safe.

Two men pushed the baby carriage up the steep gangway. On deck, the petty officer released my arm. "Do you think you can walk now, madame?" he asked.

"Oh yes, thank you so much," I said. And forgive me for lying to you, I told him without mouthing my words. He hurried back down to the quay.

The gangway was immediately pulled away. I felt a tremor run up from the lower decks as the ship's propellers started turning and the DEUTSCHLAND began to move, pulled by two tug boats. A long, deep, gut-shaking tone -- B-flat two octaves below middle C -- boomed from the horn of the ship, announcing its departure.

The little boarding group had disappeared, including Vanderheim, who obviously didn't want to be part of my stowing away. I didn't care. I was on board and we were sailing.

In the snow storm, pushing the baby carriage between steel booms, winches and huge ventilator outlets, I looked for an entrance. Finally I noticed an oval-shaped, water-tight steel door and opened it, but the gale slammed it shut again. The second time I held my back against it and little by little squeezed the baby carriage through the small opening.

Inside, I saw a different world.

THE VOYAGE

I stood in the middle of the enclosed Promenade Deck -- a longish, parquet-covered gallery. Wide, square windows shut out the snowstorm, while round portholes allowed a peek into the cabins on the other side.

Warm air surrounded me, gently penetrating my thick clothing. I put Lili down, removed our gloves and unbuttoned our coats. Soft radio music -- Mozart's serene *Eine Kleine Nachtmusik*, A Little Night Music, enveloped us. What a welcome! Moreover, the vital signs of a moving vessel outweighed all its comforts: it hummed and quivered like a woman in love. I suddenly understood why Manfred often likened a ship to a woman. Indeed, in the middle of the ocean it was Mother Earth, carrying us all to safety.

I wasn't alone on the Promenade Deck. Women walked with their children and busy sailors hurried back and forth.

As I approached a door, I saw a brass plate with an English engraving. I grinned: the Nazis' mania to remove anything foreign hadn't reached this ship. I read:

TURBINE STEAMER DEUTSCHLAND
HAMBURG-AMERICA LINE
20,607 GRT   CAPACITY 1,600 PASSENGERS

So, before the war, this German oceanliner had sailed to America. My thoughts flew over to that remote country, wondering what it was like in the USA. They, too, were at war, but they had kept it outside their land. Their women and children didn't have to flee. Their homes weren't destroyed. But back to here and now. Helmut Kalmbach was supposed to be on this ship. How could I find him on this floating island?

Out of a swinging double door came a short, jolly- looking petty officer. I stopped him. "Could you tell me where Lieutenant Kalmbach is?"

He looked at me in amazement. "I'm sorry, Madame. There are ten thousand people on board. You'll have to look for him yourself."

Ten thousand people! An overload of eighty-five hundred. Where in the world were they all accommodated? With the buggy I pushed the swinging door open and entered a large, brightly-lit salon, paneled in rosewood. A sparkling crystal chandelier and wall-to-wall red plush carpet indicated this was the room where peacetime's parties and entertainment had been provided for rich first-class passengers. Now the room was filled with women and children, sitting or lying on the carpet. All furniture had been removed to make room for the refugees. The carpeting pleasantly deadened the sound of the people's chatter, but the air was hot and heavy with the smell of the crowded bodies.

Finding it impossible to walk between the huddled people, I stepped into the narrow passageway that led to the first-class cabins. All the cabins I opened were occupied. No one paid attention to me. The adults were busy, unpacking food, consoling children, looking for toilets.

When a middle-aged officer strode by, I quickly took note of his rank and promoted him to a higher one. "Herr Kapitän, I need a space to stay."

He saluted me. "Excuse me, Madame. Who checked you in? Everyone has a place."

Holy German bureaucracy! I looked at him pleadingly. "I think I'm lost."

He shrugged. "Well, Madame, this ship has five decks. There should be a place for you. But you must excuse me, I'm in a rush. Good luck, Madame." He saluted me and left.

Frustrated I started wandering through the crowded corridors, as Lili began to cry. I gave her a pacifier with a little polar bear at the end, but Lili shoved it away with her tongue. My spirits sank. Fighting desperation, I pushed myself forward. Ten thousand people aboard and I was a stowaway!

Soon I found another spacious room, surrounded by large vaulted, stained-glass windows -- possibly a former dining salon. Gilded sconces on the wall gave the impression of a *Ratskellar*. So many women and children sat on the patterned linoleum floor I could barely squeeze in. Bending down to a gray-haired woman huddled on the floor, I said, "I have to look for a place. Could you take care of the baby carriage and my suitcase for a while?"

The woman nodded. "Try E Deck."

Lili cried louder. She needed fresh diapers and food. Where in the world was E Deck? I took Lili in my arms and hurried through the labyrinthine passageways until I saw a sign "To decks B,C,D,E." I followed the signs downstairs. The lower I got, the warmer the air became and the louder the engine noise. It was as if I was descending into hell itself.

At last, we arrived at E Deck, which lay below water level. I felt my senses violently attacked. Sticky hot air filled my lungs, making breathing a chore and the unflagging rumbling of the ventilator fans deafened my ears. The entire E Deck seemed to shake with fury. Modern hell, I decided. Let's find a place in hell! I opened several cabins and found them all overcrowded, one bunk only per family, reminiscent of the PREUSSEN. Finally, Cabin 66 had a free bunk. I sighed and slumped on the bare mattress.

During all this, Lili had been crying. Now, she screamed hysterically. Neither the diaper change nor the bottle nor cradling calmed her, and I began to realize how much the constant commotion had finally upset the child.

A woman with a motherly face turned to me. "It sounds as if she won't stop. Give her a sleeping pill. Ours are all drugged." As my shock showed in my face, the woman added, "One pill won't hurt the baby."

Searching through my cosmetic bag, which I carried instead of the drowned handbag, I found a sleeping pill, broke it in half, dissolved it in water and forced it down Lili, who struggled violently. After a short while, the pill worked. Lili fell asleep. Gently, I kissed her.

Sitting on my narrow bunk, I listened to the conversation -- mainly complaints about having to stay on E Deck. "What's wrong with E deck?" I asked.

A fat woman put a cookie into her mouth. "If the ship sinks, we won't get out of here!" she said between chewing.

"Why should the ship sink?"

"Because there are Russian submarines around here," the fat woman said with bitterness. "If a torpedo hits we'll sink."

The news shocked me as though someone had aimed a gun at me. "How do you know?" I asked.

"They shocked *us* with the news, once we were on this ship. Now we shock *you*."

I felt strangled. Russian submarines! How proud I'd been of managing to bring Lili onto this "safe" ocean liner!

"At least," the older woman said, "we're sailing."

"Where are we going?" I asked.

"We don't know," the woman replied.

Suddenly, the old nervous excitement overcame me. Since I now had a place to sleep, I could go and look for Helmut. I asked the woman to save the bunk for me.

Remembering that Manfred once said that officers usually stayed on A Deck, I climbed, the sleeping Lili over my shoulder, through the crowded D, C and B Decks, where I noticed the ship slightly listed to one side.

Finally reaching A Deck, I felt as confused by the system of passageways as on the other decks, but the lights shone brighter, the corridors were broader, the hissing from the ventilator ducts softer and the vibrations thinner. However, the slight slant of floor and walls appeared the same as on the other decks. Strange, I thought, always to the left side, or portside, as Manfred would say. I wandered between women and children, sailors, ensigns and officers until they all looked alike to me.

After a seemingly endless time, my attention was drawn to a half-naked man, who came along the passageway, dressed only in dark blue uniform trousers, with a towel dangling from his arm, apparently just coming from the shower. Incredulously, I stared at his tall, slender figure, as he approached me. His pitch-black hair, still damp, lay straight on his head but curled on his chest. "Helmut!" I cried out.

He stopped, obviously shocked, his handsome face showing mild embarrassment. I had found him! A miracle had happened. "What -- how -- how in the world did you get here?" he stammered, his huge brown eyes wide with astonishment.

"You won't believe it. I smuggled myself on board."

"Through the two controls?" He stood spellbound, obviously trying to imagine my daring intrusion. "Typically Eva," he finally stated. He shook his head, then asked, "Where's your cabin?"

"On E Deck."

"For godsakes, you have to get out of there. It's too dangerous."

"Because of the Russian submarines?" I enjoyed displaying my new sophistication.

"Yes," he said with a lowered voice. "They are around. The ship crew is handing out life vests now. We're supposed to wear them all the time."

I didn't see one on him. "Is *that* necessary?"

"Well, three torpedoes are enough to sink the ship. At least we want to be able to swim for a while. But first you. I guess the bundle over your shoulder is Lili?"

I chuckled. "She sleeps like a hibernating bear."

"Let me put a shirt on," he said. "*Mensch*, I can't believe you're here!" He led me down a corridor, pulled me into his cabin and then introduced me to his three roommates, two young women and a middle-aged fat man. The elegant one with pitch-black hair, Charlotte, said she knew me from my frequent piano playing in town. The pale woman in a colorless suit was Marion. The fat man was called Dr.Ball. I suppressed a chuckle when I heard his name. Under normal circumstances, the women would hardly have tolerated men in their cabin. Yet in the chaos....

While Helmut put a white shirt on, I scanned the room. This cabin was indeed first class. A blue-carpeted, teak-paneled stateroom, quite different from the no-frills cabins on E Deck: two bunks on either side -- complete with white linen and brown blankets. One large wash basin with a big mirror was fastened against the wall. Four armchairs stood around a square wooden table. An enormous globe, suspended from the ceiling, radiated light far better than the tiny porthole could provide.

Helmut turned to me. "You can have my bunk. I can sleep next door with my colleagues."

I put my hand on his arm. "Is there an extra bed for you?" I could easily imagine him sleeping on the floor for his buddy's wife.

"Don't worry about me," he said warmly.

"I have to get the baby carriage and my suitcase from the dining salon," I said to him.

"Let's go there," he said, putting his navy tunic on. He took the sleeping Lili in his arms as if she were his own baby. I was sure he missed his little daughter. Physically, I felt relieved; Lili was heavy.

Walking through the passageways, we once had to squeeze along a line of mothers and children who stood in front of a large pass-through. I breathed in several scents -- spice cake and onion soup. "The galley," Helmut explained. "Hot oatmeal for the children, potato soup for the adults." Only faintly I remembered we'd been without food for some time. We stopped and moved to the side while two sailors passed by, carrying a huge reel of cables. Our fragmented telephone conversation came to mind. "You told me Irene left the countryside with your baby. She was teaching school, wasn't she?"

"Yes. And they left on a trek four days ago."

"A trek?"

"Yes, remember what we learned in high school about the pioneers of the American West? Their long wagon trains? In Irene's case there were twelve people. On foot. Their belongings were on a horse wagon."

"Oh my God, why couldn't she take a train?"

"There were no trains anymore. The Russians had already pushed through. So they started on foot."

"In this sub-zero weather?"

"Anything is better than falling into the hands of the Russians."

The thought of the ordeal of wandering through the ice-covered roads of Europe with a small baby enraged me. "This damned war! Why don't we do something about it?"

He turned to me, grinning. "Do you want to take off and proclaim peace for all times?"

"I wish I could," I said angrily.

Back in the cabin with buggy and suitcase, I sat on Helmut's lower bunk, while he pulled his suitcase out from under it, ready to move out. My co-passengers had gone out to get food. Lili, lying next to me, had already stirred several times and, to my relief, seemed to be waking slowly.

Still, I yearned for information about our situation. "Helmut, what's going on?" I asked as he placed his large suitcase on the bunk. "Why are you naval architects leaving Danzig?"

He took his toiletries from the wash basin and put them into his suitcase. "Our new subs are being sent to the West before the Russians conquer all the ports." His voice sounded bitter.

"So our super-modern submarines are fleeing the Russians? What an irony!"

"The new subs are desperately needed in the West."

"Why then were they in Danzig at all?"

He folded his pajamas together. "To be outfitted. And the crews to be trained. At the safest place possible. The area around Danzig was the dead corner of the war. British and American bombers couldn't fly that far. But now, the Russians are advancing and we have to save what we can."

This hit me like a thunderbolt. That's why Danzig and almost the entire East of Germany had been spared by air raids during the last five years! "We all thought Danzig was protected on purpose. That no one wanted to destroy it."

"I know. I've heard that so often." He shut his suitcase with a bang. "But you were just in a dead corner."

A short knock and a sailor walked in, carrying four orange life vests. He saluted Helmut. "Excuse me, sir," he said, putting the life vests on the table. "Everybody is supposed to wear them day and night."

Before he could leave, my three roommates returned from the kitchen, loaded with bowls with potato soup and hot oatmeal. The sailor repeated his message and left.

The three stared at the orange monsters. "Why should we wear them?" Marion asked. "This is a safe ship."

"Russian submarines are around," I said automatically.

Charlotte pushed the life vests from the table to make room for the food bowls. "But the Red Navy doesn't even exist!"

"Unfortunately, it does," Helmut said. Decisively he pulled his suitcase from the bunk. "I'll come from time to time to see if you're behaving," he joked to me and left.

We greedily ate the potato soup. It was delicious after the dry food of the last few days. After that I stepped over to the porthole. In the gray dusk I recognized the distant coast -- about eight miles away. I tried to imagine myself swimming to the coast with the life vest on, my small child in my arms. I turned to Dr.Ball. "How long would it take to swim to the coast?"

"Maybe eight hours."

"How could I even attempt to survive with Lili? I'd rather not wear the life vest at all." I returned to my bunk and hung the life vest on the bunk post. My roommates' silence seemed to signal their agreement.

As I turned to Lili I saw she had finally wakened. Her blue eyes wide open, she stared, fascinated, at the giant lamp globe. "*Icht*," she called out.

First, I didn't understand her. Then Lili repeated the word over and over again, "*Icht. Icht.*" What a moment! It was her first word -- "*Licht*," light. The "L" would come later, no hurry. How proud her grandfather, owner of a lamp factory, would be of her.

I kissed my little daughter. The child smelled fresh and lovely. I took the bowl with the now lukewarm oatmeal from the table and started feeding Lili.

Suddenly, we heard three muffled booms. They sounded like cannon shots from far away. Everyone stopped eating. "A battle on land?" Charlotte asked. We all strained our ears. Still, we heard nothing but the usual hissing and humming of the ventilators.

Dr.Ball shrugged. "*Quatsch*. Some maneuvers."

I tucked Lili into the baby carriage for the night. Adjusting to the listing of the ship, I put the buggy against the wall across from my bed, Lili's weight holding it in place. "The bunks are also tilted," I said out aloud, while preparing for the night.

"This ship doesn't roll left to right as they do in rough weather," Ball replied. "It just remains listed to port side."

"I'll ask Helmut about it tomorrow," I said. Soon I fell asleep.

Then all at once, I jolted awake amid falling objects and shattering glass. Horrified, I sat up. I saw Charlotte's cologne bottle crashing into the sink, an ashtray and a deck of cards sliding from the table. Lili's buggy trundled toward my bunk, crashing into its post -- as if a poltergeist were haunting the cabin.

Lili, awake, sat upright in her carriage, looking at me with big questioning eyes. Marion, paler than usual, cried out: "My God, what happened?" Charlotte's sleep-fuddled face bent down from the top bunk. "What's the matter?"

"The ship has listed from port side to starboard for a change," Ball explained. "But we're still sailing."

"Everything's fine, Lili." I hugged her. "Just go back to sleep." I tucked her in and kissed her.

But I couldn't sleep; I just lay there in my slanted bunk. What in the world was wrong with this ship? "The sleeping giant turned in his slumber ...." I recalled a fairy tale, feeling the awe I'd felt as I listened to the story. Now, instead of awe, there was only fear.

Next morning, after a knock at the door, Helmut, wearing a large blue life vest, walked in. "*Guten Morgen,*" he said. His face looked grave. He sat down on my bed. "Why aren't you wearing your life vest?" he asked sternly.

"What for?"

"I'll tell you why." He turned to the others. "Have you heard the news? It's spreading like wild fire. Remember the ship GUSTLOFF that left Danzig a few hours before us? We've been following it West?"

"Yes. What about it?"

He seemed to brace himself. "The GUSTLOFF was torpedoed. Did you hear what sounded like cannon shots last night? They were three torpedoes. The ship sank in fifteen minutes. There were ten thousand women and children aboard."

A deadly silence followed. Lili, cheerfully beating a teaspoon against the metallic bunkpost, made the only noise. It took on enormous dimensions in the hush.

I reached for Helmut's arm. "Oh my God," Marion whispered.

Charlotte, clutching the corner of the table, cried out: "Did they all drown?"

"All but a few who were picked up by minesweepers."

I felt my throat tighten. When are we landing? I almost screamed. Dear God, how long will we be targets?

"How many did the minesweepers pick up?" Ball asked with a controlled voice.

"The figures aren't in yet," Helmut replied. "But, of course, the percentage can only be small. Those who could swim away fast enough to escape from the suction were the only ones rescued." He looked at me. "It pays to wear the life vest."

With feverish haste, I tried to grapple with reality. A time-bomb was ticking. We're on A Deck -- just run up to Boat Deck and jump into the water -- we can't swim to the shore, but a minesweeper may pick us up -- we might survive...

As if reading my thoughts, Helmut took my life vest from the bunk post and passed it to me. I put it on. "Only those on the upper decks got them," he said in a low voice. "Those who can get off the ship if it sank."

"And the people on E Deck?"

"No one down that far would have a chance to clamber up in time." Horrified I closed my eyes.

I noticed the cabin had become hot and sticky. Dr.Ball pulled at the porthole, hammering his fist against it. "Can somebody open this stupid thing!" he shouted. The good chance of being blown up any minute had disturbed even this placid man.

Calmly, Helmut went over to the porthole. "You just have to turn the knob and move the lever."

"*Herr Leutnant,*" I heard Ball ask. "What's the listing about?"

"The ship's overloaded. The captain is trying to balance it once in a while, preferably at night."

That was the reason why the ship turned over every 12 hours or so! Overloaded and chased! "Come on," I said to Charlotte. "Let's go out for a walk."

As I opened the door to the corridor I saw the passageway clogged with people sitting on the bare, slanted floor. I almost fell over a woman. "I'm sorry," I said. "But why aren't you in your cabins?"

The woman laughed bitterly. "Do you think we want to drown on the lower decks? Like the people on the GUSTLOFF?"

I turned to Charlotte. "Shouldn't we take one or two into our cabin?"

"It wouldn't give them any advantage," she replied. "If the ship sinks, escape will be easier from the passageway."

With the sleeping Lili over my shoulder I stepped over the huddling women towards one of the crowded red-carpeted salons. I heard a radio. I strained to hear. It was Hitler. There was no mistaking the loud, evangelistic delivery. He shouted and barked in the agitated tone that had become so familiar to us.

About a hundred women sat, devotion and expectancy in their expressions, with their children on the red plush carpet, faces turned up to a loudspeaker hung from the ceiling. Attentively, I searched the sea of faces. Literally, they were all in the same boat and could experience a disastrous fate any moment, but with eyes glued to the high hanging loudspeaker, the women listened to Hitler's words like desperate worshippers before a saint's statue.

As women, hadn't we all been brought up to accept the superiority of men's decisions? Why didn't we all rebel against the tradition that glorified war and mass slaughter?

Suddenly, Hitler's barking rose higher.

"...our brave soldiers' spirit of sacrifice
irradiates them like a halo. And you, my
dignified mothers and women, whose sons and
husbands have given up their lives for our
Fatherland, be assured, it has not been in vain.
Within a short time, the new powerful weapons I
have promised will be put into action
and will change the course of the war.
They will destroy our enemies and bring
    us the final victory!"

Cheers, fanfares, marching music. The women on the plush carpet clapped. "That was reassuring," a woman with a madonna-like face said. "Now we know we'll win the war."

I was furious. Turning to Charlotte I asked with irony: "I didn't listen to the whole speech. Did he say anything about our ship being safe?"

Charlotte laughed. She nudged me in the side and replied, "Yes! And he said Eva Krutein should now play the March of Triomphe from *Aida*."

I felt relieved by Charlotte's joke. Most musicians and artists put Hitler on the same level as any other authoritarian, and ridiculed him. We turned to go back to our cabin.

Just then, the floor rocked, the walls tilted and the crystal chandelier swayed, its pieces of glass jingling. A hysterical outcry broke loose and spread into the corridors beyond. Everywhere, mothers grabbed their children and ran toward the door. "Help! Help!...I want to get out!...I don't want to drown!...Mommy, Mommy!" Pushing and shoving, our bodies squeezed together so tightly we couldn't move, babies crying, children screaming, the women struggling to escape.

In the middle of the panic, I had the strange feeling of being in control. Realizing that the vibrations of the ship hadn't changed at all, I shouted to the panicking women around me, "The ship wasn't hit! We're sailing as before!" No one seemed to hear me. I tried it again. "The ship has only listed to the other side!"

Gradually, the crowd realized the ship was not sinking, but only exhibiting its strange listing pattern, and the panic subsided. Most people, faces drawn from emotional exhaustion, squeezed themselves back inside, stepping over women and children who were huddled in the passageways again.

Back in the cabin, right in front of the open porthole, as though nothing had happened, Dr.Ball did breathing exercises. "Don't cry," he said to Marion. "We'll make it. We're cutting through the Baltic at eight to ten knots. I'll eat a broom if we don't reach some Western coast by tomorrow."

Almost all of the ten thousand women and children had drowned. What must they have felt in their last moments? Help us, God, I prayed, one more night. I was terrified of the night. Manfred had told me that most submarines attacked in the darkness. The day dragged on endlessly. That night I tossed back and forth in my bunk. Every minute I thought: now it's going to hit -- no, not now -- but now.... Would this night never end?

It did come to an end. When gray dawn fell over the Baltic Sea something suddenly changed. I strained my ears until I realized it was the cessation of the mute humming of the turbines that had alerted me. Suddenly, the propellers restarted, ran even faster, then halted again, then continued in irregular rhythm.

"We're landing! We've made it! We've arrived in the West," we shouted to each other. Charlotte jumped up and down and Lili yelled happily, clapping her hands together.

All four of us hurried to the porthole, Marion the first to see. "We're already in a harbor. Look at all the war ships."

"God knows what harbor this is," Charlotte said.

"Who cares?" I asked. "We are out of reach of the Russian submarines."

In our euphoria we didn't hear the knock at the door. Helmut walked in with a smile that enhanced his face. "They didn't catch us. We made it."

"Where are we?"

"Kiel." Schleswig-Holstein, Northwest Germany.

"Can we leave now?" I asked.

"Patience," he grinned. "It takes two days to disembark ten thousand passengers. My group is leaving first. I came to say good-bye."

"*Auf Wiedersehen*." We shook hands. "Till after the war." The door closed after him.

As Helmut had predicted Lili and I had to wait another night, but that night, at least, was restful.

Next morning, I felt excited and impatient. I was ready long before my turn came to disembark. As I pushed the baby carriage onto the long, steep gangway, I saw a crowd waiting down at the quay. Although the DEUTSCHLAND's destination had been secret so far, yesterday's disembarkation apparently had become the talk of the town. I was sure of one thing: no one waited for *me*.

I had almost arrived at the bottom of the gangway when I saw a tall naval officer standing before me. Helmut! His face strained with concern.

"Helmut, what is it?"

He hesitated for one moment, then asked gravely, "Didn't you tell me you were on the PREUSSEN?"

"Yes."

"The PREUSSEN has been torpedoed and sunk. There are no survivors."

KIEL

Trudging through the slush of Kiel's harbor streets, I tried in vain not to think about Ruth and her twins and all the others whom the PREUSSEN had dragged down into the abyss. But I, for disobeying orders was rewarded with Lili's and my life. We were in the West, out of the Russians' reach, and whatever else awaited us would be bearable.

In the gray drizzle the fields and barracks looked desolate. I was only one of the large crowd of women in heavy winter clothing; some were pushing baby carriages, others had children in their arms or were holding their hands, all had rucksacks and suitcases dragging along.

"I'm soaked," an older woman moaned.

"Here in the Northwest it rains three hundred and seventy days a year," another one said.

"Stop!" a military voice cut into their talk. "Get on the trucks! Don't push!"

I saw an endless row of trucks, canvas tops dripping rain. Women and children climbed up into the first one and within minutes the truck filled. Lili's baby carriage was already in but there was no room left for me. I ran to tell the driver.

From the height of his driver's cabin a young, white-blond army soldier listened to my plight. "There's a very simple solution," he answered cheerily. "Sit next to me."

"Please wait for me. I'll just get my baby." I ran back, took Lili out and left the buggy in the back of the truck. Climbing into the driver's cabin I put Lili on my lap. "Thanks. I got the best seat. With a view."

"I don't know if you'll like the view," he warned me. It would be my first sight of a destroyed city.

The country road running between abandoned-looking fields was muddy from the eternal rain and the driver had to pay all his attention to guiding the truck through the sludge. A mile ahead of me, I could see Kiel's broken skyline, a result of the five years of bombing the Baltic naval base had sustained. Entering the suburbs, the truck hit several potholes, clumsily bumping up and down. But I hardly felt it. I was totally absorbed in this strange, new world of destruction. Every third house was either damaged, burned or totally destroyed. "In the desolate windows' hollows dwells horror ...." Schiller said in his poem 200 years ago. I saw how bomb blasts had ripped off only a front wall, leaving an open view into rooms with remnants of broken beds and cabinets. They upset me more than the heaps of rubble. "Where are all the people? Where do they live now?" I asked.

"Most are squeezed into other people's homes. Some live in basements. They've become cave dwellers."

I was horrified. "Children, too?"

"Of course. Half of Kiel's population has been bombed out. In any untouched buildings the police assign rooms to the bombed-out people."

"How often do you have air raids?"

"Every night." Nowhere was safety.

A block farther on, we drove through a district with four-to-five story Victorian row houses, all painted gray, apparently the favorite color of modest Kiel. "This area is hardly damaged at all," I said, surprised.

"That can change tonight."

A twinge of fear in my stomach made me clutch Lili tighter.

Soon, the truck left the densely populated area, arriving at the far edge of town. We stopped in front of a three-story red-brick school building. "Everybody out!" commanded a military voice.

I thanked the driver, picked up my buggy and joined the other women who had jumped out into the rain.

"In here!" A short, bow-legged petty officer shouted, herding us into the school building. From the high-ceiling entrance hall we were led into a spacious classroom with large, drapeless windows. All desks had been removed and replaced by military bunks. I chose one of the lower empty bunks and placed the buggy next to it.

In the middle stood the longest table I had ever seen, almost completely covered by a jumble of clean, empty cups, coffee pots, plates and bowls, all arranged in small groups. "Put your things over here," an energetic matron pointed. I took out my cup and plate, placing them on the table. It smelled so good of coffee.

Soon the school bell rang, telling us to line up for dinner.
Everyone walked with soup bowls to a door. At the door to the
kitchen young girls gave out cabbage soup, black bread and hot
oatmeal. After the mass feeding most people went to bed
immediately. So did I, fully-clothed, arranging myself on the
hard bunk. Lili slept in her buggy.

In the middle of the night, the loud wailing howl of the air-raid
siren jerked me awake. I jumped up, grabbed for Lili and ran
with the others to the entrance hall.

"Down into the cellar!" a man's voice called. The crowd pushed
down the narrow staircase. "Hurry!"

The cold, damp cellar had apparently been a storage room
before, with empty shelves dividing it into sections. Now
converted into an air-raid shelter, it contained benches and
chairs which provided seats for at least some. Women with little
children were given preference. I sat down, the sleeping Lili on
my lap. A carbide lamp, which hung from a nail in a wooden
post, spread a metallic odor. Its icy-white light made the people
in the large basement look like ghosts, fear and despair in their
faces.

I could barely hear the radio reports on the air situation.
There was some sporadic talking, but even that stopped when
we heard the first muffled sound of a bomb hit. Everyone in the
shelter fell silent. I tried to figure out how far away the hit could
have been. Then another and another. Some farther, some
nearer. Oh God, don't let them hit us, I prayed.

Suddenly, the roar of the bombing squadrons above us
increased and the shooting of the anti-aircraft guns became
fiercer. A thin whistling tone got louder until it turned into a
rustling, like rain on a tin roof; then a detonation and a cold
blast through the cellar. The walls shook. Dust whirled through
the air.

"Aye!" The outcry shrilled through the shelter. "I want out!...I
don't want to be buried alive!"

Most people jumped up. So did I.

A loud, man's voice, firm and commanding, rose above the
tumult. "Go back to your seats! This building wasn't hit." The

air-raid warden -- helpful, reliable, trained in handling frightened people. Everyone sat down again.

A claustrophobic feeling almost overwhelmed me. I strained my ears to hear, but the squadrons were apparently flying away -- the mortal danger of the night was over. It seemed to last an eternity before the monotone of the all-clear sounded and we could walk back to our bunks.

Next noon, lining up for lunch, I heard through an open door Hitler's voice:

"...My fellow Germans, twenty-five years ago I
proclaimed the victory of the Party. Today, I
prophesy, filled with faith in our nation, the
final victory of the Third Reich!"

Rousing cheers on the radio, supported by smashing fanfares, indicated the end of the speech. The line moved forward and I heard only the muted march that always followed Hitler's speeches. I listened to the conversation behind me.

"Too bad we heard only the end of the speech....At least we heard him say we'll win the war....Yes, if the Führer said it then it will come true....He didn't say how long the war will last....Until the new wonder weapon comes out....I wonder what it will be....Who knows....The Führer knows....And we can trust him....Yes, he's been right all the time."

So far, I had tried to shrug off the nonsense. Now, I couldn't stand it any longer. Turning around I saw an older woman, her gray hair pulled in a bun. Next to her a pretty blonde, her hair obviously bleached to agree with Hitler's idea of what Germans should look like. "Don't you think Hitler could be wrong for a change?" I asked. Dammit, I should have said "the Führer." By using his surname I had already shown them I didn't respect him.

The peroxide-blonde flared up. "Are you saying we're going to lose the war?"

I knew I was already in troubled waters. "No one can predict the future," I said.

"If we don't win, the ruins will lie there for the next ten years!" the older woman cried out.

"I'm afraid you're right," I said, then stopped, for I saw a Party-uniformed man with a swastika-band on his arm approach. "Anything wrong here?" he asked with watchful eyes.

If the women told him what I said it would be the end of my freedom.

"She's moving so slowly," the older woman answered, contemptuously pointing a finger at me.

"You'd better behave," the man said to all of us with a threat in his voice.

My shoulders relaxed and I sighed with relief. The woman had not denounced me. For the time being, the danger was over. I have to get out of here, I told myself.

Next morning, a civilian man limped into the dorm and announced, "Get ready. We're moving you into private homes. You're leaving in half an hour." We packed and boarded the trucks again, driving through the rain under covers, seeing nothing. We only heard the roaring of the engine and smelled the stench of diesel oil.

Eventually the truck stopped and a military voice shouted, "Everybody out!"

I found myself in the middle of the city, at the corner where two only half-damaged streets met. A Party worker gave every woman a slip of paper with an address, directing us to our new quarters. As I trudged along the row of houses, some untouched, some in ruins, I thought of my parents and Manfred and wondered how we would ever find each other in the chaos of Europe.

The house I sought was a four-story Victorian, untouched by bombs. On the third floor I rang the doorbell. A shriveled black-clad old woman opened, saw my slip, said, "Come in," and led me to my new room. There were no windows. Cold, damp and mouldy-smelling, like a cellar, it looked like a nun's cell. It had a single wooden bed with a chamber pot under it; a chair served as wardrobe and night stand. Well, at least we had a roof over our heads.

That night and the ones after, I ran, Lili in my arms, into the nearby giant public shelter as soon as the siren howled. The huge cement colossus stood above ground, exposed to the falling bombs. But when the immensely thick walls muffled the noise and stood perfectly still, I began to feel more confidence. Through all the bombings we huddled with hundreds of strangers, sitting on wooden benches until the all-clear.

"Is it really safe in here?" I asked a young mother of two, next to me.

"Oh, yes. The walls are reinforced. Nine foot thick. They resist every mass bombing." This calmed me down somewhat. But the missed hours of sleep made me walk around in a daze.

"I can hardly keep my eyes open during the day," I complained to another woman.

"You'll get used to it."

"Are *you* used to it?"

"For the last three years."

I soon discovered I got accustomed to the nightly alarms, too. Most of my waking hours I spent standing in lines: one for bread, one for shortening, one for fish, one for meat, one for vegetables and all other necessities. Fortunately, the city hall had replaced my lost ID and food coupons; without them I couldn't have bought anything.

I cooked in the old couple's kitchen. In the sink, I washed myself, Lili, our clothes and the diapers. Sharing the single community toilet with four families, I found this to be one more place where standing in line was the rule.

Somehow, in all this insanity, a sane thing happened. Lili learned to walk, her wobbly gait amusing. She even added one word after the other to her vocabulary. In the loneliness of my room, I hugged and kissed my child -- an attitude frowned upon in the stiff atmosphere of Schleswig-Holstein. "We don't spoil our children," a matron, standing in line with me, once scolded. "Only apes do that." So I contained my "apish" behavior in the solitude of my bare room.

One morning, after seven days, I woke up to realize I would suffocate if I continued the monotony of my life one more day. As I stood in line in front of the community toilet on the staircase landing, a young woman asked me, "May I go first, please? I'm already late for work."

Work! It sounded like a magic word to me. When the woman came out I buttonholed her. "Where did you get work?"

"At the employment office. Adolf-Hitler-Street."

To my surprise, there were many jobs open. People were badly needed to help organize the many refugee camps. I was hired immediately and sent by bus to the camp.

Located between barracks, the main building looked like the school building where we had spent the first night in Kiel. My supervisor, Martin Rogge, was a diminutive, one-armed man. "The rescue ships are now coming in every day," he explained. "They're so packed with refugees that some make the trip on deck, outside. The exodus is immense." He paused to sigh. "I need more people working in the reception office. Some refugees may need hospitalization. Some may have lost their ID's. Some may not have eaten for days. You have to sort them out and decide where to send them: to the nurse, the police for registration, or the employment office. You'll have to use your own judgement."

He had organized a kindergarten there, which a friendly grandmother conducted. I also could eat one meal there every day and stretch my coupons. "The easy times with the first-comers from the East are over. The ships arrive with ten times more people than all the camps can accommodate. Most refugees have to be transported to cities nearby."

"How many have come from the East so far?"

"Half a million. And there's no end in sight."

With sudden enlightenment I saw the great crowd of war victims, now and in the past, that no history book ever talked about. The suffering women, children and old people, whose families and homes had been destroyed. Why were they never included in the final summary of a war's costs? Only soldiers and weapons were accounted for.

Next morning, Lili and I took an early bus from our shelter area to the camp. "Mommy's working nearby," I told Lili. "You can play with all the other children and sing with grandma." Lili clapped her hands, smiling. Gregarious by nature, she waddled off without a single tear.

The reception office was a corner of a large dining room with two desks, one for me and one for the other social helper, sweet red-haired Marie. The hollow-eyed, rain-sodden new arrivals went first to the dining hall with its delicious smells, where young girls ladled out hot stews. Sitting crammed on the benches, the refugees, exhausted and silent, ate at long wooden tables. After finishing their meal, the newcomers were interviewed by Marie or me.

"Where are you from? What's your most urgent need?" were my routine questions.

The answers varied so much that I often wondered how people, fleeing under the same circumstances, could have such different needs.

"All I want is sleep....My boy's nose is bleeding.... I lost my ID....Where could I get dry shoes?...Could you get me a room for a thousand cigarettes?"

I listened to each of them, searched out their problems, answered their questions and then decided where to send them. To the nurse. To the police for registration and allocation. To the trains for transfer to other camps or cities.

Most ships came directly from Danzig, the only escape corridor. They described their ordeals. "We'd been sitting on our suitcases at the quay for days....The Russians had already taken half of the city....The last ship came.... We could take nothing along....We had to stand on deck. There wasn't a square foot of empty space....The ship almost rolled over...." Some cried. Some reeked. Some fingered rosaries, their lips forming words.

Some mothers had been separated from their children in the throng. "The ship was taking off and I saw my child standing on the quay crying for me." All I could do was take the woman's hand in mine and hold it for a while.

Three weeks later, when the morning sun had burned the fog away, allowing precious rays to fall through the dining room windows, a little girl, about two, got lost in the dining hall. Her parents had gone to the kitchen for seconds, and the child couldn't see them anymore. She screamed hysterically.

Since the stream of refugees had died down, I walked over to her. The parents waved from their place in line, but the child didn't see them. I bent down to calm her.

"Shoe! Shoe!" the little girl cried.

I looked and saw that one shoe lace was loose. I put the unhappy child on a bench and started tying the lace for her. Immediately, the girl stopped crying.

Still crouched before the child, I suddenly noticed a pair of black shoes on the floor beside me. Had Martin Rogge come to speak to me? There was nothing unusual about that. But a strange breathlessness overcame me. My eyes moved up dark trousers, up a dark coat, along a golden dagger, up golden uniform buttons -- my heart began pounding so wildly I could barely lift my head to see his angular chin, his smiling mouth, his perfect nose, his radiant blue eyes, his daringly slanted wide Navy cap -- and to my immeasurable joy I recognized the beloved face of my husband.

THE CONQUERING HERO

He pulled me up and took me in his arms. "My Little Bear," he murmured in my ear. "I'm holding you at last."

He pressed my head against his chest and I closed my eyes. Wasn't it just a dream? I looked up at him. "Manfred, is it true? I can't believe it!"

He laughed. His welcome, long-missed laughter enchanted me again. "I'm here. Real and genuine. Just arrived from the Atlantic coast."

Exhilarating music roared in my head, *Aida* and its jubilant reception for the victorious hero coming home from the war -- with chorus, trumpets, drums and all. He was alive and with me. His famous smile was as radiant as ever, the warmth in his words and the tenderness of his touch, deeply missed for so long, engulfed me again.

Holding his hand, I pulled him over to Marie's desk. "This is my husband. I may not be here tomorrow. Can you take over for me ?"

A shadow darkened Marie's face. Her husband, I knew, was missing in action. But Marie managed a smile. "Enjoy," was all she said.

Manfred helped me into my coat, then put his arm around my shoulder. He was home, we were together and all problems were now solved. As we walked through the dining hall, I wished I could keep walking with him forever.

But the walk through the hall was short and led straight into reality. I asked the question that puzzled me most. "How did you find me?"

He still had his arm around me -- oh, this wonderful touch, sending waves of excitement and desire through my body! "I knew about the gigantic rescue operation in the East. Most ships were landing in Kiel. Knowing you, I thought you'd be one of the first on a ship. The rest was easy. I asked the police if you and Lili were registered. You were, thank old Bismarck for such a regulation, and I came. But where's Lili?"

"In Kindergarten." I pointed. "How in the world did you get here from Saint Nazaire? I thought you were surrounded by the Americans."

We walked through the sunshine, the first I'd ever seen in Kiel. I felt light as a bird, and the jubilant music was still ringing in my head. His voice sounded above the music: "The Navy sent a plane to Saint Nazaire. I was ordered to the Navy Headquarters here. But back to you. Are you all right?"

"Yes, yes." How could it be otherwise? He was with me and the world was perfect. I put his hand to my face and held it there. A promise. A commitment. A thanksgiving.

He pressed me tighter. "Have you heard from your parents?"

"Not really. But I'm hoping they are on their way here." He didn't ask more questions. I was thankful, I didn't want anything to mar my present happiness.

Reaching the school building, we entered the kindergarten room. Lili, seeing me, got up and ran to me. I picked her up, kissed her and showed her the handsome uniformed man at my side. "This is your daddy."

Before the child could comprehend, Manfred took her in his arms, looked at her bewildered face, kissed her and said tenderly, "My little Lili, you're the most beautiful girl in the world. I missed you so much. I love you." Lili did not understand his words but perceived his message, smiled and kissed him, pressing her little mouth against his cheek.

Hand-in-hand, with Lili in the middle, we walked out of the building. I bubbled over with plans. "You must see where we live. Now, it will have to be something bigger. Or will we leave Kiel?"

"Don't give anything up," he warned. "I don't know what Headquarters wants me to do. All I know is, we have this night to spend together."

The war came flooding back, with all its demands and uncertainties. I sighed. As long as I had known him, I'd felt I had him only on loan from the Navy. Nothing had changed. On the other hand, he hadn't changed either. As always, he stormed into my life, swept me along, then chased his Navy rainbow, leaving me behind. How much did I yearn to be with him forever! Maybe after the war ....

"Hurry up -- there's a truck," he said. "It can take us downtown to your room." Typically my hero-husband, using the world as his vehicle. After one look at Manfred's U-boat insignia and Iron Cross, the big-eared Army driver readily agreed to take the three of us downtown.

Manfred, Lili on his lap, sat in the middle. He held my hand. I caressed his lively profile with my eyes. "How was life in Saint Nazaire? Did you have enough to eat?"

He chuckled. "Way too much. I even gained a few pounds. You'll see later." He turned to me, winking.

The driver cleared his throat. "*Herr Leutnant*, you come from St. Nazaire? Weren't you surrounded by the Americans?"

"For six months."

"Did you have many air raids?"

Manfred shrugged. "We are hard to hit. The big shipyard is built under a massive concrete deck. Twenty-five submarines can move into the docks at once. It's safe under the deck." He was using the present tense -- his mind was still at the Atlantic coast.

"How did you get out?" the driver asked, circling a bizarre debris formation.

"The Navy sent a plane to St. Nazaire to deliver medicine and pick up three others and myself."

"How many are left?"

"Thirty thousand."

I couldn't hold my curiosity any longer. "Why were you chosen to be flown home?"

He grinned. "No idea. But believe me, I was glad to get out of the pit. I had no desire to fall into French hands." There was no trace of hatred in his voice. He didn't seem to consider the Frenchmen his enemies, just admired game partners.

A moment later, as the truck drove around a corner, we arrived at the now familiar four-story house. "This is my place."

Manfred said to the driver, "Leave us here, please."

"*Jawoll, Herr Leutnant.*" The truck stopped and we climbed down. Manfred took a pack of cigarettes from his coat pocket and gave it to the driver.

The ensign's eyes widened. "American cigarettes?" he stammered. Then a great smile broadened his face, his wide ears

enlarging the grin even more. "*Danke, Herr Leutnant*," he said
and saluted. With a magnificent salute, Manfred greeted him
back.

"Where did you get American cigarettes?" I asked with
astonishment.

"In St. Nazaire," he replied lightly.

We walked upstairs to the third floor. I hesitated before
opening the door of the small, dark, windowless room. There was
nothing romantic about the hard bed and single chair. The
naked 15-watt bulb weakly lit the poor scenery. Yet in spite of
it, I felt elated. It was wonderful just seeing my husband move
around -- hearing him whistle the theme of a Bach fugue with
ease as if he were a trained musician. I could never have married
an unmusical man.

From his small suitcase he produced food, luxury food, which
people in the West hadn't seen for years: canned ham, white
bread, oranges, chocolate and red wine. He even provided a can
opener. I couldn't believe my eyes. "This all comes from France?"

"We are on pretty good terms with the French people. We
exchange everything. We keep their electricity going and their
hospitals and they give us the surplus food they get from the
Americans." Still in present tense! Using the chair as a table,
he spread out the little feast.

Lili, not sure about the strange food, ate standing, while her
parents, sitting on the bed, had no qualms about tackling the
French-American delicacies. Manfred washed down a ham slice
with red wine. "Imagine my flight," he said, excitement making
his blue eyes darker. "We flew close to the ground at night over
France to Germany."

"Why close to the ground?" I asked, peeling an orange. I
offered Lili a section.

"Under the radar. Since the Americans couldn't locate us with
radar, they couldn't shoot at us with anti-aircraft guns." He
smiled, triumphant.

"You are always touched by luck."

Lili put her hand out for more orange.

Manfred broke off part of his bread slice. I had never seen
him using this French custom before. "I'll never forget that night
flight," he said. "What a pilot! We were chased by three

American fighters but he shook them off. Once we climbed up to over 20,000 feet, and no heaters, no pressurization ...." his voice trailed off.

"First your U-boat patrols in the Atlantic," I said. "Now your French adventure -- it's a miracle you came out of all of it without a scratch."

"Just as you and Lili have done."

I stopped eating to tell him my story. "Imagine ..." I started, but he had no ear for it. He grabbed my arms. "Hold it for a minute, will you? You know what I want to hear? What I have missed so much in St. Nazaire? Music. Good classical music."

I smiled. "Do you want to go to a concert tonight? I hear they start at 7 p.m. because of the air raids. I'll ask my landlady for a newspaper." I left and returned with a current paper. He thumbed through the pages. "Here's something good. A piano concert. All-Chopin program. Hey, that's something, let's go there."

"Who's playing?"

"Alexander Miroshnikoff," he read aloud.

"Sounds Russian."

"Probably a Ukrainian," he said. "Many are fighting on the German side."

"How's that?"

"They want to end the Stalin regime. What a treat to hear a piano concert."

The way to the concert hall led through streets littered with mounds of debris in place of the former buildings. We walked, arms linked, with Lili on Manfred's other side. I knew that a man in uniform, officer or not, was not supposed to walk arm-in-arm with a woman. Manfred chuckled. "Navy men have the privilege to do so." Obviously, he himself was the authority who gave this permission. I happily gave in to his lightheartedness. I was sure he could overrule the Commander in Chief of the Navy with his self-confidence. I began to tell him about our escape from Danzig. As I tried to recall the anxiety I had felt, the fear and terror, I realized my outlook on the world had changed. I could tell my story only as a hilarious adventure. His presence had changed everything into bliss.

Manfred listened attentively. As a naval architect, he understood the DEUTSCHLAND's listing situation immediately. "The captain was a noodle," he said. "He didn't know what he was doing. He should go back to school and learn about stability."

"I always felt *you* should have been the captain."

"Better not. I'd have kept you in my cabin and forgotten where the ship was going." We laughed together, Lili rejoicing with us, so that passers-by looked with surprise at our merriment.

Soon, we arrived at the concert place. People were pouring into yet another old school building, which, after the destruction of the concert hall, served in its place. In the large auditorium, the audience of about two hundred sat on wooden benches. Manfred had Lili on his lap. The stage was slightly raised and without any decorations. The lid of the black grand piano was open.

When the tall, black-haired pianist walked out on the stage and bowed to the applauding audience, I leaned to Manfred. "This is the way a Chopin pianist ought to look. Hands large enough for Chopin's wide chords."

"He looks as pale as Chopin during his consumption," Manfred joked.

I submerged myself in the music. The pianist interpreted Chopin's music with charm and elegance, his technique clean. For me, classical music was the beauty of life, an intoxication unmatched by anything else. Knowing that Manfred felt the same way only magnified my pleasure. We sat hand-in-hand, feeling a wonderful current flowing between us.

When the pianist was in the middle of his last piece, the A-flat major Polonaise, the lights went out. But he continued playing. As he came to the passage where he had to jump back and forth in octaves, where every human being *must* look at the keyboard, the young Russian kept playing in the dark without hitting any wrong keys. He was phenomenal. After a seemingly endless time someone produced a candle, lit it and held it close to the keyboard.

But it wasn't needed any longer. The pianist had finished his program. The audience rose to their feet, applauding enthusiastically. "Bravo!" many shouted.

As we walked home, the night rainless for once, both Manfred and I were in high spirits. "It was wonderful," he said, carrying Lili. "All the music is still in my head."

"If anything is a candidate for the redemption of this mad world, it's music," I said.

"If one could only stop this war and replace it with music."

"Oh, I wish we could," I said. "Imagine. We're fighting the Poles and Russians, but tonight there was Polish music played by a Russian pianist. I wonder if anyone in the audience was thinking of national differences."

"There's hope in a world that makes music."

Back in my Spartan room, Manfred embraced me, held me close and kissed me. "Let's go to bed now," he urged. Melting under his desire, I forgot all except him. He put Lili to bed, right next to the wall so she couldn't fall out. He lay in the middle, I on the outside edge. "Lili," Manfred said seductively, "could you fall asleep quickly?"

Of course, she couldn't. Blue eyes big open, she sucked her thumb.

"God, I missed you," Manfred said, kissing me passionately.

"I missed you terribly," I gasped.

"How long has it been since we made love?" he asked.

"A year and a half. But it seems a hundred years ago."

Suddenly, the murderous up-and-down howling of the siren cut into our excitement. Louder and more obtrusive than ever. Right into our very marrow.

"*Verdammte Scheisse!*" Manfred cursed.

"So early tonight!" I shouted.

In a great hurry, we dressed and rushed along the block to the giant public shelter. Hundreds of hastily dressed women, crying children and calm-looking Navy people squeezed through the steel doors, everyone trying to be first. No sooner were we seated on the wooden benches than we heard the muffled sounds of dropping bombs. I took Lili in my arms as I did every night during the air raids. But tonight, I wasn't only a protector, I also was protected, in Manfred's arms. Happily, I leaned against his strength. Besides, I had come to realize this gigantic, reinforced concrete shelter was indestructible. Oblivious to the two thousand people around me, I held still as Manfred softly

caressed my cheek. A blessing, a gift from heaven. Even the
one-hour mass bombing was easier to endure with my beloved
man at my side. Then, the all-clear sounded and the crowd, tired
and relieved, began to walk out.

The night was lit by the fire of burning houses. In its
uncertain shine, dark-brown smoke wallowed over the skyline
of the intact buildings. Soldiers and civilians were clearing
narrow pathways through the ruins.

Back in our room, Manfred and I undressed, putting our
clothes into the corner. I saw Manfred forming his Navy coat
into the shape of a boat. "Can't you live without building ships?"
I asked, amused.

"I'm making a bed for Lili," he answered, putting his
daughter into the makeshift crib. As soon as he'd covered her
with my fur coat, Lili fell asleep.

If the night outside was lit by the fire of the burning houses,
so was this room filled with the flames of our unleashed passion.
Never before had I felt the intoxication of surrender and
exultation as in the remaining hours of this wonderful night. I
was a woman in love and blessed by being loved with the same
intensity.

Now my life could begin again.

IN LIMBO

We spent the rest of the night making love as if we could catch up on all the time we'd lost being apart. But before reaching the point of exhaustion we had to get up. Lili had wakened. "Thank you for not waking up," I said to her as I dressed her. With a sad smile, I turned to Manfred, "Do you *have* to go to Headquarters?"

"That's why they flew me out of St. Nazaire, my love." I resented the vibrancy of expectation in his voice.

Once on the street, he stopped a military truck and persuaded the driver, with American cigarettes, to drive Lili and me to the refugee camp. "I'll pick you up as soon as I'm through at H.Q.," he said. He kissed me quickly on the cheek.

I took Lili to the kindergarten, went to the barracks and became submerged in the world of refugees who were arriving in ever greater numbers. Besides Marie and me, there were now two other women interviewing the newcomers. I arranged with them to take over my work load when Manfred came to pick me up.

This time, I saw him as soon as he entered the dining hall -- swift commanding, his head erect, his wide Navy cap daredevil-slanted, his deep blue eyes radiating self-confidence -- a flagrant figure against the drab background of tattered refugees.

I turned to Marie. "I'm leaving now. I might not be back."

She nodded. "I know. Good luck, if I don't see you again."

Manfred and I walked out into the wintry-bare rye fields. The wind carried the scent of salt and seawater from the Baltic.

Feeling all the hope, the joy of being with him now, I asked: "Where are we going now?"

His eyes held mine for a moment before he said, "Here's my new order." He pulled the travel order from his pocket and showed it to me.

"IMMEDIATE ORDER TO START TECHNICAL MANAGEMENT POSITION AT SHIPYARD IN WILHELMSHAVEN," I read. I froze. He was not staying in Kiel but would move away from here. Without us.

"It's a pretty nice advancement," he said lightly. "I'll get one more stripe on my sleeve." I said nothing. "Wilhelmshaven is the largest naval shipyard," he said. "I have to supervise the outfitting of the new submarines. Wilhelmshaven is only 200 kilometers from Kiel." He put his arm around my shoulder and pulled me to him.

His touch instantly awoke me from my shock. "That means you're going to Wilhelmshaven, leaving Lili and me here in Kiel?"

He pulled me tighter to him. "You know you couldn't get permission to move -- or even visit me."

I struggled free from his arm and faced him. "And how long will this go on? How long must I wait this time?"

"Until the war is over, my love," he replied with a sad smile.

"The war! The war! We're always expected to sacrifice everything for the war. Do they know at Headquarters that wives and children exist at all?"

He took his travel order from me. "The country is at war, Eva," he said firmly. "We're soldiers first. No matter how we feel about our orders."

Authority! The mere concept aroused my rage. "Hitler commands and you blindly obey!" I shouted.

His face tightened. "We in the Navy don't follow Hitler's commands. We are the only armed force that is removed from him and we are proud of it. I'd never follow that Austrian corporal."

"Whose orders do you then follow?"

"Admiral Dönitz."

"Is he any better?" I asked contemptuously.

"He's the one who is responsible for rescuing you and Lili," he said calmly. "He stood up against Hitler's orders and directed all ships to stop fighting the Western Allies. Instead, he directed them to sail to the East to rescue millions of refugees, including you and Lili."

For a moment, I stood there, startled. Then my anger rose again. "It's men who cause the wars!"

He looked down at me. "You're not going to change tradition."

I clenched my fists. "I'm going to rebel!" I shouted. "Against the murderous tradition of war! Against its glorification. Against everyone who orders a war."

His face showed despair. He stretched out his hands, clutching my arms. "You can't do anything to eliminate wars, Eva," he said gently. "Not now and not in the future. Please be brave. I have to leave you now."

I slumped into his arms, feeling wretched and powerless. They're taking him away from me, was all I could think. "When do you have to go?" I asked.

"I just have time to say good-bye to Lili."

Silently we walked back toward the brick school building, his arm around my shoulder. I didn't know when and if I'd ever see him again.

In the kindergarten, he kissed Lili good-bye, then turned to me. In his dark-blue uniform coat, his broad cap shading his beloved face, he already seemed to belong to another sphere. How strange he could still reach me and take me in his arms! He squeezed me so hard it hurt, then kissed me, awakening the remembrance of last night's passionate love-making. "Soon we'll be together again, remember that, Little Bear," he said softly. I nodded, my throat tight.

He walked away, looked back at me and waved.

Our one-day reunion had ended.

Back in the barracks with Marie I saw the swarms of newly arrived women, children and scattered Army soldiers entering the reception office. Some had no coats, others were barefoot. "My God, half of East Europe is on the road," I said to Marie.

"No one wants to fall into the hands of the Russians," Marie replied.

A tattered Army soldier, whom I interviewed, confirmed Marie's remark. He was twenty years old, with a thin, intelligent face and observant gray eyes. "The ships can't take all of them," he told me. "I was the last one to climb up the fall net."

He was so outgoing, so overwhelmed by his experiences. "I'm glad you made it," I said.

"You should have seen what I've seen in Russia," he continued, his gray eyes wide open with horror, his blond hair falling into his tense face. "The SS have raged in the Ukraine like rabid dogs."

I was shocked. "For heaven's sake, man, be careful...." I looked around. Had anyone heard him? Had he forgotten at the front, that a remark like that could cost him his life?

Just then, the air-raid siren howled, its whining up-and-down pitch penetrating my very marrow. An air raid in full daylight! Lili! I dashed out of the barracks, toward the red-brick building. People ran with me, everyone in panic. "Quickly! Into the basement!" someone shouted.

In the entrance hall, I saw the kindergartners rushing toward the staircase to the basement. Lili was crying, frightened. I picked her up and carried her downstairs. Her bottom was wet. I carried her downstairs. "Mommy's here," I consoled her. "Everything's going to be all right."

The first arrivals had already lit a carbide lamp, and it spread a garlic-like odor throughout the basement. Its crude white light fell on milling people trying to find seats on the wooden benches. This was only a make-shift shelter. There was no safety here.

Someone waved to me. "Come here." It was the young Army soldier with the gray eyes. He moved aside to make room for me.

"Thank you," I said, smiling. I sat down, putting Lili on my lap.

Lili stopped crying. She rubbed her wet eyes, smearing dirt all over her small face. I wiped the round smudged cheeks with a handkerchief and kissed her. Lili took a deep sigh, stuck her thumb in her mouth and leaned against me.

The room was packed, people standing everywhere. I wondered about the civilian men in their thirties; men of that age were all at the front. What were they doing here? There was some sporadic talking, but even that stopped when we heard the first muffled sound of a bomb hit. Everyone in the basement fell silent.

Airplanes rumbled overhead, drowning out everything else. "Where's the anti-aircraft?" I asked the young soldier.

He shrugged. "They're out of breath ...."

Suddenly, I heard radio static and a man's voice. Looking up I saw one of the civilian men fumbling with the egg-shaped radio standing on the wall. I knew radios were often put into basements so people could listen to the reports on the air situation.

At first, I didn't understand the words. Then I recognized the familiar inflection. It was Hitler. The slightly raised pitch of his voice indicated the station was playing a record of one of his speeches.

"... The dead demand us to give our unconditional constancy, obedience and discipline to our Fatherland which is bleeding from countless wounds ..."

"...soon bleeding to death," the young Army soldier said cryptically to me.

An older woman with a turban turned to him, frowning. "Don't talk when the Führer speaks."

The soldier's face reddened. His eyes flashed rage. "Frau, if you knew what the SS did in the Ukraine --"

"Oh my God, keep your mouth shut!" I whispered to him.

Two of the civilian men rushed to him. "What about the SS in the Ukraine?" one of them asked in a sharp voice.

The hot-tempered young man shouted, "I've seen them kill --"

Before he could finish they grabbed his arms. "Shut up!" one of them shouted. "Gestapo. You're under arrest."

Instinctively, I stretched my hand out to protect the young man but at the last moment controlled the motion, holding back. I knew any word or gesture of camaraderie would jeopardize my own safety.

The woman with the turban held her head high in triumph. I saw the Gestapo men push their prisoner closer to the door as they waited for the end of the air raid. The young soldier showed no resistance. For a moment, I saw his thin face, lacerated with despair.

I felt like crying. Hitler's dramatic invocations continued but I didn't listen. Frantically, I thought of how I could help the young man who had escaped the Russians, only to fall into the hands of the Gestapo. At least he was silent now. I remembered how I had kept my mouth shut when the Gestapo summoned me years ago. Silence and resignation often paid. Help him, God, I prayed, to get him out of the claws of those henchmen.

Soon, the all-clear sounded and the crowd walked upstairs.

Outside, I saw the Gestapo men shove the young soldier into a small car and drive away.

From then on, the airplanes came day and night. Worn out by lack of sleep and constant fear in the unprotected camp shelter, I found myself irritated by the slightest nuisance. Lili broke a cup and I screamed at her. A refugee lamented too much and I scolded her. When Marie said, "The Americans are on the Rhine. They've taken Cologne," I snapped, "Oh, shut up!"

Then, in the middle of March, a young naval petty officer appeared at my desk in the dining hall and saluted me. "I have a letter for Frau Eva Krutein."

"That's me."

"Lieutenant Commander Krutein told me to deliver it to you personally." He handed me a thick envelope. "May I be dismissed, Madame? I have another urgent errand."

"Oh yes. Thank you." My heart pounded in my throat. What was in the envelope besides his usually short letter? Manfred wasn't a long-letter writer.

"Marie, please take over for a while. I've got to read Manfred's letter." I rushed over to the end of the long dining table and sat down, ripping open the envelope. Inside was a long, tightly written letter.

"Wilhelmshaven, March 29, 1945

"My beloved Eva,

"You may have been waiting for my letter for days. I could have mailed you a short note to tell you my new address here, but I have so much to tell you. I am now living at Banter Way 65, where I've rented a room in the apartment of a family Kalten. But this is unimportant compared to the rest of my news. I have put off this letter until I had courage enough to write.

"After I left the seclusion of Saint Nazaire, with its artificial atmosphere of protection, I was flown, as you know, to Stuttgart and then took a train north to Kiel. On that trip we passed many destroyed or still burning cities and I had my first painful awakening to the fact that what we are doing here in Germany is senseless; that we are already on the brink of losing the war."

How much had it taken him to write this! An officer admitting defeat!

"I don't know which shock was greater, the confrontation with our defeat, or the realization that something has pushed me toward the side of the defeatists. I couldn't cope well with all this and I tried to sweep it under the rug and escape into the joy of seeing you and Lili and being home again and tried *not* to see the war situation as it appears to be. Thanks to you and Lili I managed to block out the nagging thoughts successfully. Please, darling, forgive me for not telling you sooner, but I couldn't do it face to face."

I was moved by his humbleness -- how unusual for him.

"When I took the train to Wilhelmshaven, I expected it to arrive in four hours. Instead it took *ten*. The engineer had a radio and constantly listened to the air-situation report. Whenever enemy planes were announced, he stopped the train, sounded a hand siren and called everyone out of the train to seek cover in the fields. We all ran out to lie in trenches or under shrubbery. One time there was only one plane, sometimes two. They were flying so low we could clearly see the American emblems. This happened six times in the 200 kilometers from Kiel to Wilhelmshaven. The planes fired only two or three times, but the shocking thing was that our anti-aircraft guns didn't return the fire, although there were many around. Suddenly I realized there was no resistance because the guns had run out of ammunition. Our planes were grounded because there was no fuel. That was when I knew we had lost the war."

I closed my eyes, letting the letter sink to the table for a moment. Then I picked it up again.

"Lying in the trenches in the fields, I couldn't help but see very clearly, as one sees in the last minutes before dying, that everything was lost for us. The Rhine area is in American and British hands, the East is lost to the Russians, the cities are all destroyed and Germany's military power is almost completely paralyzed. Believe me, *Liebling*, this realization was harder than anything I have ever experienced in my life. All my faith, my efforts, my personal sacrifices were totally without sense and meaning, a waste, maybe even a wrong-doing. Knowing that the majority of the German people still have to go through this

transformation is not a consolation. It makes it even harder, sort
of multiplies the burden. I don't know if I'll ever get over this
horrible feeling of being defeated, worthless, discarded."

I stopped reading because I couldn't see the words any longer.
I wiped my eyes and nose with my sleeve.

"I feel sorry and helpless for having to drag you with me into
hopelessness and resignation. I know you depend so much on
my judgment and my trust in politics. You never bothered much
with politics, and as soon as we committed ourselves to each
other, you left our political views to me. I believed we would win
-- to be positive is still expected of all of us. I can't tell you how
it saddens me to shatter your world, my love."

I clutched the corner of the table as if it were a life saver.

"What I have to say now will even be more devastating than
all the rest. I don't know if the electricity is working in Kiel, so
you can listen to the news, but Russian troops are fighting in
Danzig. Two days ago a single heavy air raid destroyed 95% of
our beloved city."

"No!" I whispered. "Not Danzig!" Frantically, I kept reading.

"You'll never see the cathedrals, the wonderful Renaissance
buildings and the Medieval towers again. They're gone forever.
They say Danzig is a hell of smoking ruins. There's heavy street
fighting going on and it's predicted the city will fall within the
next few days. I only hope your parents escaped before the
destruction and are on their way to the West."

In my mind's eye I saw my home destroyed, my parents
homeless. Had they left in time? Were they still alive?

"*Verdammt*, in the middle of this dreadful war we have to
prepare for the future. There's probably very little time left until
the British enter Wilhelmshaven, Hamburg and Kiel. Although
we don't have to anticipate inhuman cruelties from them, as we
would from the Russians, a fighting army is a fighting army.
They shoot to kill. You must protect yourself and Lili! Try to get
out of the city into open country, Eva. Get away from the street
fighting. If you hear of women and children evacuating to the
countryside, report for it immediately. The countryside *is* safer.
Should fighting troops approach wherever you are, don't stay in
the house. Dig a hole in the ground, deep enough for yourself
and Lili to hide in as long as necessary. Not only do you have to

protect yourself from the enemy but also from our own retreating soldiers. Hitler has ordered all retreating soldiers, on penalty of death, to leave nothing standing. That means they have to burn all bridges and buildings to delay the defeat. The rule of the day is survival. Do whatever you must to survive this awful war. It can't last too much longer. *Be sure to get out of Kiel immediately*!

"My treasure, how I yearn to be with you. I love you so much. Please, please, take care of yourself and Lili! All I can do is write you this miserable letter. God, how I wish I were there.

"I take you in my arms and kiss you.

Manfred."

My hands let the letter sink to the table. The words I had just read droned through my head, growing to shouts of horror. I covered my ears, but the shouting continued. I felt as if someone had cut the ground from under my feet and I was losing my balance. The war was lost; my home destroyed; my parents' fate uncertain; worst of all, Manfred, my symbol of a secure and powerful life, had lost his faith in the future. I managed to get up from the table and go out into the rain. There, I broke down, crying uncontrollably.

After a while I began to think of what I had to do -- again, it was just Lili and myself, without Manfred. The struggle for survival would go on. Clutching his letter, I walked back to the barracks.

OFF THE TRACK

WOMEN AND CHILDREN MUST LEAVE KIEL, the newspapers said. I read the headlines in Rogge's office. "Where do we go this time?" I asked.

The one-armed supervisor held his pencil upright. "To the countryside. After all, Schleswig-Holstein is our richest province, agriculturally. In the country it's easier to feed two million refugees." Our exodus hadn't ended yet. "In the country you'll have quiet days and nights," Rogge said. "No air raids." Unimaginable.

Next day, the train took me, Lili in her buggy, and hundreds of other refugees from Kiel into the flat open country of Schleswig-Holstein, Germany's northernmost province which bordered on Denmark. After 40 kilometers of riding west through flat country with rye fields and woods beyond, the train arrived at a hamlet and spilled out its horde of women and children. A lame young man with a swastika band around one sleeve approached us. "Follow me," he said.

We began to march. The mild spring air smelled of moist soil. I breathed a deep sigh of relief when I saw wide green meadows with grazing cows -- the famous black and white Holsteins. How refreshing to see live creatures after the depressing atmosphere of ruined Kiel.

As the women trudged through the tree-lined dirt roads, past clean one-family homes, I heard the birds sing. Even a cuckoo, the mystical prophet of the aviary world, called from far away. I counted six calls, then it stopped.

"I counted six," a teenaged girl said. "Six years until I get married. "

It was traditional that the number of cuckoo calls tells you either how many years you have to wait to marry or how many years you will live. I didn't fit into either situation. Maybe I should treat the six calls as the months I would have to wait until I could see Manfred again. *Ach*, the cuckoo myth was nonsense like everything else we used to believe in.

Occasional troop trucks hurtled past, interrupting my gloomy thoughts.

One woman said, "This is where we have to hide out from the enemies when they attack the village."

"What's the name of the village?" another one asked.

"Buxheim," the swastika man replied.

I wondered if our migration would end here. Suddenly, I realized that we, the East Germans, weren't the only ones who had fled. Where had the French women gone when the German soldiers broke into their country, the Polish women who had tried to dig themselves into the soil but then had run away? And what had happened to the Russian women when the German troops suddenly fell upon their land? Those women had gone through their ordeal long before me. Had I ever thought of them? I remembered the young Army soldier whom the Gestapo had arrested. "The SS raged in the Ukraine like rabid dogs," he'd said. My God, what had they done? And then, what did I feel when our submarines torpedoed British ships with fleeing children? Who heard their cries in the icy waters of the North Atlantic? Who thought of their parents' despair? Who would ever give a thought to the German refugees? Or any refugees in the world? How long, oh God, would mankind continue to glorify war and its horrors?

"*Halt!*" The swastika-man stopped us. "The first woman in the row goes into *this* house." He pointed to a one-story home. One mother and her two children walked toward the house.

The troop marched on. From now on, they stopped at every house to release one mother after another. When we turned into another road, I read the sign: PETERSILIEN WEG -- Parsley Way. At number 3 it was my turn.

3 Parsley Way was a small white one-story house with the usual attic and a green pointed roof. The brown-framed windows had their shutters wide open as if inviting newcomers. In the tiny garden surrounding the house, crocuses and tiny leaves on the beech-trees showed the beginning of spring. I pushed the buggy toward the house and knocked at the door.

A small, portly woman in her forties, dressed in the old-fashioned style of village women, opened the door only a crack. Her gray eyes peered suspiciously out at me.

I swallowed, then said my name. "I'm supposed to stay with you. My child and I."

Without expression, the woman answered through the crack. "I have no room for you. I've already taken in my cousin and her husband. Go somewhere else." She shut the door.

I stared at the closed door. Nothing in my past had taught me how to react to doors closed in my face and being chased away. Helplessly, I turned around to the small group, which was still waiting. The swastika man, who had been watching the scene, limped to the peasant woman's door. "Frau Poppenbüttel," he called in a threatening voice. "I'll call the police if you don't let this woman and her baby in."

As if she'd been waiting for this threat, the landlady opened the door so that I and the baby carriage could enter.

Her straight blond hair was pinned up into a bun -- Schleswig-Holstein's common coiffure, matching her outmoded dress. "My cousin and her husband live up there in the attic," Frau Poppenbüttel said, resentment in her voice. She pointed to a spiral staircase, which led up into darkness. She ushered me through the dining room, where Hitler's large framed picture overshadowed the simple standard furniture.

We entered a small room. "You can use this," my new landlady said. It contained only a simple military bed and a chair. But it had one feature that surpassed luxurious furniture: a window to the back yard. A late birch tree stretched out its still leafless branches toward the window; it wouldn't be too long before its tiny toothed leaves would emerge. When Frau Poppenbüttel put a crib for Lili into my room I thought I could hardly wish for more. Otherwise she turned out to be a real Holsteiner who didn't communicate.

After my first night, pleasantly uninterrupted by air raids, I went into Frau Poppenbüttel's kitchen; I noticed a loosely crumpled newspaper in the garbage can. Smoothing it out, I read its date, April 19 -- three days ago. I read the headlines. "AMERICAN, SOVIET TROOPS CONVERGED AT ELBE, SHOOK HANDS ... BERLIN STILL UNDER HEAVY FIRE ... ROOSEVELT DEAD ... "

I looked up from the newspaper and out into the back yard. Fresh green leaves covered the shrubs and trees, wildly contradicting the hopeless war situation.

Above where the newspaper had been torn off, I read the words: " ... now, Americans will join the German forces, as the Führer has prophesied for years -- our great hopes are coming true ... "

I looked up as I saw a thin man walking down the spiral staircase. A gray felt hat half-covered his face. Frau Poppenbüttel's relative?

Down at my level, with sloppy posture, he barely overtopped me by one inch. His age seemed indeterminable. His face ran down to a point like an inverted triangle, his gray, fast-shifting eyes were constantly on the alert. The face of a movie thief, I thought, fascinated.

He tipped his hat upwards, revealing a low forehead. "'*n Morgen*. Are you the new one?" he asked.

I nodded, said my name.

He didn't say his. Dragging his feet, he entered the kitchen. "Where are you from?"

"Danzig. And you?"

"Cologne. Bombed out." His thumb pointed upstairs to the dark attic. "We live in that hole. Me and my wife."

With ease, I adjusted to his standards. "What's your name?"

"Albert." He picked up one of Frau Poppenbüttel's frying pans and returned to the spiral staircase. "If you're bored, come and see us."

"I will." As I watched him ascend the spiral I stood nailed to the spot, elated. I was invited! There was someone to talk to! The world looked much better now.

A few hours later, I picked up four potatoes from under my military bed and walked into the kitchen to start mine and Lili's evening meal. "May I use this pot?" I asked Frau Poppenbüttel, whose potatoes were already boiling over the coal fire. The landlady nodded.

"May I use this plate?" Again, nodding.

"May I use this fork?" Nodding.

Verdammt, I cursed silently. Is there any place in the world where I could get things for myself? Maybe Albert and his wife had some ideas. I took Lili's hand and walked up the spiral staircase in search for humans who talked. At the end of the dark attic with its steeply slanted roof I noticed a door and knocked.

"Come in," a woman's voice called.

When Lili and I walked in, I saw that the 20x20 "hole", as Albert had called it, really was nothing more than a wooden room with a slanted ceiling and a tiny window, cut out barely above the floor. Two single beds, placed in L-shape, dominated the room. An overweight matron with gentle brown eyes and tightly combed-back gray hair ending in a small bun sat on one of the two beds. Seeing us walk in, she got up with visible difficulty.

After introducing myself and Lili, I asked, "Are you Albert's wife? I met him in the kitchen the other day. He said I should come and visit you."

The woman nodded, smiling. "He told me. I'm Ida." She pointed to the bed. "Sit down. As you see, we have no chairs." I sat down and Ida walked to the corner, where a one-unit Bunsen burner stood on a wooden box. Beside the two beds and a wash stand in the other corner, this was their only furniture. "Come here, little girl," she called.

When Lili waddled to her, Ida took a sugar cube from a bag and gave it to the child. With lightning rapidity, Lili put the rare delicacy into her mouth.

"How do you say?" I asked.

"*Danke*," Lili answered, chewing.

"That was a great gift," I said to Ida.

The matron stepped over to the other bed and sat down. "Well, after we were bombed out in Cologne we learned to appreciate every little bit. My husband is so good, he brings in all kinds of things. I can't leave the house anymore. I'm too ill."

"I hope it's not serious?"

"My heart doesn't make it anymore. And nothing in here works." She patted her stomach.

"Do you have a doctor?"

She shook her head. "They all say the same. I should stay in bed. But how can I? One has to cook and wash ..."

"Do you get any help from your cousin?" I asked.

Ida's lips curved down. "That woman downstairs? She hardly remembers that we live up here. All she does is dig in her garden."

"Let me know if I can help you in any way," I said.

Steps came up the staircase. "I wonder what he brings home today," Ida said. "He always brings something."

The door opened and Albert walked in, carrying a huge cardboard box. His felt hat cast a shadow over his thin face. His alert eyes checked out the room. There was no greeting nor words of recognition. He put the box on a bed. Ida opened it carefully and took out one item after the other.

Amazed, I saw a hairbrush, a flashlight, a pair of children's shoes and a nice, fat, gray, mouth-watering liver sausage. Where did he get all this? None of these things were officially available.

As if he guessed my thoughts, Albert explained casually, "I exchanged them." Against what? There was nothing valuable in their room. Albert, still with his hat on, said to his wife, "I'm hungry."

Ida shuffled her feet to the corner with the Bunsen-burner and returned with half a bread loaf and a knife. Holding the loaf against her bosom, she sliced the bread with great skill. Albert took a pocketknife from his trousers and began to spread the slices with liver sausage; one for himself, one for Ida, one for me, one for Lili.

Instantly I felt part of the family. "I haven't seen *Leberwurst* for a long time," I said. It tasted as good as at home.

"Want some for tomorrow?" Albert asked me. Without waiting for my answer he cut off a thick slice of *Leberwurst*, put it on a slice of bread and passed it to me.

"A great gift," I said. "Thank you so much."

Carrying my treasure down to my room, I felt beside myself with joy. I'd made some friends who treated me as if I belonged to them, no matter the circumstances, no matter Albert's mysterious business. Both were just wonderful.

Soon after, Ida and Albert proved their friendship in another way. I discovered to my horror that Lili and I had caught lice from God-knows-where. Revolted, I felt like running away from myself. Instead, I ran upstairs to Ida.

The motherly matron wasn't horrified at all. "Don't worry about it. If you live in the country, this can happen." Calmly, she picked up a small bottle of kerosene from the corner. "Take this along," she said. "Rub a half-teaspoon-full into your hair. Also into Lili's. Wrap your heads up tightly and let the kerosene set overnight."

"And then?"

"That's it. The stench kills every living thing smaller than man."

She was right. Lili and I almost suffocated from the odor, but after that, my bear-brown and Lili's gold-blond hair were clean and shiny again. I felt reborn -- until my next ordeal when I suddenly developed several dozen festering boils on my body. Again, I asked Ida for advice. It was Albert who recommended I see the doctor in the nearby village for a prescription of rubbing alcohol for disinfection.

I followed his advice. After receiving the prescription from the doctor, I went, accompanied by Albert, to the local village store. When I asked for a small bottle of rubbing alcohol, Albert overruled me and ordered, "A big bottle!" The salesman filled a large bottle.

As we walked home I asked Albert why he wanted such a big bottle.

"For making *schnaps*," he said firmly. "I've got a good recipe."

At first I was startled. I might not need the whole bottle, but who would drink stuff made of rubbing alcohol? Suddenly, I saw the humor of the situation and my lust for adventure surged up, sweeping away my scruples. Why not? This was something new. Amused, I watched Albert hurry upstairs with more than half my rubbing alcohol. In my room, attending to my boils with the pure liquid, I could smell the narcotic aroma that spread through the whole house. Albert was brewing his *schnaps* in the attic. He allowed no one except Ida to watch him.

Next day, as I went up to help Ida with her household chores, Albert introduced me to his brew. "Drink it," he urged, seeing that I hesitated. "This isn't methyl alcohol. You won't get blind from it."

Finally, I brought myself to drink it. It tasted very sweet and had the biting sharpness of heavy liquor; only a faint smell of medicine reminded me of its origin.

By and large, the rubbing alcohol was a smashing success. My boils shrank, and Ida, Albert and I spent several enjoyable evenings of fun and laughter drinking *schnaps*.

Fully aware of my questionable company, I still rejoiced. My mother couldn't see me and lament about the horror of her fallen daughter, now friends with shady people. I thoroughly enjoyed Albert's and Ida's Rheinish lightheartedness. Besides, neither the natives of Schleswig-Holstein nor the refugees who were spread out over Buxheim promised to be as interesting as my new friends from Cologne. To hell with middle-class values! I found Albert's clandestine activities fascinating, even though I was almost certain they were illegal. He was my first real con man, and a very shrewd one at that. I decided, as long as he didn't pull tricks on *me*, I wouldn't judge him harshly.

A few weeks after we met, Albert stormed into the kitchen where Frau Poppenbüttel and I were peeling potatoes for the daily meal. "Come and help! I think Ida is dead!" he shouted, his face twisted in terror. We dropped everything and ran upstairs.

To my horror, I saw Ida slumped over her washboard, strangely motionless, a terrifying picture of helplessness. We carried her heavy body to the bed. "Go get a doctor," Frau Poppenbüttel told Albert, who stood helplessly between us, his teeth chattering.

Buxheim had no physician. So Albert would have to look in the nearby village for the doctor who had prescribed my rubbing alcohol. Until then, there was nothing we could do for Ida.

Two hours later, when the doctor arrived, he declared Ida dead; she had suffered a heart attack. I was heartbroken. I had lost a real friend. Ida's warmth, her camaraderie, this all had made me feel at home. Now, this motherly person was gone. Tenderly, I passed my hand over my dead friend's graying hair, silently saying farewell to her.

Albert cried vehemently -- a reaction I hadn't expected from this puzzling man. But the day of Ida's burial in the village cemetery, Albert was his old self again. He invited the neighbors who had attended the ceremony to a funeral banquet in Frau

Poppenbüttel's dining room. He obviously adhered to the old custom of pulling mourners out of their sadness and back to the joys of life. Indeed, the guests seated under Hitler's portrait feasted on six decorated cakes Albert produced, and his *schnaps* raised our spirits to unexpected heights.

The next day, I heard Albert rummaging in the attic. Bewildered, I went upstairs to see him sorting out Ida's few clothes. "I'm going to exchange them for better things," he told me. "You have first pick."

I didn't trust my ears. "How can you be so happy? Yesterday you cried."

He kept shuffling things around. "Oh, that was yesterday," he replied contemptuously.

I was angry. I hadn't exactly expected him to mourn for months, but his sudden change from grieving to trading was too much for me. I couldn't forgive him.

A few days later, he came home from one of his mysterious errands. "Hitler's dead," he said.

THE CHAOS

Hitler dead! Because of the way Albert said it --nonchalantly, almost incidentally -- I couldn't believe it. "Who said that?" I asked disdainfully.

"I know someone who has a radio. The radio said it."

"Rubbish."

"It's true. He shot himself."

"Why?"

"I don't know. Maybe he felt like it. There was a woman he married a few hours before."

"And you believe that nonsense?"

"Who knows?" Albert said lightly. "I never believe what the radio says anyway."

I was getting used to the idea. Somehow it sounded believable now, and my resistance vanished. I felt a sense of relief: the man who had kept all Europe under his jack-boots was dead. Would everything change now? Or had the destruction gone too far? Was Germany a sandcastle collapsing under the waves of invading soldiers?

I had one burning wish: if only the end of the war would come! Being without a radio, I felt suffocated in this isolated village. Even newspapers seldom reached Buxheim.

"Who will be Hitler's successor?" I asked Albert.

"I don't know," he said, "but who cares? They're all alike."

I yearned for a meaningful conversation. If only I could pick up a phone and call Manfred! Impossible. I knew his number but there was no phone in Buxheim. I had received two additional letters from him, telling me briefly about his new responsibilities at the shipyard. He directed the outfitting of the new submarines at a rapid pace, in a desperate effort to prolong and win the war. His life seemed so far removed from mine, not only geographically, but in life style as well. Gone were the enchanting hours in his arms, along with the hope of winning the war.

To my unpleasant surprise, a new element intruded on the silence of the house: Albert's whistling. Off-pitch and incessant, a torture for my ears. "What about this new habit?" I asked Frau Poppenbüttel, for a moment forgetting the woman's taciturnity.

For a change, the landlady gave me an answer. "It means he's up into something."

Before I could discover what he was up to, Albert played the role of messenger one more time. Passing through the kitchen, he interrupted his whistling, tipped his inevitable hat upwards, and said to me in his nonchalant way, "Guess what. The war is over."

I slumped into the kitchen chair. Nothing more profound came to my mind than to ask, "What day is it?"

He simply pointed his thumb toward the calendar at the wall and walked out, whistling. May 8, I read.

The war was over and lost, lost! But it was over. The killing had stopped, thank God in all eternity. But what would happen now?

Unable to cope with the uncertainties, I looked for Albert again. I found him with Frau Poppenbüttel in the dining room; they were removing Hitler's picture from the wall. My landlady was in tears. Like all the others who had seen the dictator as the answer to Germany's misery, a messiah, her life would now be without meaning.

Not so Albert. Although not whistling -- which I interpreted as a sign of respect for his relative's tears -- his body movements indicated alertness and excitement. Whatever his state of mind, he was still a reliable news reporter. "Do you know which troops have invaded our area?" I asked him.

"The British," Albert replied, suddenly whistling.

All right, the British. As long as it wasn't the Russians, the nationality of the invaders wouldn't make too much difference. "But now what?" I asked him.

He interrupted his whistling. "Back to business as usual." I wondered what his usual business was.

Soon I saw myself confronted with the most profound change of the era. On the day of Germany's surrender, all protection and organization vanished. Grocery-store shelves emptied overnight. The owners hid their merchandise because a supply no longer came in. The local people hoarded as much as possible. Because they owned their homes and lands, they were in a position to exchange clothes or hardware items for food. In one day, the peasants became the wealthiest people in the country.

The refugees had nothing to offer or exchange. "How can we survive?" they asked. But no one answered -- the authorities were gone. Every woman had to look out for herself, stretching out her meager stock as long as she could. So far, no one had physically suffered, there'd been sufficient food, although distributed with difficulty because of the unexpected two million refugees. Thank goodness, Lili's state of health was excellent. But for how long? Now, there was no milk for her.

One day, Albert knocked at my door and invited me to come to his attic. "I have company."

Upstairs, two strangers sat on Albert's bed. Both were young men in their twenties. One was very tall and already balding. The other was shorter and had a scar on his cheek. They didn't rise as I entered the room.

Albert said, "These are my friends." He mentioned no names.

"*Guten Tag*," I said, shaking their hands.

"*Dzien dobry*," both said in Polish. I looked at Albert in surprise.

He explained in his nonchalant way, "They're from the Polish prisoner-of-war camp. The minute we surrendered they were freed."

With a feeling of camaraderie I said in German: "Welcome to freedom."

"Uh?" the taller man said.

"Don't they understand German?" I asked Albert.

The bald Pole laughed. "Sure we understand," he said in German. "Have you ever met a Pole who didn't speak two or three languages?"

I sat down on the other bed and listened to their strange conversation. Albert spoke the dialect of Cologne and the Poles spoke German with Polish grammar and syntax. Nevertheless, they seemed to understand each other well. I learned the Poles were here to do some exchange business. Together with their freedom they had received large CARE packages from America. Now, they had more to eat than they could consume and so they were ready to enter the black market.

The conversation was interrupted when a Polish woman with a round Slavic face came up to tell them to hurry back to camp. The three Poles departed, leaving Albert and me alone.

One thing had become very clear: no one would care in Buxheim if Lili and I starved to death and Manfred might hear about it only six months later. So, our survival was up to me. "How can we survive?" I asked Albert.

"Go and loot!" he said.

"Loot what?"

"Army warehouses. Anything. Don't sit around here. Loot or go *kaputt*."

What a choice. Loot or Lili and I would be without food. Resolutely I decided to get out of the house and see what other people were doing for their survival.

With Lili, 19 months now, sitting in her indispensable baby carriage, I walked through the village. On the far side the flat green meadows, heavily dotted with yellow dandelions, expanded into the distance. I saw a huge barn and crowds of people. Some were walking away, dragging full sacks. One man even carried a mattress on his back.

"What is this building?" I asked a bystander.

"An army supply house," she said. "Yesterday, our army guards officially gave up the warehouses. Now, everything is unclaimed goods and there's no authority to stop us."

"Can you simply go in and take things?"

The woman shrugged. "I'm a refugee with nothing. Besides, if *we* don't take the stuff, the enemy soldiers will." As if encouraged by her own words, she entered the warehouse.

All my values fought against looting, but I had to feed Lili. I parked the buggy at the entrance, where other babies' vehicles stood, told Lili to stay there, and ran into the warehouse.

I stopped abruptly, staring at the chaotic scene. In the huge, barn-like building people climbed over trunks and crates, pulling things this way and that. Many items had been thrown to the ground and trampled. But the general mood was merry; it was as though everyone was playing a wild game at a party. I felt the mob's strange euphoria kindling my own lust for adventure and when I saw a staircase I ran upstairs. No one was there. An open box attracted me. It contained light-blue silky blouses reserved for the women auxiliaries who did signal duties. But there were no armed forces any more. If I didn't take them, the enemy would. The blouses were light and I took about two dozen of them. They were also slippery and I lost four of them on my way back to the baby carriage. The rest I threw into the buggy and started for home, jubilant. What could I receive in exchange for them? First of all, milk for Lili.

Never in my life had I taken anything that wasn't mine. But who was the owner of the blouses? An army that no longer existed? Who was the judge? There were no judges in a survival situation. Should Lili go hungry? No, and three times no! I would go on "looting" until law and order returned to the country.

Very quickly I adapted to my new career in "organizing," as the ambiguous activity was called. Always being around and keeping a sharp eye on what was happening were prerequisites for success.

Once, I pushed Lili in the baby carriage to a nearby village. A truck suddenly stopped in the middle of the street. Someone from inside opened the rear flap, and huge boxes marked "Oleomargarine" became visible. A man on the street quickly climbed up and threw the margarine boxes down to the people. "Hand *me* one!" I yelled at him.

He threw one to me.

The minute I had the heavy box in my arms, a man in a strange uniform shouted "Stop!" in English, raising his gun.

Everyone ran away, including me. I heard one shot. Clinging to the fervent hope that the soldier had aimed at the sky, I ran to the baby carriage. That's when I saw the five-tipped star on the truck. Oh yes, the British had come. I threw the box into the buggy, covering it with Lili's blanket.

She started crying. "Push your legs in, "I told her in a whisper and helped her to adjust to the new object in the buggy. Then I slowly walked away, playing the role of an innocent mother. I made it! We had food!

At home, I saw that the margarine box contained 20 pounds of American oleomargarine. Thank you, Lord, I prayed -- only to recall how Gypsies prayed to special saints before stealing. What had become of me? But "organizing" wasn't the same as stealing. I had to survive. For Lili. For Manfred. No, I would not think of it as stealing. It was survival.

And so, working day by day, I soon had a nice supply of food, top quality military clothes, even a small carpet and a radio. "The radio isn't working," I complained to Albert.

"Didn't you say your husband is an engineer? Let him fix it later."

Albert had an even more flourishing trade than mine going. With the help of his Polish friends he supplied the attic with every imaginable piece of merchandise. One day he said to me, "Tomorrow we'll have lots of chicken."

"How's that?"

"The Poles know of some peasants who are hiding their chickens."

"How will the Poles get the chicken?"

"Somehow," Albert replied and walked away.

I forgot the conversation as Lili and I retired for the night. The June evening was warm and I opened the window wide to let the spicy scent from the garden flow in. The room was on the ground floor and my bed next to the window. Now, in midsummer, darkness lasted for only two hours. A soft wind soughed through the trees, crickets chirped and a dog barked in the distance. Soon I fell asleep.

Suddenly a noise woke me. Horrified, I saw a man hovering on the sill of my open window, his stooped body silhouetted clearly against the faintly growing light. He carried a sack on his back. "Watch out," he whispered. In one leap he jumped over my bed and made it to the door, which was unlocked as usual. He opened it carefully and vanished.

I sat bolt upright in bed, my legs shaking. What was going on? And suddenly I knew; one of the Poles had stolen the promised chickens. That explained his behavior. Everything had happened so fast and so silently that Lili hadn't awakened. What had I become? An accomplice of thieves? What about the peasants who had lost their chickens? How far would I allow myself to go in this time of survival? I lay down and eventually went back to sleep.

I woke up hearing unusual activity in the house. Then, a knock at the door and Frau Poppenbüttel calling my name.

"Come in," I called.

The landlady stepped in, beaming. "Do you want to can chicken?"

I hadn't my senses quite together yet. "What chicken?"

"Albert's Polish friends brought lots of chicken last night. We can't eat them all, but I have lots of preserve jars. You can have some."

I jumped out of bed. "But I don't know how to can."

"Never mind. You pluck them, I'll can."

A new adventure. I hurried to get myself and Lili dressed. A little later, we joined our landlady and Albert in the kitchen.

His inevitable hat shadowing his triangular face as usual, Albert ordered all doors and shutters locked. The electricity wasn't working yet, so we worked by candle light, although the sun outside was shining brightly. These particulars only heightened the excitement of preserving our purloined chickens.

There were sixteen birds, dead and cold. Albert helped me pluck while Frau Poppenbüttel did the canning. We filled eighteen jars, closed the lids tightly and divided them among ourselves. A sudden thought sprang into my mind. "And the Poles get nothing?" I asked.

Albert made a contemptuous gesture with his hand. "They have plenty of food."

I was confused. "Why then did they steal the chickens?"

"Out of revenge, maybe," he replied lightly.

I felt a sharp stab in my stomach. This wasn't "organizing" anymore or even looting. The Poles were not starving. This was plain stealing. And I had been part of it. That's when I realized I had overstepped the threshold from the acceptable to the unacceptable. My dissolute life style must come to an end.

When my six jars were safely in my room, I said to Albert, "This is the last time I do business with the Poles. Don't count on me any more."

He stared at me for a moment with a calculating look, shrugged, tipped up his hat, which was more soiled than ever, and without saying a word, ascended the spiral staircase that seemed to coil around him like a snake.

Suddenly, I felt very alone.

TOWARDS A REUNION

We heard rumors that a profound change had occurred in Germany, maybe in the whole of Europe, but in Buxheim, we were cut off from the world. Heated discussions were going on everywhere. "We'll have another war soon," some said. "This time we will fight with the British and Americans against the Russians."

"*Verdammt, nein,*" others said. "Germany will be dismembered and assigned as war loot to the Russians, the British and the French."

"And the Americans will take nothing?"

"They're still at war. With Japan." At least, *we* had the war behind us.

If I could only talk to Manfred! I dreamed of going to the shipyard where he reigned over 1,200 subordinates. The shipyard was his empire and I longed to be one of his subjects.

I took Lili's hand and walked into Frau Poppenbüttel's tiny back yard. It was a balmy day, and I delighted in the azure blue sky, the comfortably warm July sun on my skin. I inhaled the garden's sweet smells of jasmine and honeysuckle and listened to the melodious symphony of birds chirping, warbling, and trilling, celebrating the glorious day.

Lili ran to the small sandbox to play with a battered tin cup and a rusty teaspoon. I joined her. Soon we were deeply involved in sand play, building castles and moats, filling and refilling the moats with water from a bucket.

"Let's find some 'trees' for the 'woods'," I said. Looking around I saw the berry shrubs -- red currants, gooseberries and raspberries, all ready to be eaten. I picked some. Lili popped them into her mouth by the chubby handful, smearing the red fruit juice all over her face. As I cleaned her up with the water of the castle moat, the ancient nursery song of the toadstool popped into my head. I sang it to her:

"*Ein Männlein steht im Walde,*
ganz still und stumm.
Es hat aus lauter Purpur
ein Mäntlein um.

A little man stood in the woods,
quite still and mute.
He has a little coat of pure
bright crimson on."

As I sang, yellowhammers, blackbirds and finches chirped along.

The concert was suddenly interrupted by Frau Poppenbüttel's voice from the house. "It's so warm. We should wash today so the clothes will dry quickly."

"You're right," I called back without any enthusiasm. "I have to wash my bed sheets. Do you want to be first?"

"You can be first. I'll get the fire started."

While the landlady started up the coal fire, I put the washtub onto two chairs in the garden and started scrubbing on the washboard. I used the American lilac-scented soap I'd traded with the Poles.

The soap reminded me of Albert and the Poles. Albert had returned to Cologne. The Polish camp had been dissolved. I only hoped they were able to return to Poland.

Half-way through the wash, I heard a noise at the garden door. Looking up I saw a tall, lean man come in. His cap cast a shadow over his eyes; his pants and shirt were a mismatch. He held a letter in his hand. "*Guten Tag*," he said, "I'm looking for Frau Eva Krutein."

A messenger from Manfred! I approached the man, rubbing my wet hands on my skirt. "It's me."

"I'm *Kapitän* Horten from the buoy carrier SYLT." We shook hands.

"I bring you a letter from your husband."

I tore open the letter. It was short.

"Dearest Eva,
"Checking the list of outgoing ships this morning, I discovered one sailing to Schleswig-Holstein to pick up buoys. I asked *Kapitän* Horten if he could bring you and Lili to Wilhelmshaven on his return. He readily agreed. Hurrah! I'll have you here within a few days. Can hardly wait. Have a good trip.

    Love, Manfred."

Overjoyed, I looked at Horten. "When?"

"Tomorrow morning. We'll have to walk to the harbor. Can you be ready by 5:30?"

"Can I!"

After he had left I excitedly returned to the garden. The sheets were hardly washed at all. *Zur Hölle mit ihnen*, the hell with them. I took them out of the water and threw them over the fruit shrubs which usually served as drying racks. The sheets were still dripping soapy water, but I thought: I don't care if Frau Poppenbüttel has to wash them again or if the wind blows them all over Schleswig-Holstein. Out of here and off to Wilhelmshaven!

Suddenly, a shock curbed my euphoria. How would I carry my accumulated stuff to the ship? Simply bribe the hostler across the street; he had a horse cart. As usual in emergencies, my brain worked at its best. Rummaging through my booty I came across a man's felt hat, old fashioned and of uncertain color; I'd traded one of the two dozen silk blouses for the hat and a towel. Now I'd bribe the hostler with it. With a few pops and puffs I made the hat acceptable and ran over to the stable.

The hostler, tall and stoop-shouldered, was brushing his horse. "*Guten Tag*," I said.

He turned around. His deeply wrinkled face could have been a model for an artist painting an allegory of drudgery. "'*n Tag*," he answered.

"Giving your horse a good treat?" He nodded. "How about yourself?" I asked, starting my enticement.

He gave me a dull look. "Uh?"

"How'd you like to have this hat?" I felt like a siren. "I think you'd look very handsome in it."

He stared at the puffed-up hat. Should I put it on his head? No, then he couldn't see it. So I put it on my own head, slightly slanted, knowing all hats looked good on me.

He had enough sense to realize it, too. A faint glow rose in his eyes.

"See?" I smiled and turned in front of him like a model. "You'll like this, too."

"Can I try it?"

"Sure." I took the hat off and put it on his head. He looked like a clown in a circus. The dignity of his lined face had become a caricature.

"What do I look like?" he asked.

For a second I hesitated. What would Albert say, my teacher in survival? "Great," I lied.

The hostler grinned. "What d'ye want for it?"

"Could you take me and my stuff to the harbor tomorrow morning?"

He nodded. "What time?"

"5:30 AM."

"All right. Cart and horse will be ready by then." He beamed with pride.

"Thank you," I said. I didn't even know his name.

I went to look for Frau Poppenbüttel. I found her in the dining room, abandoned like an orphan, before the empty spot on the wall where Hitler's picture had hung.

I interrupted her vigil: "I came to say good-bye. My husband has sent me a ship to Wilhelmshaven."

Without expression she looked at me. "Oh," she said, relief in her voice. We shook hands.

Sleeping without an alarm clock was a rather difficult matter. Fearful of oversleeping, I woke up every half hour. Still, I was ready for the departure on time. At 5:30 the horse cart stopped in front of the house. *Kapitän* Horten had also arrived exactly on time. German punctuality hadn't changed a bit.

The captain seemed bewildered when he saw the many cardboard boxes to be moved onto the cart. His eyes widened. "I thought you were a refugee?"

"I traded a few things," I murmured.

He watched in disbelief as the hostler loaded boxes, items wrapped in blankets, suitcases, a mattress (traded for two silk blouses), a radio and Lili's baby carriage, which was packed like a stuffed egg.

I disregarded Horten's astonishment and lifted Lili up to pet the horse. Actually, this was an excuse to pet the horse myself. I seldom resisted caressing a furry animal.

Sandwiched between the two men, with Lili on my lap, I watched Schleswig-Holstein's landscape pass by for the last

time. The fields that had just begun to sprout when I arrived
three months ago, had now transformed themselves into a green
and yellow chessboard, abounding in fertility. Green stood for
potato fields, covered with fully grown plants, and yellow for the
rye, swaying in the ever-present West wind and sending off its
cereal scent. The beech trees were heavy with dense foliage and
had become much-desired shelters from the sun at midday.

Singing birds were everywhere. I listened for a cuckoo call.
Would the legendary bird prophesy my future? And there it was
-- calling only once. One year or one day until I would be reunited
with Manfred. Tomorrow I would be in his arms.

HURDLES

After a long day's tempestuous sailing over the raging North Sea, the small buoy carrier at last moored at the berth in Wilhelmshaven.

Relieved, I stepped onto the quay -- a broad, flat place with a jumble of oversized lampposts, a control tower and a small cottage. The sun had just vanished below the horizon. Ruffled by the wind, a few scattered trees looked like forgotten stage decorations in a shut-down theater. No human being was in sight. Lili and I were alone on the deserted wharf. It was only 9:30, not too late to call Manfred's number. Still a little seasick, hand-in-hand with Lili, I approached the cottage in hope of finding a telephone.

"Stop!" The English command immediately made me turn. A British soldier was pointing a gun at us.

"No!" I screamed in terror. Frantically, I turned my back to him and crouched to protect Lili. Was there still war here? Why didn't he shoot? Had he gone?

"What are you doing here during curfew?" I heard him shout -- the first English words I had heard since high school. "Get up! Turn around!"

I rose and turned to him, pressing Lili against my legs. In horror I saw his gun still pointing at me. In the uncertain twilight I couldn't make out his face.

"What are you doing here during curfew?" he shouted again.

"Curfew starts at ten. It's only half past nine." To my surprise I found the right words in English.

"Curfew starts at half past nine," he snarled back. "I could shoot you, you know that?"

My ear, sharpened by the tension, registered a slight diminishing of his threatening tone. Maybe he wouldn't shoot.

In fact, he lowered his gun.

I quickly took my stand. "I'm coming from Schleswig-Holstein. Curfew starts at ten there."

"I have to take you to the military police," he said calmly. His greenish-brown fatigues were very different from German soldiers' uniforms in shape and color, but equally proper and unobtrusive. Yet his wide smooth cap sat slightly slanted on his head, projecting boldness and frivolity -- almost as daring as Manfred's.

As we walked down the quay, the soldier asked casually, "Does your baby like chocolate?"

"Oh yes," I answered mechanically.

He pulled from his pocket a chocolate bar, wrapped in aluminum foil, and gave it to Lili.

Surprised by his change of behavior, I looked sideways at him. Our eyes met.

"Did I scare you?" he asked.

I realized my advantage. "Yes, you did."

"I'm sorry." He sounded really sad. "Your English is very good," he added, obviously trying to keep the conversation going.

"You're very polite. Are all Englishmen polite?" What in the world do you talk about with a victorious enemy soldier who's arresting you?

He ignored my question. "Where did you want to go when you left the ship?"

"To my husband."

At this moment, we arrived at the cottage which apparently served as the British military police-station. My new friend motioned us in.

Three blond young British soldiers sat at a long table covered with office paraphernalia and one telephone at each end. The men looked relaxed, almost bored. When they saw Lili and me they leaned forward with obvious interest.

My guard told my story to his apparent superior, a blue-eyed petty officer with a friendly face.

How similar they all looked; each of them tall, slim, blond -- and relaxed. My God, they were in uniform; they should be stiff, impersonal and deadly serious. That's what I was used to. They seemed to be discussing the situation, but I couldn't always follow.

Lili's face was totally smeared with chocolate. She smiled at her new friend. Obviously charmed by her, he said, "She's cute," and produced another candy bar.

Lili grabbed it with delight. And for a moment, I forgot that Britons and Germans only recently had killed each other by the hundred thousands.

The petty officer turned to me. "How long has it been since you've seen your husband?"

"Five months," I replied, alarmed. Why did he ask that?

"What's his address?" he asked again.

"65 Banter Way," I answered hesitantly. A discussion followed, unintelligible to me.

The petty officer turned to me again. "We'll take you to your husband right away."

I was sure I misunderstood. "Pardon me?" I stammered.

"It's against the rules," he continued, "but if you haven't seen your husband for so long we don't want you to wait any longer." He looked through the open door. "It's getting dark." He turned to my guard. "Be careful." And to me, "Good night, madam."

I couldn't move.

"Anything else, madam?" the petty officer asked.

You're so wonderful, so noble, I wanted to say. You're not an enemy, you're a friend. War is the greatest crime in the world; we should never have one again. Tears came into my eyes. I searched for English words but this time I found none. But the petty officer must have perceived my silent message. He nodded and smiled as if he understood.

Outside, twilight was already turning to darkness as we left the military station and went back to the buoy carrier to inform *Kapitän* Horten. I thanked him for the trip.

"Lucky lady," Horten said warmly, as we shook hands. "Do you have all your things together?"

If my British companion was surprised at the mound of clutter he was supposed to transport, he didn't show it. Instead, he put two fingers against his teeth and produced a loud whistle.

A military truck which hadn't been there before drove closer to the gangway. My guard talked briefly to the driver who jumped out to open the rear of the vehicle. Then he started hauling my booty and the carriage from the boat to the truck while my guard lighted the scene with his flashlight. When everything was stowed away, there was just enough room on a bench for Lili and me to sit.

The guard said to me in a lowered voice, "Madam, you've heard this before, but what we're doing here is against the regulations. We'll take you home on one condition. You have to keep absolutely silent. We have to cross two bridges and pass two military controls. Any noise from the inside of the truck and we'll all end up in jail." He left to join the driver.

I sat in the darkness, filled with gratitude and excitement. Holding Lili tight, I listened to what happened outside. The truck stopped -- apparently the control point at the first bridge. English voices, short questions and answers I couldn't make out. Silence. I visualized papers being checked. "All right," I heard. A few more words and laughter. How they all joked and laughed on duty. I'd never seen any German man in uniform, military or Party official, smile -- let alone joke while on duty. As a matter of fact, I'd always identified deadly seriousness as a condition for effort and achievement. But the joking British had won the war and the serious Germans had lost it.

At the second bridge, I heard the same sequence of conversation, silence, "All right," jokes, laughter, then departure.

After a seemingly endless ride in the darkness, the truck stopped. My guard opened the door. "This is Banter Way. What was the number again? 65?" I nodded.

He let his strong flashlight play over the house numbers. Then I saw the number. "Over there's sixty-five!" I burst out. I jumped down and took Lili out.

The guard walked us to the three-story row house. It was midnight and the door was locked. The soldier let his flashlight go over the name labels and bell-buttons. None bore Manfred's name. "Which one?" the Briton asked me.

"I don't know."

"I'll ring all of them." With the butt of his gun he pushed every button twice. I heard different bell pitches all over the house. Lights went on, windows opened.

An idea flashed through me. I whistled the motif from Beethoven's Fifth Symphony -- Manfred's and my identification whistle.

We waited. Then the door opened and a slightly different Manfred stood before us.

UNITED

Astonished, I saw my husband turned into a civilian. Without a uniform, he no longer represented the State. His aristocratic appearance, his well-shaped face and figure were the same, but his posture had slightly, very slightly, stooped and his smile had lost its overwhelming radiance.

I heard the British soldier say, "I'm bringing you your wife."

Manfred bowed politely to the Briton and said in English, "I'm much obliged..." It was the first time I heard him speak English! Even his language had changed.

How different this Manfred was from the lighthearted, confident Naval officer I'd dreamed of for so long. I turned to my guard. "Thank you so much, sir."

"I'll help your husband with the luggage," the soldier said. Both men went to the truck and hauled my numerous boxes, sacks, blankets, suitcases, mattress, radio and baby carriage into the house and upstairs to the landing of the second floor where Manfred had a rented room.

"Would you like to come in?" I asked the two soldiers-turned-movers, trying to keep them around a little longer.

"I'm sorry, madam," answered my guard, "but we aren't allowed to enter German residences."

Disappointed, I said, "I understand. But thank you so much for your help."

"Our pleasure, madam." They saluted me and left. I saw them walk downstairs and felt sorry to see them go. Weren't these my friends who were leaving? I hesitantly closed the door and turned around.

And there he was: the object of my long desire, my husband and friend, my lover of one precious night four months ago. I rushed into his arms. He held me tight and kissed me longingly. "I've been waiting so long!"

I inhaled his clean, sweet scent. "And I, I've been counting the weeks, the days, today, the hours." I looked up at him. "Your eyes still have the color of the sky."

He hugged me tighter, brushing my cheek with a kiss. "And you look beautiful. Enchanting. Radiant." He mocked a thorough search of my hair. "Is the thick fur still there? And the green dots in your eyes?"

I chuckled. "They survived the war."

Smiling, he released me to lift Lili high up above his head. "My little Lili has become a big girl, but she's still the most beautiful girl in the world." Lili wiggled with joy.

I rejoiced. I'd been wrong, very little had changed. His warmth, his charm, his tenderness were enchanting me again, making it easier for me to face the poverty.

As we carried my booty into our room, Manfred asked, "How in the world did you get all this stuff?"

"I looted and traded."

Stowing away my many boxes, he said, "We'll leave your stuff right here in the corner. The mattress comes in handy; Lili can sleep on it. We have no furniture to put things in. I didn't know you'd bring this much stuff with you."

I looked around. The room was sparsely furnished, but it looked acceptable. Two single beds, a bare table with two chairs, and a small bookcase filled with books. White lace curtains hung over the windows -- a sight that transported me back into pre-war times.

"The furniture belongs to our landlady," he explained. "By the way, three bombed-out families live in this apartment in addition to the landlady and us."

"Kind of a mass meeting, right?"

Soon we put Lili, already half asleep, on the mattress. He sat on a chair, pulled me on his lap and kissed me passionately. Shivers of excitement swept through me. Gently, he said under his breath, "Let's wait a bit until Lili is in a real deep sleep."

I got up. "You're right." I sat down opposite him on the other side of the bare wooden table. Curiously, I looked at Manfred's dark blue civilian suit. "Where did you get that?"

He laughed. "Don't you recognize it? It's my old Navy uniform. Minus the stripes and gold buttons." I stared at the black buttons. "I carried a suitcase for an old lady and she gave these to me. Times change, buttons change."

"What happened to your dagger?"

His face froze. "All weapons were supposed to be delivered to the enemy." How hoarse his voice had become! "But like most officers I threw the dagger into the North Sea. To avoid the humiliation of the delivery." His eyes studied the bare table top, his face an unreadable mask.

"What happened at the shipyard when the armistice came?" I avoided the hated word "surrender."

His face lit up. "No problem and very little change. Armistice happened on a Tuesday. On Wednesday, the British came into the shipyard and told us to go on with what we were doing. Instead of reporting to a German admiral, I reported to a British commodore."

"That was all?"

He shrugged. "Yes."

"You didn't mind the change of superiors? From German to British?"

He shrugged again. "Why should I? I speak English. No trouble understanding the new boss." His voice sounded as though it were just an everyday matter. Did he take the lost war so lightly? His long letter three months ago had sounded so different from the way he talked now.

He got up. "Let's go to bed right away." We hurried to undress and turned off the light.

Where our lovemaking four months ago had been wild and carefree, so this night's encounter was filled with tenderness and gratitude for being alive. I intensely felt that we were walking hand-in-hand into a somber future, prepared to take its hurdles together.

Meanwhile, Lili, 19 months old, had developed into a smart, lively toddler. She was cheerful, healthy and able to play with whatever was around. There were no dolls, no toys. All she had were chestnuts I had found on the street. She never tired of moving them from one box to another. Besides playing with the chestnuts, Lili and I used the furniture as toys. The table, laid upside down, became a car; the two chairs, put side by side, became a tunnel. Lili's cheerful nature made it easy on all of us.

She also was eager to learn new words.

One day, I stood waiting for the butcher shop to open. The row houses in whose shadow we stood were an island in an ocean of rubble. For long stretches, I could see only ruins; their irregular, ugly shapes projected into the clear sky in disturbing contrast.

Lili, practicing her new running skills, dashed back and forth along the queue. I stopped her running, took her hand and entered the seductively fragrant realm of the butcher.

A row of gray, pink and red sausages of different sizes hung on hooks from an iron band. I bent down to Lili, pointed to the sausages and said, "*Wurst.*" I was sure Lili's mouth was watering just like mine.

The butcher with his huge belly under a blood-smeared apron was the absolute master of his exclusively female customers. His opulent appearance showed there was no meat shortage in his home. Yet this was his shop, not his home.

I passed my meat coupons to him. "*Wurst*, please."

Majestically, he shook his head. "You've already used up your sausage coupons for the month."

Verdammt, I hadn't noticed. "Then some meat, please."

He supported his weight on his hands on the empty counter. "I haven't had meat for weeks." Now what? "Want some bones and udders to make a soup?" the blood-smeared master asked. "No coupons necessary."

So I took the bones and udders home, added potatoes and simmered them for three hours. I got a relatively good soup, as good as *Wurst*.

That night, we were getting ready for bed and Manfred stood naked for a moment.

Suddenly, Lili pointed at him and called out with delight, "*Wurst! Wurst!*"

Manfred hastened into his pajamas.

While Manfred was more than busy at the shipyard, overseeing the proper repair of the ships and often bringing home stacks of work lists, working on them into the night, I felt unchallenged and yearned to do something besides housework, standing in line and reading the landlady's books in our room. Three months after the armistice, public life had come to a standstill. No mail, no buses in service, no libraries or theaters open.

One evening in August, when Lili was already asleep on her mattress, Manfred and I sat at the small table. He had brought some papers home from work. The window was open, and the white lace drapes waved in the mild summer breeze, fanning in the salty aroma of the North Sea.

"What are you reading?" I asked.

He looked up, bewildered. "Work lists."

"What work lists?"

"Items for the repair of mine sweepers. They're coming in tomorrow." His eyes returned to the papers.

I knew the shipyard was his sacred world. "Can I visit your shipyard?"

He looked at me, probably saw the restlessness in my eyes and pushed his work lists aside. "There isn't much to look at besides the ships you can see in the harbor. Or is there something else you want?"

"Maybe just talk. Can't we go out for a walk?"

We left the door open, so the co-tenants could hear Lili if she should awake. We began to walk in the mild summer night, carefully avoiding the heaps of rubble and the holes in the street.

"At the shipyard, have you heard anything about Danzig?" I asked. "Will it become Polish?"

He put his arm around my shoulder. "It already has."

I had feared it all along. The Poles had finally received what they wanted for years, but what would the mountains of rubble mean to them now? Oh God, where were my parents now?

"There's something else extremely important," he said. "The Americans have dropped an atom bomb on Japan."

I forced my mind onto the other side of the world. "They're still fighting in the Pacific?"

"That's not the point. Imagine, one single bomb was able to kill hundreds of thousands of people at once. This is technology applied for political purposes on a scale unheard of." His voice sounded agitated.

"Misery everywhere, without end."

"But this atom bomb may bring the war to an end."

We were walking among the frightful ruins. It wasn't dark yet; we still had long hours of daylight. Only a few people strolled through the streets. The night breeze fanned a sweet scent around us, which came from trees and shrubs that had survived the destruction. I inhaled the aroma as if it were life-giving.

As we passed by a half-destroyed church, I saw a white poster on its wall. Hungry for something to read I walked closer. It was a Catholic church announcing its services. I glanced over the poster and discovered on the bottom a notice:

"Choir rehearsal, Tuesday, 7:30 P.M.
Anyone interested in singing is invited
to attend. On Christmas, choir and
orchestra will perform Mozart's Great
Mass in C minor."

I was thunderstruck. Mozart's C-minor Mass! I'd sung it in a concert performance in Danzig when I was sixteen. As if someone had turned on a record player I heard the double chorus in my head: "*Qui tollis peccata mundi*. Who taketh away the sins of the world." The music rang around me and enlivened me. I turned to Manfred who had read the announcement too.

"It sounds good. You're thinking of joining, aren't you?" he asked, smiling.

"I don't know yet. You never know how good these church choirs are. It all depends on the choir director." Maybe the choir director would be good. Then I would be back in the music world. I made sure to remember the time. Tuesday, 7:30. Two more days.

I felt Manfred's arm around my waist. "I can hardly wait till Tuesday," I said.

MUSIC!

Ten minutes early, I stood, excited and impatient in front of the bombed red-brick church. Its large Gothic entrance and side towers showed only minor damage while the massive main tower protruded like a useless broken pencil into the blue evening sky.

I saw people pass by the damaged church and enter the adjacent brick-red two-story building. Probably that's where the parochial activities took place. I stopped a middle-aged man, asking for the choir room.

"In the rectory, first floor," he answered. "I'm going there myself." I followed him.

In the rehearsal room about fifty chairs were lined up for the choir members. Some singers had already arrived and stood around chatting with each other. I saw an upright piano against one wall. In front of it, a tall, skinny young man thumbed through some sheet music -- apparently the choir director. In his worn-out clothes, he looked rather dilapidated, but his curly brown hair and rimless glasses gave him the appearance of a scholar. "*Guten Abend.*"

He looked up. "*Guten Abend,*" he answered with fleeting politeness, then looked back to the sheet music. I noticed one earpiece of his eyeglasses was fastened with a rubber band passing around his ear. I introduced myself.

"Emmerich Smola," he replied without looking up.

"May I sing in your choir?"

"Have you ever sung in a choir before?" His voice still sounded indifferent. He kept sorting out the music.

"Yes."

"Soprano or alto?"

"Alto. I've sung the Mozart Mass."

Immediately, he looked at me with obvious interest. "You have? Where?"

"In Danzig."

He seemed to contemplate, then sighed. "Danzig is lost, isn't it?" His eyes looked into a great distance. "I'm from Bohemia. The Russians are there too. I guess we can't go home."

I still didn't have my answer. "May I sing in your choir?"

"Of course. Take a seat over there with the altos."

I was accepted! Happily I sat down. Soon, all the choir members had taken their seats and the rehearsal began.

The choir was an unusually large group, but the singing only average. I heard some good sopranos and saw the director had little trouble with them. But the altos were shaky. I sang as loud as I could so they could follow me.

In the middle of the *Gloria*, Smola interrupted the singing. "At this point you'll hear a short interlude from the organist, whom I still haven't found yet." Standing, he played the interlude on the piano.

This was my challenge! I could hardly bear my tension, and the duration of the rehearsal seemed endless. Finally, he shut his music score. "That's it for tonight," he said. "See you next week."

While the choir members left the rehearsal room, I approached Smola again. "I heard you say you need an organist."

"Very much so." There was hope and curiosity in his voice. "Do you play?"

"Yes, I do."

He put sheet music on the piano rack. "Can you play this?"

I sat down and played the interlude by sight. A spark of excitement flew through me, as I had experienced so often when I made music together with a good musician.

"Excellent sight reading," Smola said. His voice sounded animated. "Let's go to the organ right away."

I got up to follow him, trying to calm my euphoria.

He walked with long strides through a corridor that led directly into the dark church nave. Incense filled the air, awakening a faint memory of Danzig's cathedrals. But there was no time for nostalgia. By the light of a low emergency bulb, I trailed Smola up a winding staircase.

"You know," I heard his voice in the half-darkness, "we'll have a twenty-five piece orchestra for Christmas. But you'll have a lot of solo-organ parts to play." His program planning now obviously included me.

When he switched the lights on I saw we had arrived at the large organ balcony. Organ pipes, descending in size from left to right, covered the huge wall, dwarfing the instrument itself which had two keyboards and about fifty stops. No problem with the two keyboards, but how could I handle all the stops? I had never bothered learning them. "Make yourself familiar with the stops," Smola said.

Hesitantly, I pulled out a few stops. He obviously noticed I had little idea what combinations to use. But he said, "Don't worry about it. Someone can help you with the stops." He pulled some out, others in. "Try this."

I pressed down an F-major chord. Immediately, the tonality evoked Handel's organ concerto in F in me; I started to play it from memory. The echo came back from the dark nave just in time to enhance the music. What a tremendous sound the organ had!

Smola listened. "Good memory. Do you know the B-flat major? It's my favorite."

"Handel?" I asked.

He nodded.

Playing the beginning of the concerto, I looked at him, smiling in triumph. Did he have another request?

But Smola didn't smile. He was already in the middle of arranging the Christmas program. "We could put this at the end of the program. Do you want to play the whole thing?"

I stopped playing. "Wouldn't it be too long? People may get tired of that much music."

"*Quatsch*. When people put green stuff in the offertory bag they want to get their money's worth. If you want to play all three movements, you may."

I liked this shop talk. But I hated long concerts. "How about playing only one?"

"The first movement then," he decided immediately.

There seemed to be no further need for discussion. It was as if we had known each other and worked together for a long time. I sensed his genius and his total dedication to music. And he must have recognized that, musically, he could count on me. Deep gratitude filled me. I had arrived where I belonged. I was home.

Smola turned off the organ switch and the lights. The first act of my new great adventure had ended. Still half-blind from the lights on the organ balcony, we groped our way down the winding wooden staircase. Down in the church nave, I recognized the red glimmer of the Eternal Light. Spellbound, I remained on the spot.

As Smola opened the door to the rectory, light fell into the nave. I saw him holding the door open for me. He must have sensed my hesitation and asked, "Do you want to stay here for a while?" I nodded. "See you next Tuesday then." He closed the door.

Wonderfully alone, I felt immersed in the mystery of a Catholic cathedral. All sensory perceptions were reversed. My ears, used to music and noise, readily filled with stillness and the quiet soothed my nerves. A fleeting memory of Mozart's words passed through my mind, "Silence is the best part of music" -- a sentence I'd never understood before but did now.

After a while, a wonderful feeling of relief settled within me: music had saved my spiritual existence. How wonderful life had suddenly become. Now, I was ready to face the world again.

Only fifteen minutes later, I arrived at home to find my family in bed. Switching on the dim ceiling light, I saw Lili, thumb-in-mouth, lying on her mattress in deep sleep. Manfred, curled up in bed, his head almost entirely covered with his quilt seemed asleep, too -- probably dreaming of seas and ships. But to my surprise, his voice, muted by the comforter, asked, "Well?" I sat down on his bed and told him about my new musical activity.

He pushed his covers away and emerged from his underworld. "Music -- that's where you belong," he said. He really supported me! "I don't want you just sitting in the house, cleaning and boiling potatoes."

"You don't mind if I go to rehearsals every Tuesday night?"

"Not at all. On the contrary, I'd be very proud of you if you played the Mozart Mass."

I stared at him in awe. "What a rare man you are. All the others never 'allow' their wives to do something outside the house."

"You know I always felt men and women have the same rights."

"I know. You're so exceptional. That's why I married you."

He smiled -- his well-known, radiant smile, which had always enchanted me. I bent down and kissed him. As he embraced me fully, I felt the warmth of his body and my own desire. "Hurry up and undress," he urged. "I want to have a musician in my bed."

I laughed, joyfully giving in to his demand. Under the dim ceiling light, we made love. After it, when he was long asleep, I lay beside him, filled with physical gratification and exultation, knowing I'd arrived in Eden.

Before the second choir rehearsal, Smola said to me, "Sorry to take you out of the altos. They really needed your support. But it's more important to me that you accompany us on the piano. Later on, on the organ, of course." Although this meant the end of my singing, I felt happy to be needed.

Smola didn't seem to be the only one to tap my sources. At the rehearsal break, a bald man from the tenor section approached me. "Would you like to work with a professional singer?"

"Of course," I rushed to answer, not wanting to lose any opportunity.

"It's Angela Rymann, an opera singer from Berlin. She's been stuck here in Wilhelmshaven since the end of the war. She's desperately looking for an accompanist. Would you be interested?"

Would I! I gave him my address. Things were looking better every day.

As if in protest, my stomach growled. No meat, no fat, just dry bread and cabbage soup every day weren't exactly filling. I was thankful I could always get milk for Lili.

So the rehearsal nights became increasingly important to me. I also made new friends.

At a rehearsal break, a middle-aged man with a large, beaky nose approached me. "My name is Hans Müller. I want to tell you how glad we all are that Herr Smola found you. It was very tiring for him to conduct *and* play at the same time." His gentle dark eyes looked at me in admiration.

"I'm glad I can help," I said.

Stroking his receding brown hair, he started asking me detailed questions about myself, my family and my parents. "The reason I'm asking is to find out if you need any help." What kind of help?

"As a refugee you probably lost everything," he continued. "You're part of our church now. Maybe we could help you here and there."

As the rehearsal continued I took my place at the piano. While I was playing, my mind produced a list of needed things. Manfred badly needed a pair of shoes. His soles had several holes and he always came in from the rain with wet feet. Would Müller be able to get Lili warm pants and shoes for the winter? She had outgrown almost everything and clothes weren't available anywhere.

After the rehearsal, I raced home to tell Manfred the news. I found him sitting at the table, reading under the insufficient ceiling light. He looked up from his work sheets and smiled at me in welcome.

"Good news!" I burst out. "A charity man from the choir wants to help us out with things."

His smile vanished and he remained silent.

"Aren't you glad?"

"About what?"

"This man may help us! Maybe he'll get you new shoes. Maybe Lili will get warm clothes for the winter."

"I'd rather walk with holes in my shoes," he said.

I felt a shock. Then, all at once, I understood. "Are you still obsessed with pride and honor?"

"I'd rather die than lose them," he said.

"Centuries-old German ideals. Luxuries we can't afford in a survival situation."

"There's no reason to become a beggar."

I was angry. "You'd rather let Lili suffer from the cold than abandon your old ideals?"

He sat there, his head, once so proudly borne high, bent down in conflict and helplessness, and a great compassion for him overcame me. "It's hard to possess nothing, isn't it?" I asked softly. I had struck his sore point.

He got up from the table, undressed, went to bed and fell asleep immediately.

I envied him for being able to escape into sleep. This gift I did not possess. My worries, stronger than my slumber, often kept me awake in the darkness for hours. But tonight they were swept away by music and hope, hope for friends and help. Next Tuesday, I'd be there again. I turned on my side and fell asleep.

The following Tuesday, during rehearsal, the door opened. The singing stopped abruptly and all choir members got up. When I saw Smola bow slightly I turned around to see the honored newcomer.

A man in his forties stood at the door, both hands in the pockets of his dark-gray suit -- an unusually sloppy attitude and totally in contrast with his round white priestly collar. His dark eyes scanned the choir, Smola and then myself. "You folks sound pretty good. I heard you two blocks away," he said jokingly. "Please be seated."

As the choir members sat down again, I realized I had remained on my chair the entire time. This had to be Father Sylvester, the pastor.

The priest smiled at the choir director. "Herr Smola must be an offshoot of the Toscanini family."

Even Smola smiled. I understood: the priest had hit on his dream to become a famous conductor.

With a quick side glance at me, the priest jokingly said to the choir, "I heard the new accompanist is as good as a full orchestra. We could save the money for the musicians at Christmas and give it to charity."

The choir laughed.

Hanneli, a pretty dark-haired girl called from the soprano section, "But we know you'd rather pay the money and have a spectacular show for Christmas."

The priest laughed. "And we'll exhibit Hanneli as the Queen of the parish. With her, we could raise high fees." He came across like the director of a cabaret. He opened the door. "Before I'm attacked again I'd better leave." He waved good-bye to the choir.

Smola instantly recovered his serious demeanor and continued the rehearsal. But the priest's lighthearted remarks had enhanced the atmosphere.

After the rehearsal Müller stepped over to me, telling me that the charity committee had found two available rooms for our family and my parents. We could move in within a few days.

I told him we had absolutely no furniture, but he said I shouldn't worry. "You make me feel at home," I said.

"We want you to feel at home," he said warmly.

I rejoiced and rushed home.

To my surprise, Manfred didn't object at all. "All right," he said.

As we were preparing for the night, I said, "I thought you'd reject the whole idea."

He just shook his head.

"What made you change your mind?"

With a trace of bitterness, he replied, "I still hate the idea of being a recipient of charity. I'd never accept anything for myself alone. But I can't reject things given to you and Lili." It must be a hundred times harder for him than for me to go through these times. "But I have good news," he went on. "The German Red Cross has started a huge project to help displaced people find each other. You should go and register our names and address tomorrow. When your parents come they'll go through Red-Cross camps. Right away they'll find out where we live."

When I went to the Red-Cross station next morning to register, I learned that only adult names were put on the lists. So only Manfred's and mine. After that, I went over hundreds of listings, searching for my parents' names but didn't find them. Instead, I discovered those of Helmut Kalmbach and his wife, Irene, and their address in Wilhelmshaven.

SNOW BABY

When I told Manfred the good news, his face lit up. "Let's go see them tonight. I don't want to wait another day."

The overcrowded state of the apartment came in handy again. I asked the bombed-out family in the adjacent room to leave the door open and watch over Lili's sleep.

Then Manfred and I began the long walk through the expanse of Wilhelmshaven's ruins. The days had shortened and the first signs of autumn had appeared; the wind from the North Sea, grown colder, chased yellow leaves through the streets. Because of low clouds it was almost dark; whatever light could filter through the cloud cover was on the brink of fading. Still there was enough light to make roads and ruins visible.

We walked silently through the streets lined with heaps of rubble and damaged buildings. The sky darkened completely.

Suddenly, I heard a faint sound, like children singing. I looked at Manfred to see if he heard it, too.

He smiled. "How wonderful, the lantern song. The children walk with their paper lanterns again."

The singing became louder. When we reached a corner, we saw a group of about twenty pre-school children, singing and marching through the street, followed by adult chaperones. The children held colorfully-lit paper lanterns on sticks in front of them. The round lanterns swayed gently, and the candles within them flickered and illuminated the various designs on the lanterns. In the magical light the children's faces looked devoted and enchanted. I heard them sing:

"*Laterne, Laterne,*
Sonne, Mond und Sterne.
Brenne auf, mein Licht,
brenne auf, mein Licht,
aber nur meine liebe Laterne nicht.
Lantern, lantern,
Sun, moon and stars.
Burn, my light,
but don't burn my beloved lantern.
Boomela, boomela, boom, boom, boom."

We stood still as the children marched toward us. Enchanted by the magic scene, I said softly: "Out of the ruins come children, carrying the light of promise." As a child Manfred had lived in the Northwest. "Manfred, what's the meaning of this custom?"

"It's held at Equinox. It's a symbol of replacing the fading light. Candles and lanterns substitute for the vanishing sun." His eyes followed the children who were marching on.

"Did you walk with a lantern when you were a child?"

"Oh, yes. Holding my mother's hand."

When the charming parade was gone, we continued our walk through the darkness, following the beam of Manfred's flashlight. As we approached the area where Helmut and Irene lived, Manfred said, "I'm really looking forward to seeing Helmut again. God, what fun we had together!"

"I've seldom seen either of you speak one serious word to each other. You were always kidding and joking." I added, "Remember? Irene was our matchmaker. What a smart idea."

"She was right, we are a good match."

Arriving at the area where Helmut and Irene lived, Manfred let his flashlight play over the gray town houses. I saw this area had suffered only mild bombings -- roofs missing here and there. We found the house and their name on the door, walked upstairs and rang the doorbell.

A moment later, Helmut, with his strong, disciplined face and bushy brows, opened the door. He wore, like Manfred, his former Navy uniform without the stripes and golden buttons. "Oh my," he called. "It can't be true! Irene, come here, quickly!" Was it really seven months ago he and I had been on the DEUTSCHLAND?

Irene appeared. "I can't believe it!" she called. Her face looked thinner than I remembered. Her light-blue blouse and dark skirt drooped on her. The couple, strikingly good-looking, dark-haired and brown-eyed, still looked like brother and sister. Someone at their wedding had cracked: "It's incest!"

Now, both smiled with joy and we all hugged each other. "How long has it been since we've seen each other?" Irene asked me, her tone of voice a shade less cheerful than I expected.

"Two years," I replied. "When you started teaching in the country."

"A long time ago," Irene said as though she hardly re-membered it, her friendly, motherly face without expression. What had happened to these formerly light-hearted people? I became concerned.

They led us into their only room. "Don't expect too much," Irene warned. "Four different families live in this three-bedroom apartment."

"Living *en masse*," Helmut said. "The anathema of our time."

The scantily furnished room looked more impoverished than our own -- the typical emergency lodging of refugees, with junk posing as necessities.

A small square table and two single beds were the only furniture, several boxes piled up in one corner, others shoved under the beds because there were no cupboards or closets. Drapes were absent, and a lonely bulb, bare of a shade, hung sadly from the ceiling.

Irene apparently read my thoughts. "This is our new standard. Poverty."

"Welcome to the club," I said.

"Come sit down on our modest beds," Helmut invited. "You found us through the German Red Cross, didn't you?" I nodded. "Tell us how you ended up in Mudtown," he commanded.

I frowned. "Where?"

"Mudtown is Wilhelmshaven's nickname. Too much rain, too much mud. We don't have much choice -- after the news tonight." Helmut's smile was sad.

"What's the news?" I asked.

"Don't you have a radio?"

"Yes and no." I winked at Manfred. "We have one but it's not working."

Helmut put his arms around Irene's shoulders, lightly massaging them. "You've probably heard that our glorious victors have decided the Poles can keep Danzig. It's *Gdansk* now. There are two and a half million German survivors in the East, including Gdansk. The Polish government has ordered them to leave the area within four weeks."

"That's impossible!" I shouted.

"I'm afraid it's true."

"Oh God, and my parents? What about their home, their business? Everything they owned was in Danzig!"

Manfred put his arm around my shoulder. "We hope they're on their way to us," he said, his voice calm. "We even have a room for them. By the way, we're moving in two or three days. This is our new address." He passed a piece of paper to Helmut. "But tell us how you and Irene found each other in Mudtown."

"I had a friend here in Mudtown and Irene had his address," Helmut replied. "So I was waiting for her here."

"What do you do now?" Manfred asked.

"I'm a janitor."

"God! I hope not for too long." I turned to Irene. "How did you get here? You trekked, didn't you?"

"Yes," she replied, almost indifferent. She sat with her husband on the other bed, strangely stiff, her face expressionless.

"Did you trek on wagon or on foot?"

"On foot." She became motionless, a statue.

"On foot from Danzig up to here?" I asked, unbelieving.

"No, only to Berlin."

"Five hundred kilometers on foot? Tell us about it."

"We wandered by day," Irene said as if she disposed of something unimportant. "We stayed overnight in whatever shelter we could find. If we didn't find any we slept in the fields."

"But it was in the middle of the winter. How could you sleep in the fields at freezing temperature?" I asked.

"You can if you're exhausted enough. We all huddled together..."

"Oh Irene." I looked about the poorly furnished room. "Where is little Hilde? She's almost a year old now, isn't she?" The joy of our reunion with Helmut and Irene had made me forget about the baby I'd never seen.

Suddenly, I saw Irene's face distort and freeze -- an expression on it I had never seen before. Tearless, her breath came in several short bursts. Helmut moved quickly and took her in his arms. She fell limp and continued gasping. At last, the tears came.

Helmut, still holding her, turned his head to us. He said quietly, "Our child died on the road. To survive, Irene had to leave her and go on with the trek."

I held on to Manfred's hand. The baby had been only a few months old.

"Oh my God," I heard Manfred whisper.

For a long time no one spoke. I felt helpless and empty.

Irene's sobbing stopped abruptly. Her red, swollen eyes looked hard and cold as she freed herself from her husband's arms and tried to regain her composure. Her face suddenly looked tired and old. She grabbed a handkerchief, wiped the last tears away and blew her nose. Staring into the distance, she said with a broken voice, "It's been ten months now, but I can't seem to adjust. I miss my baby."

I walked over to her and took her in my arms.

Helmut got up from the bed and stepped to the window sill. Taking a pill from a small box and filling a glass with water he brought both to Irene. "It's aspirin," he explained. Aspirin, the ritual panacea for everything. Irene swallowed both pill and water. Then she took several deep breaths, held them for a moment and let the air out slowly.

I sat down on the bed again. I wasn't sure if we could ask her questions now, but then I thought it might be good for her to talk. "Can you talk about it, Irene?"

She nodded. "It's all right."

"How come you trekked on foot? I thought you had a horse and wagon?"

She sighed. "We started out that way. The Russians were still far away from the village where I was teaching. There were ten of us. One, a peasant, had a horse and a wagon to haul our belongings. We marched behind the wagon so as not to overwork the horse. The road was icy and there were blizzards. Hilde was well-wrapped. And I thought I would never have a feeding problem with her. I had enough milk powder for three months."

"How in the world did you prepare the formula?"

She hesitated. "I had hoped to pass villages where I could supply my thermos bottle with warm water. But the roads were jammed. Every day new people came from the side roads and joined us, all pushing to the West. Finally, there were so many wagons and people that we were stalled for days. So I melted snow in my mouth and spat it into the bottle and shook it. Hilde was hungry and took it." She stopped, her eyes distant, the pain of the ordeal written on her face.

I was afraid she would lapse into a crying spell again, but she stayed calm. "The first days of trekking were normal. We would eat from our reserves and even fed the horse well; we depended so much on the animal. At night we climbed on the wagon and covered ourselves with waterproof canvas."

"All ten people and the suitcases and boxes?"

"Oh yes, we were glad we had any shelter at all. But we didn't stay alone for long. German troops marched in the opposite direction, so the refugees were shoved aside into the trenches. Some trucks got stuck and had to be abandoned."

Apparently, she could sit no longer. She got up from the bed and started walking around the room. "We knew the Red Army was still far behind us, but we didn't anticipate their planes. Although there were no military objectives or even villages for miles, they came over us, flying low and machine-gunning. The attack came so fast, we couldn't even take shelter under the wagons. Many people were killed. Our horse fell dead too." She paused, moving toward the window, staring into the darkness.

"Oh Irene," I gasped. Her body trembled and she folded her arms to stop the shaking. Looking at Manfred, I saw his tense face. Helmut's head was hung low; I couldn't see his features.

Irene turned away from the window. She didn't look at us but stared at some point on the bare wooden floor. When she spoke again her voice was hollow, cold and almost dead sounding. "We knew we had to leave the wagon on the road and could take only the most important things with us. Before we could do that, the Russian planes came back and dropped several bombs on us. For cover, I had thrown myself with Hilde into a ditch along the roadside.

"Hilde didn't understand what was going on but all the other children cried until their voices were drowned out by the noise of the airplanes. After the attack, it took me a while to recover from the shock. Then I went to look at the damage. Most of the adults were killed and all the children, except Hilde. She was the only child alive. Our wagon was hit. The debris was strewn all over the snow. Hilde's milk powder gone." From then on her voice became lower. "She was only eight weeks old. I tried to feed her with melted snow. But she cried for milk and there was none. We marched on but no village was in sight. She cried one more day. Then she only whimpered. At last she stopped whimpering, she didn't move. She grew cold and I couldn't warm her anymore. I was also cold." Tears slid down her cheeks.

I went to her, took her in my arms again and held her, softly stroking her hair. When I heard Manfred ask, "Did you bury her?" I released her but kept my arm around her shoulder.

Irene sighed. "The ground was knee-deep in snow and frozen. There were no shovels. So we buried our children in the snow..."

The silence of that snow burial reached into the room.

After a while she continued. "We had nothing to eat for the next eight days. We walked through small villages, but they were only ghost towns. All the people had fled. We searched the houses for food, but others before us had raided them and we found nothing to eat. But I learned one can make it without food for a long time."

"Did you have water?" I asked.

"Oh, there was plenty of snow along the road. It's as good as water. Somewhere we found a village which was still populated. That's where I collapsed. We got medical treatment there, were fed and slept in real beds. But the village people were fleeing also, and so we left again."

"On foot?"

"Yes, on foot. We were many thousands by then and there was no transportation. We made it in three weeks to Berlin. My goal was Wilhelmshaven. As Helmut told you, we had a friend here. That's how we found each other."

"My God, Irene, I don't know how I can help ..." my voice trailed off.

With astonishment, I saw Helmut smile at Irene. He got up to stand in front of his petite wife. "We've tried to make up for the loss," he said, looking with tenderness at her. "Irene is pregnant again." He took her in his arms.

I felt both their pain and their joy. I reached out and took Manfred's hand. Helmut and Irene were starting over, just as Manfred and I must do.

THE CAMPS

We were moving again. Müller's promises had become reality as he drove us to 22 Park Street, a completely intact four-story apartment building with pitched and mansarded roofs that stood out among the ruins. On the fourth floor, the attic apartment had a slanted ceiling. Two rooms were ours; one small one still unfurnished for my parents, the other one, with the slanted ceiling and a tiny window, already had two beds, a bedframe for Lili's mattress, a table and four chairs. All these gifts were more precious to me than the whole expensive dowry my mother had amassed for me.

Müller told us that two bombed-out families lived in the other rooms and we would share the kitchen and bathroom with them.

We were right in the middle of arranging furniture and unpacking our boxes when the doorbell rang. I rushed to open it. "Irene and Helmut! What a pleasant surprise."

Helmut mock-saluted me. "We've come to pay a ceremonial visit in your new home."

Observing the old tradition, they'd brought bread, salt and a *pfennig* as symbols of ever-lasting food, salt and money. "Thank you," I said. "You're marvelous friends."

Irene picked Lili up, kissed her, then held her away from her, studying the child's round small face. "My, look at those eyes!" She turned to me. "How old is she now?"

"Almost two years."

"Watch out that she doesn't get married at eighteen because of those beautiful blue eyes."

I admired Irene. There was no sadness or bitterness to show her terrible loss. She had brought Lili a small box filled with buttons of different colors -- a precious treasure. Lili beamed and turned the box over, letting all the buttons roll on the floor.

"Now you have to pick them up," Irene said. She turned to Manfred. "I want to see your entire villa."

Manfred gripped hers and Helmut's arms from behind. "Let's have a grand tour through the house," he said, leading them from one corner of the room to the other.

Meanwhile I went to the dark, small kitchen to make ersatz coffee. I inhaled the awful smell of its main ingredient, barley. But filling my recycled brown tin pot, I felt as proud as if I were serving prize-winning coffee.

When I returned to the big room I found all three in a heated discussion. As I filled their cups Helmut said angrily, "They're just plain lies."

Irene's voice sounded depressed. "I'm afraid they're true."

"It's probably all exaggerated," Manfred said.

I put the coffee pot down. "What are you talking about?"

Suddenly, there was silence. The two men wrinkled their brows. "The Allies say millions of inmates were killed in the concentration camps," Irene said.

I gazed at them. "Whaaat?" I heard Lili clatter the buttons.

Helmut continued to vent his anger. "The Allies probably think they can tell us as many lies as they can invent."

"Who exactly said what?" I asked.

"Supposedly, some of the camps were extermination camps," Manfred said. "They contained gas chambers in which the inmates were gassed to death." The image of an atrocity of such enormity could not be absorbed immediately by anyone.

"It's a bunch of lies!" Helmut yelled.

"I don't believe it either." Manfred's voice was calm but firm. "Where are those camps supposed to be?"

"In Poland and Southern Germany," Helmut answered.

"Far away from Danzig," I said. "Thank God we had nothing to do with it." Not realizing it, I was accepting the accusations. "Who did the killings?" I asked.

"The SS, Hitler's handpicked elite," Helmut replied.

The image of those black-uniformed tyrants, who'd worn a skull and cross-bones on their caps and lapels, rose before me. "Everyone feared them," I said. "But who would have suspected them of mass murder? It's unbelievable."

"There are even pictures in today's newspaper," Irene said. "People who look like living skeletons." She got up, stepping over to the corner of the room. She picked up and uncrumpled a newspaper, putting the front page before me.

I stared at the huge black letters, which seemed to jump off the front page:

GRUESOME DISCOVERY: EXTERMINATION CAMPS
INMATES GASSED TO DEATH
CREMATING FURNACES FOUND. MILLIONS CREMATED
GERMAN NATION MUST FACE TRUTH
POPULATION ORDERED TO SEE HORRIBLE EVIDENCE

Two pictures, somewhat blurred by the low quality of paper and printer's ink, showed Allied soldiers standing before collapsed but living bodies, who were no more than skeletons. Reality. Cruelty. Atrocity. "Oh my God," I whispered. No one spoke. The silence seemed to confirm the accusations. Shaking my head, I said, "I can't cope with it." I looked at Manfred. "Mass killings! No! No! I can't believe it!"

Manfred took several sips from his mug. "We don't know what's true and what's exaggerated." He put his mug down with a clang. "When we listened to enemy stations during the war the Allies broadcasted false propaganda -- like our own government. We've been lied to for years. I never heard anything about what happened in the camps. And we're supposed to believe them now?"

"But what if all this is true?" I asked.

"Everyone knew the camps existed," said Irene. "But knowing what was going on *inside* was a different matter."

"My cousin Franz was in a concentration camp for a year," I said.

"What had *he* done?" Helmut asked.

"He was a Communist, got drunk in a bar and sang the Nazi anthem in parody."

"Did he tell you how it was inside?"

"Of course not. You know yourself, everyone upon release had to sign a paper that they would never talk about their experiences in the camp. If they did, they'd be returned. Everyone knew that."

"We brushed it aside," Irene said. "'Do not trouble your head about others; what we don't know doesn't harm us.'"

"And now we have to pay for this attitude," I said.

"If it's true," Manfred said, staring at the pictures, "then we must carry this horrible crime on our shoulders until we die." Immersed in our thoughts, no one spoke.

Still shaken, I could not give up on the topic. "How much did we actually know about the camps?"

"Not much beyond that they were prisons for dissenters," Helmut said. "And that they were impossible to escape from."

"The fact that talking about what went on inside was strictly forbidden, should have told us something," Irene said.

Helmut snorted. "It did. But we had other things to do. Our mind was set on fighting the enemy."

"Our duty was to be good Naval officers," Manfred said. "Besides, curiosity was dangerous. In a dictatorship all negative information is very effectively suppressed. It never reaches the population."

"We were too intimidated," Helmut said. "All Germany was, and later, all of Europe."

Manfred hesitated. "I'm not sure I ever felt any fright."

"We just dismissed fear from our consciousness," said Irene. "Along with all the rumors we heard. That was the path of least resistance."

Manfred shook his head. "I think we treated the rumors as we treated the propaganda. We felt it was a waste of time. As children we were trained not to pay attention to our neighbors. Later, in the Navy, we were taught not to pay attention to politics. We were tightly knit groups with our interests limited to the Navy."

"Kind of living in a golden cage," Helmut said.

"Rather like in a wildlife zoo," Manfred said. "Only the bars weren't visible."

"We all lived that way, didn't we?" I said gloomily. "Well-fed and protected by the lords if we were obedient and agreeable."

"Of course. A good citizen never interfered with the government...." Helmut began, and Irene continued, "....good sheep have no responsibilities."

"I can tell you how *rebellious* sheep were treated," I said to Helmut and Irene. "The Gestapo summoned me two years ago."

"Tell them," Manfred said.

GESTAPO

Moved by the remembrance, I got up and stepped over to the window. Dark clouds were gathered over the horizon just as they had been when I walked, uneasy and puzzled, to the gloomy court house in Danzig two years ago. The Gestapo had an office in the same building. No longer could anyone tell the difference between jurisdiction and terrorism.

My heart was pounding as I entered the five-story building with its long corridors and many doors. I wished I weren't alone, but Manfred was on a submarine combat patrol in the Atlantic.

I knocked at door number 378.

Someone opened the door from within with force -- not for me, I soon discovered. A petite middle-aged woman in cheap, unfashionable coat and hat was chased out of the office, followed by an SS man who yelled at her, "You damned asshole, don't tell us any of your lies!"

The woman's motherly features were distorted by fear. How could anyone shout at an older woman -- a respected figure in our culture! I wondered. I felt like putting myself in front of her to protect her. Before I could do anything the SS man quickly took her down the hall.

The door had stayed open and a tall, black-uniformed SS officer commanded me: "Come in!" I stepped into a large room with carved dark-brown office furniture and leather armchairs of the same color. A bespectacled SS man sat behind a typewriter, motionless, apparently awaiting orders. Next to him, a young, slender SS man bent forward, staring at me, never taking his eyes off my face.

An SS officer in his tailored black uniform and red armband with swastika sat behind a huge desk and rose as I entered. Looking thirtyish, he had an almost pleasant face.

I looked at the skull and cross-bones on his jacket lapels as he asked me: "Frau Krutein?"

"Yes."

"Please, take a seat," he said, pointing to the comfortable leather chair across from his desk. We both sat down.

He hadn't introduced himself but I saw the small brass plate on his desk. "Dr.Wolf. Lawyer."

A long interview began. Wolf asked questions about my life and my education. I answered and the puppet behind the typewriter typed my answers into his machine.

The staring man became a great nuisance to me. His function obviously was to observe the delinquent persistently. After a short time I felt so nervous from his staring I had to make a strong effort to hide my irritation. I had no idea what charge they would bring against me.

After two hours of interrogating me Wolf picked up a piece of paper. "This letter has been brought to my attention. Did you write this?" He passed it to me.

I recognized my handwriting, read the words and remembered. It was a letter I'd written to my father when he was on vacation six months ago. One of my sentences was underlined with a red pencil -- by someone else.

"Yesterday, some Army shark came to our factory to draft our last workers."

Suddenly, I felt a chill colder than ice crawl up my spine and knew I was condemned. I had used the derogatory term "shark" for an army officer. A crime unheard of and unpardonable. I knew people who had been sent to concentration camps for lesser offenses -- perhaps even the poor woman who had been chased out of this office before I came in. Maybe I'd never see Manfred again, or my parents.

"Did you write this?" the lawyer asked again.

"Yes."

"Explain what you mean by 'shark'," he commanded.

I sighed. It was so hopeless.

"Answer my question!"

I searched for words. "I meant," I began, "I meant we felt terrible that he drafted our last workers. We hardly knew how to go on with production with not enough workers ...."

His hands clutched the edges of his desk as he started to shout at me. "You stubborn Frau! Do you know what you are? A defeatist! You are an enemy of the German people! With your behavior you damage the people's will to victory! You as a citizen

of Danzig should be grateful that the Führer led you back to the
mother country Germany!"

Oh, how I wish he hadn't! We would still be free. I know I was
never obedient, neither to my mother, nor at school, nor to the
Nazis. And now I had to pay for it.

"Do you know what you are?" he screamed. "An abscess that
we'll squeeze out! A cancer we'll cut out! You know what it
means -- concentration camp!"

I had known it all along. This lawyer meant business. The
end of my freedom. I became aware of the man whose job it was
to read my thoughts and emotions from my face. Powerless, I let
him see them. There was a silence in which I expected the
inquisitor to push the button to call his henchmen. I held my
breath.

Yet with a lower voice he spoke again. "There's only one fact
that might save you. Your husband is a Navy officer. He's
devoting his life to his fatherland. For this we might save you."

A straw, a totally unexpected straw! Oh dear God!

"If you sign a letter, we'll let you go," my accuser said.
Anything, I thought, just to get out of here. I nodded.

The lawyer motioned to the typist. "Write. 'Out of stupidity,
I, Eva Krutein, have used a derogatory term in regard to our
outstanding, courageous Army and I am overwhelmed with
remorse. I implore the Gestapo to forgive me and grant me
probation time, in which my future behavior will be observed. I
promise never to use subversive language again; otherwise I
shall be sent to a concentration camp.'"

I signed the letter and he released me.

Finished with my story, I returned to the table and sat down.
"I can tell you," I said, "from then on I kept my mouth shut about
criticizing the government."

Irene sighed. "That's why all of us stayed silent. People were
in an iron grip. If one opened his mouth, he could end up in a
camp. We didn't hear what we didn't want to hear. It became a
matter of survival. One survived by simply being silent."

A distant thunder clap alerted us, bringing us back to the
present. "The sultriness is unbearable," Irene said. "That's how

we felt during all those years. But we got used to it and kept functioning."

Helmut got up, walked over to my chair. He hugged me from behind, holding my shoulders for a moment. "I didn't know you had gone through this," he said softly. Then he went to Irene, stretched his hand out to her. "Let's go home before the storm breaks, my love." Irene took his hand and rose.

"When will we see each other again?" I asked.

"Soon. Can we call you somewhere?"

"Call me at the shipyard," Manfred said, giving them his number.

"Where's Lili?" Irene asked. We looked around but she had vanished.

"The door is ajar," Manfred said with suspicion. "She's getting into mischief." He rushed into the dark entrance hall. I could see the door to the bathroom half open, heard the toilet flush and Lili scream with joy.

Manfred dashed into the bathroom. I followed him. Lili was about to take the co-tenants' toiletries from the lowest shelf and throw them into the toilet. "Lili, don't!" Manfred shouted.

Shocked, she stopped, razor and brush in her hands. Manfred snatched them from her. The toilet gurgled, refilling with water.

"Have you thrown other things down?" Manfred asked in a stern voice. Lili looked like a guilty puppy. "Dammit!" Manfred grumbled. "How can we replace their things?"

Irene stood at the door. "We'll collect toiletries for them," she said cheerfully. I took Lili's hand and pulled her from the bathroom.

After the Kalmbachs left, Manfred took Lili back to the big room.

I stood still in the dark entrance hall, hearing the muted noises from the co-tenants' door. A cold and heavy feeling descended over me. The image of the mass murders sprang up with frightful clarity. Knowing I had to deal with it I went to share it with Manfred.

Back in the new room, I saw Manfred arranging our two beds in an L-shape along the walls, while Lili joyfully took wooden spoons and pot lids from Müller's box, scattering them around the room.

I sat down on one of the beds. "Manfred, how do *you* feel about the mass murders?"

"I don't know," he murmured, shaking his head.

I knew it was not his nature to reveal his innermost thoughts. "Who do you think knew about the killing -- if it's true at all?"

He stepped over to Lili's mattress, which stood upright in the corner. "You know yourself we never heard about it."

"True," I said. "But how was it possible to keep such a thing secret?"

I heard him sigh deeply. Then he carried the mattress to the bed frame along the opposite wall. "Weren't we all held at gunpoint, one way or another? Do you think anyone working in the camps would have dared to tell someone?"

I snorted. "Of course not."

"As *you* kept your mouth shut after your encounter with the Gestapo, so did everyone else -- even without being summoned like you."

"My father didn't," I burst out. "How often did he protect our Jewish and Polish employees from harassment, risking his own life?"

Manfred carefully fitted the mattress into the bed frame. "But did he actually change the course of events?"

"No, but he did take a stand." With sadness, I saw that my father's heroic attitude had accomplished very little.

Manfred turned to me. "Even the underground people couldn't help much. They were all hanged. Remember the Junkers after their attempt to kill Hitler?"

How could I *not* remember! In a flash the image of my parents' housekeeper rose before me. Had Dorothea been with the underground? I drooped, elbows on knees, and put my face into my palms, evoking pictures and voices from the past. Whom had I known who'd been sent to a concentration camp? Walter Hoffman, an old family friend, for his homosexuality. Once released, he never talked about it. Trude Unger, my good friend from Vienna, for standing up for Catholicism -- she was set free but never told me a word about her experiences....the Gypsies I'd read about....the Jews -- those who had stayed and were caught by the war. I looked at Manfred, who was putting the household things on the table. "Remember my high school friend

Hadassah who went to Palestine? Before her departure, I asked her why she was leaving. I said, 'Nothing can happen to you in Danzig. We are a Free State.' I never forget her answer. She said: 'Never hope for the best. That's how you avoid the worst.' She left and survived."

At this moment I heard the thunder again, but closer. Listening to the resounding noise I wondered why it didn't rain.

Suddenly, a horrible memory came to me. "Uncle Alex!" I cried out.

Astonished, Manfred looked at me. "Who?"

"My godfather."

"The one you loved so much?" he asked kindly. I nodded. "What about him?"

"When my mother and I went to see him and his wife, they didn't answer the door bell. Then neighbors told us they'd been sent to the East."

Manfred sat down next to me. A deep frown creased his face. "They were Jews, weren't they?"

I nodded again. Painfully I relived the event which I hadn't understood at the time. "There'd been rumors that Jews would be settled in the Ukraine. We assumed Uncle Alex and his wife were on their way to do just that. So many had plans to go there voluntarily, as Fritz and Erika did...."

"....and you and I wanting to move to Holland."

"Right. Never in my life would I have thought the SS would kill them." I shut my eyes. Oh dear God....

Manfred's head hung low, his face sad. In the silence I heard Lili happily banging the wooden floor with a big spoon. Through the small window I saw a flash of lightning and seconds after I heard the thunder. Still, there was no rain. I kept looking into the distance as if I could see the future. I asked, not only Manfred, but also myself, "If the accusations are true, won't the world think we all knew and let it happen?"

He nodded. "And we'll never be able to prove we didn't know," he said with a lowered voice. Silence spread out between us, a silence of shared grief -- different from the silence for survival years ago.

Lili's sudden crying interrupted the stillness. I went over, crouched next to her. Seeing she had hurt her hand on the sharp edge of a cooking pot, I sat down on the floor and cradled her. Wiping the tears from her cheeks, I crooned, "Shsh, tomorrow everything will be better." Lili sobbed a few more times, then calmed down, taking her thumb.

I heard a chair being moved. Manfred got up. He came over to me, putting his hands on my shoulders. "The killing is over now and the dead are resting quietly."

"Are they?" I asked. "It doesn't undo it. It's a nightmare that will never end." I sighed. "I wonder how other people feel about this horror?"

"You'll find out tomorrow when you stand in the food lines," he prophesied.

Darkness was closing in. As though to seize the fading light I looked out the window and saw the heavy, dark clouds casting a dreary pall over the ruins. When would the clouds finally burst, discharging their rain, cooling the air and the spirits?

But the clouds hung heavy, bleak and foreboding.

PUNISHED

Next morning, the gloomy dark bank of thunder-clouds still hung over the ruins, darker and lower than yesterday, the atmosphere still unrelieved by rain. Since yesterday's revelation of the mass murders, the sky's gloom reached right into my heart.

I dressed Lili and took her to our grandmotherly co-tenant, Frau Bïttger, whom we had met the night before, finding her to be an ideal baby-sitter. Then I went down to the street to join the food line that extended from one corner of the block to the other. Joining it, I saw the usually taciturn women in an uproar. They all spoke of yesterday's news of the mass murders in the camps.

"These are the greatest lies I've ever heard....It's easy for them to blame all of us for crimes somebody may have done -- *they*'re the victors...."

This outraged me. "Haven't you seen the pictures? Do you think those skeletons were manufactured?"

"I'll tell you something," a stately matron said. "All of us should be suspicious about printed news for the rest of our lives. For the last twelve years we were supposed to believe in our glories and victories. Now we're supposed to believe in our atrocities. It always depends on who's dictating the news."

"Right! We've had enough of being told what to think."

"Let's burn all newspapers."

"That won't take away the truth," I shouted. "Denying the evidence means only we don't want to admit our guilt!"

The stately matron laughed contemptuously. "I haven't done anything wrong. I don't feel guilty."

"But we all are," I said. It felt good having said that.

As the line inched forward, moving me toward the bakery, the aroma of fresh bread and buns titillated my nose. I was still hungry, although I'd already eaten my portion for the day. I had no coupons left for bread so I stepped over to the butcher line, tuning in to the agitated remarks around me.

A buxom girl's yell, "We need another war!" hit my sensitive spot.

"Are you out of your mind?" I shouted. "Do you want even more misery? Aren't we beaten as we are?"

A long roll of thunder roared through the atmosphere like a threat of doom. Everyone looked up in apprehension. There still was no rain.

With anger I realized how invigorating the idea of another war was to some people. "The next war will make *everything* better!" the buxom girl shouted.

"You are very wrong!" a calm voice said. Turning around I saw a pale young woman. "Another war wouldn't make life any better. We should strive for peace!" The most sensible words I'd heard that morning. Peace! What a wonderful word, an ideal, worth striving for. I wanted to talk to this woman, ask her how one could work for peace, but the line moved up, the crowd shifted and I lost her. I entered the butcher shop, bought my family's meat ration for the week -- four ounces of fat beef -- and rushed home to pick up Lili.

There still was no rain.

Finally, at the end of the day, the thunderstorm broke loose. Two ear-splitting thunder-claps and two lightning flashes from different directions ruptured the atmosphere, and a heavy downpour pelted the ground, cooling the air immediately. Poor Manfred, he was on his way home.

Minutes later, he stormed in, completely drenched and with bad news. "The Americans have decided to lower our food rations to 800 calories a day."

That meant slow starvation. What about children? Lili? "How did they come to that?" I asked.

"A powerful secretary in America, Henry Morgenthau, has brewed this up. It's supposed to be a punishment for the way the Jews were treated by the Nazis." He slammed the paper on the table.

I picked it up and read. Morgenthau was quoted as saying: "... Germany is a mental patient ... a whole zoo of animals, ranging from snakes to apes ... Destroy the German spirit of violence. Convert Germany into a land of farms. Regardless of starving thirty million Germans, eliminate their heavy industry ... teach them they've brought all the misery upon themselves..."

That sounded so much like the verbal bombardments of the Nazis. I looked at Lili's round baby face, and Irene's starved child came to mind. "Are they punishing *babies*, too?" I asked.

Manfred shrugged. "Apparently. There's another thing to worry about, too. The Allies reopened the concentration camps and are interning Germans with military titles."

"That's incredible!"

"But it's true. It's part of this so-called punishment." Oh, where was peace?

Manfred reached for his sandwich, which was thinly spread with lard. "I'm sick and tired of living here in Germany."

"Where else?"

He looked at the drapeless window. The gray thunderclouds had dispersed and passed to the east. White cumulus clouds, like fantasy buildings, moved majestically across the evening sky. "Far away," he said softly. "To America. The Russians are too close."

"We're trapped here as we always were. First chained by the Nazis, now by the Allies." He said nothing. I shrugged. "Go ahead and dream about the future," I said. "As for me, I have to deal with the present -- to keep Lili healthy."

He turned to me. "What can *you* do about the 800 calories?"

"I'll steal to get her fed," I said almost in a whisper. "I've done it before and I'll do it again."

But in the dim light of the room I saw his face distort with aversion.

GALE WARNING

"Look at that North Sea." Irene pointed as Lili and I walked with her along the deserted grassy beach.

I looked at the choppy gray waves that fiercely leaped over each other. "Like malicious strays, fighting for prey," I said. "Listen to the sea gulls." They screeched as they dodged and fought for food. At least the smell of salt and sea weeds was familiar and delicious.

Lili ran ahead of us, challenging the wind, throwing her small weight against its thrust. Irene smiled. "She looks and acts so much like Manfred, so cheerful."

"Manfred's not like that anymore."

"You mean he's changed?"

I nodded. "He's withdrawn, he never smiles, he seldom speaks to me, just answers questions." How good it felt to talk to an old friend.

"We all seem to be in the same boat," Irene said. "Helmut, too, has changed. He's withdrawn, never smiles, seldom speaks to me, just answers questions."

"Do you have an explanation?"

"Don't forget," she said, "our men's lives were shattered in a way we can hardly understand."

I stared at her.

For a moment Irene seemed to be lost in thought. Then she said, "They loved their country, and when it was at war they stood up and risked their lives for it. Now the values are reversed and their efforts are considered to be crimes. Who can live with that?"

With sudden enlightenment, I understood. "That's what it is! Manfred can't cope with the collapse of Germany! On the outside he's doing exactly the same as before the surrender, but on the inside he doesn't know how to handle the shambles." I looked at the waves which relentlessly pounded the shore. "So, it's not me."

Irene said very softly, "Think what Helmut and Manfred must feel when they read and hear in the news everyday that they are war criminals. Can you imagine how much energy they spend struggling for self-esteem? Struggling to hide their vulnerability?"

I nodded. "And all that even though the Navy had removed itself from the Nazis."

She sighed. "It will take a long time for our men to recover."

"What I don't understand is this: they're frustrated, and heaven knows, to live with defeat is no small matter. So they withdraw and don't talk to us anymore. Why in the world do they withdraw from their families and not from their work?"

"Don't you remember what we were taught, Eva? 'Hard work is a panacea.'"

How well I recalled my mother urging me to work twice as hard when something had gone wrong. "So, they work to escape?"

"I think so."

"Perhaps that remedy is not a bad solution. Transforming shambles into reconstruction."

She nodded. "And you'll see how fast we'll build up this country again." She stopped to put her hands against her lower back. "I'm not used to walking so much. Let's go home."

Spontaneously, I hugged her and kissed her. "You don't know how much this afternoon has meant to me. Now I have hope." I pondered for a moment. "When do I see you again? I want to give you all the things Lili has outgrown."

"Thank you. That takes away a lot of my worries." She paused for a moment. "For the time being I'm concentrating on my new baby. But afterwards I'll look forward to getting back to teaching."

"They'll need you soon."

"First I have to prove my existence. Remember I lost my handbag on the trek? I have no birth certificate."

"Neither have I."

We laughed. It sounded as if a burden had fallen from our shoulders.

When Manfred came home later than usual, Lili was already asleep. Fortunately, her slumber was so deep we didn't have to lower our voices.

He brought along a stack of papers, lists and books.

"God, are you going to school again?" I kidded.

With a bang he thumped the stack on the table. "No. But I have a new order from the British government to prepare ninety fast torpedo boats and minesweepers to go to sea again."

"To go to sea again? For what? For a new war?"

His face tensed. "There are rumors that the Western Allies are ready to go against the Russians."

"This is unheard of! We're still shattered and now they want to drag us into another shitty war?"

"Watch your language." His voice sounded threatening.

"That's what war is, shit! Shit! I'll say this as long as I live!"

He sat down, ignoring my outburst. With studied calm he started eating his radish sandwich.

For a moment, I stared at him, furious because he ignored my anger. I watched him wash down his sandwich with tea. He ignored me completely. My anger became rage. What could I do to make him see me? Feel me? My eyes fell on the stack of lists and books. I rushed forward, took a handful and threw them at him. The papers only gently touched his chest. Some fell on his plate, others to the floor. He looked startled. But he still didn't look at me. I grabbed more lists, aimed at his head and threw harder. He looked up at me, bewildered. Seeing me grabbing more of his precious papers he held up his hands to fend them off. I seized one of his books, throwing it at him.

He jumped up, rushed at me and clutched my arm. "Stop that!" he shouted.

I tried to use my other arm but he grasped it before I could reach another book. "Let me go!" I struggled to free myself from his firm grip and for a moment I caught a glimpse of his raging eyes.

Suddenly, I noticed Lili was awake, sitting up in her bed, her eyes horrified.

I rushed to comfort her. "It's all right, Lili." She started crying. I cradled her. "Sh-sh-sh." Gradually, she stopped crying. I gently put her to bed again.

Manfred picked up the book and papers that lay strewn around on the floor -- like the ruins of Germany. I stepped over to him. The papers again lay neatly piled up on the table. But his eyebrows were tightly knit. Staring at his papers he commanded: "Explain why you did this."

"All you do is work, work. You never listen to me. You don't even look at me."

Immediately, he glared at me. "Do you want me to give up work? We'd soon be beggars."

I snorted. "We're pretty close to being that anyway. No, I didn't say you should give up work. All I ask is that you communicate."

He hesitated, his face still tense. Then he said: "I told you I have a deadline for the reports."

I shook my head. "You didn't tell me that."

"I thought I did. That's all I have on my mind tonight."

I nodded. "I know, all you're interested in is your work. You don't love me anymore."

"Oh, you're wrong," he said in an imploring voice. "I love you as much as ever." Gently, he pushed me into a chair and sat down on another. "I'll tell you what bothers me." I stared at him, not believing he would tell me about his innermost thoughts. "It's a terrible feeling for me not to be able to provide food for you and Lili. I see we're starving and I can't help it. I see the winter come and there's no fuel."

I wanted to say something, but then curbed my tongue.

"Day in, day out I read and hear we're war criminals. I see nothing that I've done is wrong but I'm still treated that way. The Allies are still searching for those who've been on U-boat missions. The British are shipping them to Canada as prisoners-of-war."

"Now? After the war's over?"

"Yes. They call it retaliation. I'm trying to hide the fact that I was on U-boat patrols."

"How can you hide it?"

"I'm trying to do the best I can in managing the shipyard. To make myself indispensable to them. I keep the deadlines, try to be perfect." He paused again. "And that takes up all my energies."

Deeply moved, I rose and walked over to him. I took him in my arms, held him. "Why did you never tell me?" I asked softly.

"I couldn't."

"Now you can."

Gently, he pulled me down on his lap. He attempted a smile. "Only because you brought all your guns into play, Bear."

I kissed him on his cheek. "Promise you'll talk to me on your own? I promise never to throw books at you again."

He kissed my lips. "I promise. And I love you more than ever."

"I always loved you. I always will."

We kissed passionately. Observantly, he looked at his thumb-sucking daughter. "Is she asleep?"

"As tight as a bear."

A wild love-making ended our confrontation.

PAVING THE WAY

One morning the door bell rang. I went to open it. A dark-haired middle-aged woman of imposing stature introduced herself as the singer from Berlin, sent by the bald tenor from the church choir. With the beautiful diction of a professional singer she said, "My name is Angela Ryman. You may have heard my name before."

I had, but only from the tenor in the choir. The woman had an air about her as if she expected to be known worldwide. I asked her in and she strode into my modest room like a Valkyrie into Valhalla. We sat down at the table.

The singer looked about the sparse room. "Where's your piano?" she asked like a stage director.

I leaned back and apologized with a smile. "We just moved in."

"I realize that. I was at your old address. They sent me to this place."

My old survival instinct awoke in me, driving me on. "My piano isn't here yet," I heard myself say.

"When will it be here?"

"Soon," I said with conviction.

"I hope *very* soon," Ryman said. "I've been without an accompanist for too long. I got stuck in this dreadful town at the end of the war. As soon as I get a travel permit, I'll go back to the Berlin State Opera. I have to work up a new repertoire. I'm sure you do classical songs as well as operas?"

"Yes, of course."

"I want to learn *Madama Butterfly*. Have you done it?"

I shook my head. "No."

"Do you want me to leave my score with you so you can practice?"

"It's not necessary. I sight-read well."

For a moment, the prima donna raised her beautifully-shaped eyebrows. Then she lowered them. "Wonderful." She rose. "Let me know as soon as you get your piano. Here's my address."

She went, leaving me aghast. What had I done? I let this imposing, egotistical woman push me into creating a piano. So, get one!

In the evening, I arrived early enough before the rehearsal to discuss the matter with Smola, who was shuffling sheet music as usual. The choir members hadn't come in yet. I told him I needed a piano urgently. "Do you have any idea where to get one?"

He stopped shuffling, looked into the distance and grinned. "At the end of the war I was sheltered by a peasant for a month. Believe it or not, he had a piano which he never used."

A piano was about the last thing a peasant would have acquired in normal times. "Someone had probably traded it for butter and bacon, right?"

"I suppose so. The peasant may have thought owning a piano meant being able to play it. What a disappointment when he found out he couldn't."

"What condition was it in when you saw it?"

"Sound did come out. It was terribly out of tune, but all the keys worked."

"Do you think I could possibly trade him something for the piano -- provided that it's still there?"

Smola scratched his curly brown hair. "I don't know. There was a special problem with its location."

"What about it?"

"The peasant put the piano away in his goat stable."

"You must take me to this peasant," I said. "I want that piano."

"Ready for the great adventure?" Hans Müller asked. Our well-proven friend stopped his battered pick-up truck before us. Manfred tossed my precious trade item, the rolled-up stair-carpet and several leather straps into the back of the truck. Off we went. Müller cautiously drove his rattling vehicle around the debris on the streets -- twisted metal, girders, broken plaster. "When are they going to clean up the city?" he yelled.

"They'll soon get us 'war criminals' to do it," Manfred said.

Müller stopped to pick up Smola, who swung himself onto the open back of the truck.

Leaving the city behind, we now drove on a bumpy country road lined with beech trees. The flat green scenery was dotted with grazing sheep and white and black Holsteins, their noses deep in the grass. Through the open window flowed the aroma of dry, crisp hay. At last we entered a village with low brick stone peasant houses with attics and pointed roofs and stopped at a house with many-colored autumn flowers in its front yard. Smola knocked at the door.

A white-haired, blue-eyed giant of majestic bearing appeared in the doorway. After a long look at us he recognized Smola. "Our music master! Come in."

After introducing each other we entered a small living-room-cum-kitchen with a wood-burning iron range and a scrubbed wooden table. "Herr Andersen," Smola said cautiously, "we need a piano. I remember you once had one and never used it. Do you still have it?"

Andersen nodded. "Yes."

"Do you want to sell it?" Smola asked.

Andersen scratched his head. "Sell it?" He seemed to calculate. "I dunno. For how much?"

Smola looked at Manfred, who said, "150 marks."

"Not enough."

"Well, 200 then."

Andersen stood there like a pillar. "Money doesn't buy much these days. What else did you bring?"

"A beautiful rug," I said quickly. "Just made for this room." I could no longer curb my impatience. "Where's the piano?"

Signaling us to follow him to the back door Andersen opened it. We stepped directly down into the stable.

From the dimly lit room came an awful smell. About two dozen goats were chewing diligently.

Seeing no piano, I whispered to Smola, "Where is it?"

He pointed to an object in the farthest corner -- an oversized, chocolate-brown upright piano. Its surface was scratched, edges chipped off -- but it was there!

Smola opened the keyboard lid and started playing. Jazz! The rhythms immediately electrified me. I saw Manfred thumping his foot to the music. He never could stand still while jazz was played. Suddenly he rushed to the monstrous piano, picked up two wooden pieces from the floor and, using the top of the piano as a percussion instrument, started drumming, blending perfectly into Smola's rhythms -- a born jazz drummer. As for the piano, it was so badly out of tune, it could make a dog sick, but what did it matter? It just added humor to the strange concert.

Suddenly, the jazz performance was rudely interrupted. "I forgot what good music this piano can make," said Andersen. "It's 250 marks now. 250 marks and the rug!" He walked back into the kitchen.

Manfred quickly produced two handfuls of crumpled bills and laid them out on the table.

"Where's the rug?" Andersen asked.

Müller rushed out to the truck and brought in the rolled-up carpet. "Put it in the goat stable, right where the piano is," Andersen commanded. Müller obeyed.

Now the chore of moving the monster began. Half pushed, half carried, it made its way through stable and kitchen. Outside, the three men, puffing and moaning, heaved the monster onto the truck and laid it down flat to prevent it from overturning. Smola sat down next to it, looking like the sad guard of a felled tree. Off we went again.

Half-way back to Mudtown, Manfred pointed into the distance. "Now look at that! This is an historical occasion!" Looking up I saw a large, gray-and-blue painted autobus, swaying with dignity, coming toward us. "The first bus after the war!" Manfred said in mock-solemnity.

When the bus was closer, Müller rolled his window down and waved at the driver. He waved back, as though aware of his importance to Germany's revitalization. "Mail service is starting today, too," said Müller.

"Germany is risen from the dead," Manfred parried.

"You can beat the Germans, but like a toy jack-in-the-box, they'll pop up again," Müller said.

At home, after the Sisyphean task of lifting the monster piano step by step up to the fourth floor, it was finally rolled into our room. We sat down and celebrated with ersatz coffee, its typical odor, as if burnt, mingling with the smell of the cabbage soup the other tenants were cooking. I wished I could have cooked for all the men tonight, but the times when anyone had food for others were over. All I could do was thank them for their kind service, for providing me with a bridge to my new professional life. Then, hunger drove them in different directions, each to his own home kitchen.

With the new piano I felt like a knight who had found a horse. I charged into battle as fast as I could -- first to a tuner, then to the opera singer.

At our first session, Angela Rymann strode across the room -- like Brünnhilde ready to kindle the fire as she approaches Siegfried's dead body on his funeral pile. "My dear," she said, opening the session, "we'll have our hands full. We'll start with *Madama Butterfly*. I'll need it for the State Opera in Berlin. But before then I want to give several concerts with classical songs here in Wilhelmshaven and in neighboring cities. Later on I want to do joint recitals with a flutist. He and I have several programs in mind."

I felt at home. This was the kind of shop talk I loved. "You want to start with *Butterfly*?"

"Yes. I'd like to work with you every day. Could you do that?"

Could I! I was so excited I forgot to ask Rymann how much she would pay. Never having made music for money, I didn't put the two together.

As we worked, it turned out Rymann had a wide vocal range, pleasant in both high and low registers. She had musical sensitivity; whenever I had to correct her for rhythm or pitch Rymann sang it right immediately.

My rusty voice also came in handy. As Rymann sang her part, I sang the other roles. This, of course, required my full concentration. To handle the three different levels was challenging; I had to control Rymann's part, sing another one and play the orchestra part, all at the same time. Although this was a highly specialized form of accompaniment -- professional opera coaching -- I felt I was in my element. I was glad I'd studied opera scores on my own all those years.

After two hours Rymann closed her score. "That's enough for today. Thank you, my dear. I think we're doing quite well. I'll come tomorrow at the same time. My husband should have dinner ready." She strode to the door.

"Do you have enough food?" I asked the usual question to everyone. "Did you have a chance to 'organize' things?"

The prima donna majestically continued to the door. "Are you implying we would participate in vulgar scavenging? I'd rather starve!"

Suppressing a grin I changed the subject. "Is your husband a musician, too?"

"No, he is not. But he's my concert agent. He is very devoted to me and my art. He does all the house chores, shopping, cooking, washing." She raised her chin a little higher. "But sexually he's been a failure for years."

I was shocked, never having heard anyone talk like this before. "Does it bother you?" I managed to ask.

"Not anymore. I had a great love affair when I was eighteen. Then I burned out totally. Now, twenty years later, nothing can disturb my equilibrium anymore." She paused on the spot like a statue, then stalked downstairs.

At the evening table while we were chewing our meager sandwiches, I told Manfred about my first session with the singer. "She has a good voice and learns fast. Her husband is impotent but she's through with love affairs just the same."

He looked up in amazement. "Who told you that?"

"She did."

He shook his head. "Maybe theater folk have different ways. How much does she pay you?"

"Sorry. I forgot to bring it up."

He frowned. "After all the fuss of getting the piano, and spending your time with her?"

My elation evaporated. "I'll talk to her tomorrow," I promised.

But within the next twenty-four hours, my world, as I had known it, was shattered.

THE HURRICANE

A sudden gust of wind, warning of an impending storm, rushed through the open window. As I hurried to close it I heard an unusual noise from the entrance hall, as if the mail slot had flapped. The first mail after the war? The newspapers had said only postcards would be allowed, to make censoring easier on the Allies who wished to control German minds. Curiously, I walked into the dark entrance hall, leaving the door open to lighten the darkness.

There it lay, like a gift from heaven, a simple white postcard, postmarked Hamburg, addressed to me, written by Dorothea, my parents' housekeeper and my dear friend. I read:

"Liebe Frau Eva:

"Today I found your address in the Red Cross lists. I'm in the Holy Cross hospital in Hamburg. Has your father arrived? Please write.

Dorothea."

My father was on his way! But what about my mother? My God, what had happened to her? I read the scanty text over and over. I groped for an explanation. Maybe mother was very ill and with Dorothea, who was taking care of her as servants always did when their patrons became ill and helpless. They were in Hamburg, only a few hours away by bus. But Dorothea said she was at Holy Cross hospital and I wondered what illness my mother had that made her too sick to travel. So I would have to go to Hamburg myself -- no easy task with all the restrictions on traveling.

My next impulse was to reach Dorothea immediately. Long-distance calls were still forbidden, so the fastest way would be to mail Dorothea a postcard, too. Taking Lili's hand, I walked down the street, every now and then struggling against the gusts of wind. On the way I discovered a new store had opened: a radio repair shop. That would be my next job, to take our radio there for repair.

I found the newly opened post office located in a former military barracks. Only one postcard was allowed for each customer. I bought one for five *pfennigs*. I saw the imprinted

stamp still bore Hitler's portrait but was printed over with
"Germany's Demon" -- a smart combination of frugality and
reeducation.

I took out my pen, crouched down using my knees as a desk,
and wrote to Dorothea that the three of us were in good health
and she should visit us as soon as possible. "WHERE IN THE
WORLD IS MY MOTHER?" I wrote in big letters.

Returning to the apartment, our friendly co-tenant, Frau
Böttger, said, "Listen to the radio. There's news about refugees."

My egg-shaped radio! I rushed over to the junk corner of the
room and pulled it out from under the blankets. When I plugged
it in, it was dead. I shook it, hoping the coils and wires inside
might somehow fall into place, but it stayed dead. Time to get
to the radio repair shop four blocks away.

The young square-built repairman immediately checked the
radio and after only a few minutes of working with the interior,
he turned the knobs -- and Mozart's Jupiter Symphony
resounded.

"Great," I said. "At last I'll have music in the house."

The young man's face stayed solemn. "You may want to listen
to the news as well. The Allies are carrying out what they agreed
to do in Berlin." He started cleaning up the table.

"You mean the dismemberment of Germany?"

He snorted. "That has already been accomplished. Now
they're busy with the expulsion of millions of Germans still in
the East."

I swallowed before I said, "Oh God, my parents haven't
arrived here yet."

"Neither have mine. I've heard that the expulsion is being
carried out with inhuman cruelties." He stopped rearranging his
tools and shrugged. "Let's hope our parents will be spared."

Shocked, I rushed home, struggling against the wind. It had
grown to a howling gale that swept dust and debris through the
cluttered streets.

Back in our room, I plugged the radio in and turned it on. The
last movement of Mozart's Symphony filled the room. When the
Symphony ended, the newscaster came on, announcing an
eyewitness report from Berlin. There was a strong background
noise. It sounded like a crowd of excited people. The reporter's

words were terse and to the point, and his voice transmitted his agitation at what he saw.

"This is Berlin. I'm standing on the platform of a railway station where trains with freight cars from the East rolled in a few minutes ago."

The background noise of the people grew louder.

"Red Cross nurses and male helpers with stretchers are ready to receive the human load. At this moment, railroad workers are opening the freight cars. People will probably start disembarking in a minute -- I'm standing next to the second car from the engine. The door is open now, but no one's coming out -- I don't know why. I can see the people crowded in the stock car -- a nurse is talking to them, making inviting gestures. I get the impression they're afraid to come out -- but now a young woman is stepping to the edge of the stock car."

The reporter's voice darkened.

"She is dressed in a strange fashion; some kind of sack is wrapped around her and it looks as if she isn't wearing anything under it. She's talking to the nurse -- she seems to be making sure it's safe to come out. The young woman is turning around, talking to the people inside the car. Maybe she's reassuring them of a friendly reception."

What had happened to those inside the stock car? Like mistreated animals, too shy to come out. The reporter continued.

"Some people who had been sitting on the floor of the car are getting up and stepping forward. I see that none of them are fully dressed -- a few very old men are in their underwear, some half-naked; the same with the children."

His voice rose.

"The Red Cross helpers are rushing toward the stock cars -- I see the same thing happening at the other cars -- they're helping the people out, wrapping blankets around them -- the children refuse to be touched by the Red-Cross helpers, shying away from them, clinging to the rags of the adults."

I closed my eyes as if not wanting to see more. Yet my ears heard more.

"I'm trying to get closer to them -- I can see their faces now. The faces of the adults reflect an expression of total apathy and exhaustion, their hair is unkempt, many have dark rings under their eyes. The children are crying."

I could hear them.

"The Red Cross helpers have entered the freight cars now. They're putting people onto stretchers, covering them with blankets up to their chins -- a cold wind is blowing from the East."

There was static.

"I've climbed up on a bench. As far as I can see, these people coming out of the freight cars are predominantly women of all ages and children. Only here and there I see an old man or two -- the same with the sick people on the stretchers. The platform is crowded now; all are walking to the staircase -- the Red Cross will take them to the hospital. They're taking dead bodies out, putting them on stretchers, covering them completely -- they're leaving the platform."

Silence. The report had ended. In disbelief, I stared at the brown egg-shaped radio that had magically brought me into contact with the world. Yet what a world! Who were those miserable fugitives? Oh God, had anything like this happened to my parents?

Unannounced, a Mozart concerto sounded from the radio, probably intended to soothe, to comfort the listener after the horrible report.

Angrily, I switched the radio off. The war, my old arch enemy, even now, five months after its end, kept breeding violence, its ugly poison flooding over innocent women, children and old men. Danzig and other areas were given away and to silence any protests the populations were simply thrown out! I saw the men of the world, of all ages and races, their minds infested by the tradition of war, their military leaders boasting of their murderous achievements. The generals, conducting the war theater, diligently counted soldiers, tanks and bombers but never asked or considered three quarters of the population, the women, the children, the old. As these were killed, burned, raped, starved or maimed, the reports left them out. How long would the survivors remain silent?

I tried to find the reason for the continuation of this primitive thinking; that mutually slaughtering each other was the solution of problems. Who in the world prepared male minds for destroying the world? Since Adam and Eve, mothers had raised their sons to be boys who could fight their way through life. Then later, when national problems arose it took only a small step to transform the tough boys into tough soldiers. Hadn't all the mothers I'd known raised their boys to become soldiers? To fight for their country and fight till the end? When would the time come when women would implant in their sons the message of peace? It was then that I promised myself: if I ever had a son I would teach him there should be no more wars.

Later than usual, Manfred came home, his hair disheveled. "The gale is so strong it's almost a hurricane!" he exclaimed.

While we were eating I showed him Dorothea's postcard.

He stopped eating. "She doesn't mention your mother at all!"

"I know," I said miserably. I told him about the repair of the radio. "I heard an awful radio report about the arrival of refugees in the East."

"I heard it too. In the shipyard. These people coming out of the East now are called expellees, in contrast to the refugees, like you, who left of their own volition."

Expellees! That's what the miserable people in the boxcars were called. "What did you hear about them?"

"An average of 25,000 arrive in Berlin every day."

"My God, what is this? What's going on in the East?"

In a low voice, trembling with controlled anger, he said, "The Poles are expelling all remaining Germans from the territories they've taken over, and they're doing it in an inhuman way."

"Why doesn't the Red Cross interfere?"

"They didn't during the Nazi time either."

"For God's sake, can't we get help from the British and the Americans?" I shouted.

"Remember? Russians, Americans and Britons agreed to the expulsion and signed the agreement in Berlin-Potsdam this summer. The papers reprinted it today." He took the newspaper from his briefcase. I read:

THE POTSDAM DECLARATION

Orderly Transfers of German Populations

The Berlin Conference reached the following agreement on the removal of Germans from Poland, Czechoslovakia and Hungary: The three governments recognize that the transfer to Germany of German populations remaining in Poland, Czechoslovakia and Hungary will have to be undertaken. They agree that any transfers that take place should be effected in an orderly and humane manner.

Approved:

J.V.Stalin

Harry S. Truman

C.R.Attlee

I threw the paper on the table. "They call it orderly and humane? But they're committing atrocities! How come the Western Allies don't interfere in the East?"

Manfred shrugged. "They've lost their lever on the Russians. They're powerless in the East."

I felt my rebellion collapse. "Can't we do anything about it?"

With a bitter snort Manfred replied, "We're the most powerless of all." His voice sounded heavy with hopelessness.

I rose and went to his side of the table. Standing above him, I silently put my hand on his. He lowered his head, laying his forehead on my hand. I put my other hand on his smooth ash blond hair. "I love you," I said softly.

Suddenly I felt my hand, on which his forehead rested, getting wet. Manfred was crying. I heard him sob and saw him fumbling in his pocket for his handkerchief.

I smiled as I said, "Good, you found your handkerchief. It's our only one."

Energetically he wiped the last tears from his face. "One day we'll have more."

"It may take a while. But I'll always be with you." He pulled me down on his knees and held me tight.

PRELUDE TO AN INFERNO

During the next days I arranged with Frau Böttger to take care of Lili while I was busy coaching. I also had to talk to Angela Rymann about money. I had promised Manfred.

The prima donna strode into the room and with an inflated gesture placed sheet music on the top of the piano. "My dear, are you ready for good news? Ulrich von Gonsenheim will be in Wilhelmshaven this week to rehearse with you and me."

"Who is Ulrich von Gonsenheim?"

"The famous flutist, my dear. Haven't you heard his name? That's unforgivable! He's an old friend of mine and we want to do a recital. With you as our accompanist, of course." And as if she realized money was a burning issue between herself and me, she came up with a glistening promise. "We'll split the income." That was more than I had expected. "We'll meet at the city theater. Saturday, ten a.m."

Three more days to wait.

A second postcard from Dorothea arrived.

Liebe Frau Eva:
Glad you all are well. You *must* come to Hamburg. Please come as soon as you can.
    Dorothea.

A mystery! Why didn't Dorothea say the most important thing: how my mother was? No matter, I had to go to Hamburg. How was I going to get official permission to take the bus?

My stomach growled. "Drink a glass of water when you're hungry," Frau Böttger had said the other day. I did.

I heard the doorbell ring. Let Frau Böttger open it this time, I thought. A moment later, there was a knock on the door and Frau Böttger's voice said, "There's a gentleman at the door who wants to see you."

Father! it screamed in me. I rushed to the door.

A very tall, thin man -- *not* my father. My spirits crashed. The man in the somewhat crumpled greenish-gray Army uniform with all the military buttons removed carried a small suitcase.

I saw his slick black hair, his dark-rimmed glasses riding on his Roman nose -- it was Fritz, my girl friend Erika's husband, who had spent his last night in Danzig in my apartment on Lili's mattress!

We hugged each other for a long time.

"Where in the world have you come from?" I asked.

"American captivity."

As we walked into our room, his first question was, "Have you heard from Erika and the baby?"

Sadly, I shook my head. "Have you checked the Red Cross lists?"

"I found *your* address but not hers."

"You have to check the lists regularly," I told him. "30,000 people arrive from the East daily."

"I know." He sat down on a chair. "I've decided to go to Lübeck. That's where most people from the East arrive. I hope to find Erika and Helga there." His voice sounded hopeless. As he adjusted his glasses, I remembered he'd always done this when he felt anxious.

"How will you get to Lübeck?" I asked.

"In two hours, a friend of mine is picking me up with his car."

"A friend with a car? Who in the world is that? Having a car?"

"An American," he said. "A doctor from the POW camp hospital. He officially asked for my assistance in surgery and we became friends."

At this moment, Lili walked in. While she hugged and kissed me Fritz rummaged in his suitcase. He produced a huge number of candy bars and put them on the kitchen table for Lili. She unwrapped one with the speed of a pickpocket. Fritz took her on his lap and hugged her. I could feel how much he missed his own little daughter.

"Helga must be two years old now, right?"

"A little bit over."

Silence. I thought of the atrocities which were going on in the East at this very moment; he must be wondering if his wife and daughter had been spared.

Fortunately, Manfred's arrival interrupted our uncomfortable silence. He was as glad to see our old friend as I was. We all stayed in the kitchen to give me a chance to watch over the boiling potatoes, serve tea and to prepare a raw cabbage salad.

Meanwhile Fritz briefed Manfred on his captivity. "We all were fed quite well. We were supposed to be shipped to America, but four days after they captured us, the war was over and we had to stay."

"You were lucky."

"I felt the opposite. I would have loved to see America."

Manfred smiled. "I agree. It would have been an incredible experience. Just to see their technology. When I think of the way the Americans built ships on the assembly line while we were still wasting our time with our ancient methods ..."

Fritz pulled a handkerchief from his trouser pocket and cleaned Lili's chocolate-smeared face. "As far as technology is concerned, I imagine that you'd like America. My American friend and I spend a lot of time together discussing our two countries. In medicine they're also way ahead of us. But as far as prejudice is concerned, they're our equals."

"Prejudice? Against the Negroes?"

"Against the Germans! You won't believe how the propaganda machine has worked in America. People over there think all Germans were SS puppets."

"I can't believe it," Manfred said.

Fritz adjusted his glasses. "One man on the surgery table asked me how many Jews I'd killed. A communication clerk asked me if I'd been a stud."

"What's that?" I asked.

"A male animal kept for selective breeding. Some American newspapers told their readers that men of certain height and stature were used as studs to breed a special race."

Manfred burst into laughter. "What a great idea! To spend a life just doing that!"

I slapped his arm. "Come on, you boaster!" I got up to check the potatoes and put them on the table. We started peeling them. "I wonder how the Americans are behaving in Southern Germany," I said. "Are they as nice as the Britons in our zone?"

"They're all so very different. Most are nice." He hesitated. "Unfortunately, they have reopened concentration camps."

"Whaaat?"

"Don't you have them here in the British zone?" Fritz asked. "The British have the honor of inventing them half a century ago, and from what I've heard, they were the first ones to reopen our old concentration camps and put Germans in. The Americans followed suit."

Manfred finished peeling. "Yes, they did it here, too. They've even put a very dear friend of mine in one."

"Who?" I asked, horrified.

"Helmut Kalmbach," he said.

I stood petrified. "For what?"

"For having been a naval officer of a certain rank."

"But that's incredible! Nine months after the end of the war?"

Manfred leaned back in his chair. "In the last war days Helmut was automatically promoted to Naval-*Bau-Rat*. The British and Americans rightly translated it to mean Naval-Construction Consultant. In their wisdom they came to the conclusion that, whoever was a consultant counseled the Nazi government and therefore is a villain. He had to be put in a concentration camp."

I was thunderstruck. "And how are they treated there?"

"Not exactly nice from what I've heard," Manfred said.

Fritz frowned. His glasses slid and he adjusted them. "It probably depends on the boss. Some are fair, others are brutal. Like in the Nazi concentration camps, it's the sadists who are responsible for the brutalities."

Manfred got up. "Let's clear the kitchen for the others. It's ten to seven. We'll listen to the news."

Fritz looked at his wrist watch. "I still have half an hour."

I rinsed the dishes under running cold water before going over to the big room.

Manfred had turned the radio on and we sat, facing the egg-shaped set as the music of Strauss' *Death and Transfiguration* sounded through the room. Immediately after the last notes came the voice of the newscaster:

"*Guten Abend*. The stream of expellees from the East is flooding into Berlin day and night. Of the more than 30,000 arrivals ten percent are dead. Another ten percent die within days after reaching Berlin. The remainder are half-starved and ill. Ninety-five percent are women and children, and five percent of the men are over seventy years old. Almost all women have been raped by Russian soldiers repeatedly and are receiving medical treatment to prevent the spread of venereal diseases."

There was an unusual pause before the newscaster spoke again.

"The practice of raping women has no age barrier. Women of eighty and children of six years have been violated. The number of suicides among these women is in the thousands."

Again, a pause. I put my hands over my ears. Mother, where are you? What has happened to you?

"The expulsion of fourteen million East Germans had been agreed to by the Allies in Yalta and in Berlin."

Manfred turned off the radio.

"It's unbelievable!" I burst out.

Manfred got up and walked to the window. Holding his hands together behind his back, he seemed to speak to himself. "This savagery is going on over there right now and nobody is stopping it."

"Why don't the Allies stop it?" I asked.

"They're the ones who are doing it."

"The Anglo-Americans aren't," Fritz protested, "the Russians are."

"They're Allies," Manfred said.

I flared up. "How can they be?"

Manfred shrugged. "They're strange bedfellows, to say the least."

Silence.

Manfred slowly turned around. "We're defeated. There's no way we can ask for justice."

I heard Fritz's dry voice. "When we were victorious, we were no angels either."

Angrily, I asked him, "Did you or your friends rape children and eighty-year old women in any country you conquered?"

"I didn't," Fritz replied. "But I can't speak for the others."

"Do you think any German man has behaved as the Russians are doing?"

Fritz adjusted his glasses. "I can't speak for the SS in Russia."

"We'll never hear what happened over there," I said. My immediate problem made me change the subject. "I have to go to Hamburg as soon as possible." I showed them Dorothea's mysterious postcard.

"Do you know the train to Hamburg starts tomorrow?" he asked. "I just heard it at the railway station." He told us that everyone could go now without a permit.

"Fantastic!" I burst out. "Do you know what time the train leaves?"

"They said ten a.m."

"You should go," Manfred said. "Then you'll have peace of mind."

After a look at his wrist watch Fritz rose. "Time for me to leave. I don't want my friend to wait. Americans are usually on time. By the way," he added, "I want you to meet him."

"Tell him to come up," Manfred suggested.

"They're not allowed to enter German residences. But why don't you come downstairs and meet him?"

"Let's see what an American looks like," Manfred joked. "I've never seen one."

Arriving at the dark street, I saw the clear, star-bedecked sky, with its crescent moon hanging over the phantom-like ruins.

An open jeep stood in front of the house. In the dim light from a gas lamp on the street I could read the white letters below its windshield: MILITARY POLICE. Inside sat a young American Army officer, his capless head turned toward us. Seeing Fritz, he jumped out and approached us. He was of Manfred's height, but with a paunch and a cigarette in his mouth. "There you are," he said to Fritz.

How strange the words sound, I thought, almost not English at all. His blond short-cropped hair looked a bit ridiculous to me, but as far as I could see his features were as handsome as Manfred's -- I wondered if he had blue eyes, too.

"Eva, this is my friend Jim Porter from Los Angeles, California," Fritz said.

The American threw his cigarette away. "Hi, Eva," he said in a friendly, strangely nasal voice. "Nice meeting you." The man called me by my first name! How did he dare?

When Fritz introduced Manfred, the American said, "Hi, Manfred, nice to meet you." Manfred bowed slightly, the American did not. The defeated and the victor! I thought.

Fritz seemed to sense my bewilderment. "Americans call most people by their first names. And they don't bow."

My astonishment grew when I saw the American bend down to Lili and pat her cheek. "What's your name, honey?" Was he going to give her honey? I thought. The British often carried sweets along, too.

Fritz translated. "This is Lili, two years old."

When I saw him crouch before her I expected the American to produce a can of honey. His face even with Lili's, he said, "You're a cutie-pie. Just like my own little daughter at home."

I didn't know what cutie-pie meant but I understood he was a father, missing his child on the other side of the world. "How long has it been since you have seen your daughter?" I asked.

"Seven months," he replied, still looking at Lili. He turned to me. "Would Lili like a short ride in my jeep?"

"I'm sure she would." I asked her in German. Lili, easygoing with friends and strangers alike, wiggled with joy. "*Ja!*" The American seemed to understand that much German. He put Lili on the seat, jumped in beside her and drove away.

While we were waiting in the dark, Manfred said, "Look at the boards over there." He was staring at the ruins of a house across the street. "It's good fire wood."

"It's wet from the rain."

"It could be dried..." His voice trailed off.

I forgot his remarks as a minute later the jeep appeared from the other side and stopped in front of the house. Lili beamed. "*Noch 'mal!*" she screamed.

"Once more," Fritz translated.

Jim, as though waiting for her command, drove away again.

I felt excited. "What fun for Lili! He's really a nice person."

"I told you so," Fritz said. But his face reflected concern. "We have to be in Lübeck tomorrow morning. So I'll have time to search for Erika and the baby."

"I wish you all the luck in the world," I said warmly.

"And I wish you luck with your mother," he replied.

The jeep returned, stopped. Jim jumped out and took out the beaming Lili. She ran into my arms.

"Thank you so much, Dr.Porter," I said.

"It's Jim," he said. Then he added. "I pretended she was my little girl." I realized that even in his strange uniform and with his unfamiliar American accent, he was a human being who loved his child and longed to be home. I now felt he was one of us. The world was small and people were reaching out for each other. I had to restrain myself from hugging him. "Thank you, Jim," I finally said, using his first name easily. We shook hands, saying good-bye to each other.

Suddenly, Jim ran to the jeep and rummaged in his travel bags, looking for something. He came back with a large red apple. "For Lili," he said.

What a treasure! "It's Lili's first apple," I said to him. How much would I love to hug him for this! Was this done and understood in America? Instead, I lifted Lili up to him. She hugged and kissed him.

Fritz and the American drove away under stars and a crescent moon that hung so low it looked reachable. The world seemed wondrous and tranquil.

Climbing the stairs with Manfred and Lili, I realized it had been only a small break in the horror. Not far away, the world was in turmoil.

AWAY TO HAMBURG

We looked at the room we'd reserved for my parents. In two days, I'd be back with my mother. My father could arrive even before us! Then I'd move heaven and earth -- the charity committee -- to get furniture for them.

Manfred gripped my arms and said gently, "Keep up your courage, Little Bear. Your trip won't be easy. You'll probably see and hear horrible things. Try everything to bring your mother home." I nodded.

Lili was going to stay with Frau Böttger. "Only one time night-night," I told her, "then Mommy will be home again."

I took my overnight things and two days' supply of dry bread, which all fit into my shopping net.

Driven by travel fever I arrived early at the railway station, realizing how much I enjoyed my freedom from the confinement of our room at the apartment house.

The rectangular, sandy-colored train station had been a frequent target of British bombers and all the residential buildings of the surrounding neighborhood had been razed. Ironically, the station itself remained untouched.

After buying a round-trip ticket to Hamburg I walked to the roofed platform. I breathed in the odor of metal and coal dust, smells that reminded me of childhood vacation trips.

Soon, the chugging of the locomotive, far away at first, then growing louder, aroused my excitement. As the train rolled in, the waiting crowd became tense as usual; each traveler wanted to climb on the train first. The moment the cars came to a shuddering halt, people started elbowing and pushing, yelling and calling each other names. War or peace, German travelers hadn't changed a bit.

Once in the passenger car, I looked into every compartment, but found them all full. I had to stand in the corridor until, some 45 minutes later, we arrived in Bremen, the only stop before Hamburg. Passengers got off and luckily I found a place in a non-smoking compartment. Above the two wooden benches colorful pictures of scenic vacation resorts reminded travelers of dream places, now as impossible to reach as the stars.

Taking my place at the window, I looked at my companions, a girl in a *dirndl* dress, a chic woman and two men, the older one smelling of fish.

Soon, the routine game of train conversations started, progressing from trivia to camaraderie. Today, it opened with gloomy remarks about Germany's collapse.

The fish-smelling man said, "It was wrong to surrender. We should have held out until England and America found out they were fighting on the wrong side." Oh, an unbending Nazi.

The younger man reddened. "Are you one of those they're looking for these days? I'm talking about denazification."

"I've never been a Nazi!" cried the Nazi.

"But you sound like one."

Suddenly, a conductor opened the door, asking for our tickets. As he checked and punched them laboriously, it turned out the hellhound had no valid ticket; he was playing the favorite game of travelers in Germany. A routine dispute arose. When the conductor asked the Nazi to follow him he just shrugged, realizing he'd lost the game. Both of them left the compartment. So did the smell of fish.

Immediately, the chic woman pulled a silver box from her handbag, which bore the initials M.D., and offered English cigarettes to all.

Soon, the empty seat beside the young man was occupied by a fat man in clerical garb and Roman collar. Seeing the majority in the compartment smoking, he pulled snuff from his pocket and sniffed the powdered tobacco from his hand.

M.D. blew several perfect rings into the air. The entire compartment was filled with blue smoke, and I began to dream of a place and a time where no one smoked. Shangri-La!

Looking outside, I took in the monotony of the foggy scenery, the flying telephone poles and the knocking rhythm of the train wheels. Turning around I saw the girl in the *dirndl* dress arguing with the young man, who said he was a Marxist. Marx or not, at least this follower didn't smoke. Communists are marvelous people, I concluded with inner sarcasm.

"The Allies prohibited the Red Cross from delivering food to the interned Germans in the camps," M.D. said. "The Allies feel the Germans have to be punished."

No one asked, "Why?"

"But who are the Allies?" I asked. "Those millions of Americans and British or a single person? Who makes a decision like that?"

M.D. deeply inhaled cigarette smoke and said, "From what I understand, Henry Morgenthau is mainly responsible. He has an enormous influence in the American government."

"What does Morgenthau want?" I asked.

"To reduce Germany to an agrarian state," the priest answered.

"We all are supposed to become peasants?" I asked.

"Since we don't have enough arable land," the priest said. "That would mean death by starvation for us all."

I shook my head in disbelief.

"There is a way out!" The young Communist rose to new heights of oratory. "If we all unite and go the Communist way we will have the Soviet Union behind us. We would be saved."

Rage shot up in me. "Saved by those mass rapists?" I shouted. My mother came to mind -- my throat choked and I searched for my handkerchief.

The country girl put her arm around my shoulders and asked tenderly, "Did you have bad experiences with the Russians?"

I blew my nose. "I'm afraid something has happened to my mother."

The girl hugged me tighter. "She'll recover, they all do."

She was right. No matter what had happened, my mother would recover. "Thank you for your words," I said.

The girl opened her handbag, unwrapped a round golden-crusted bun, and offered it to me. It was sliced, yellow cheese and pink ham visible at the edges. It smelled delicious. Am I in the land of milk and honey? I asked myself. I saw the girl conjuring up cookies, candies and American cigarettes. I devoured the bun. The combination, cheese and ham, was new to me. I wondered if it was what the Americans ate.

The young Communist finished his portion of American food -- smooth yellow butter cookies. "You must have very good friends in Southern Germany," he said, eyeing her green *dirndl* dress with its close-fitting bodice and full skirt.

"I know the American soldiers well," she answered calmly. "I was starving, and they were lonely. I'm not starving anymore. And they're very nice and generous." All of us here had just profited from American generosity.

The air was so smoky I could hardly see the people I faced.

"You're from Nürnberg?" M.D. asked the country girl. "I noticed your accent."

"You're thinking of the Nürnberg trials?" asked the girl. "They're a shame, aren't they?"

The young Communist braced himself. "They're very just trials!"

The country girl's voice was full of irony as she asked, "Is that your party line?"

"The Nazis have to be punished!" he cried.

"But not by the enemy!" the country girl countered.

M.D.'s calm voice sounded in the airless compartment. "There's no doubt about the humiliating effect of the Nürnberg trials. Of course, you realize the court's authority has no basis in international law. It is very arrogant of the Allies to set up the trials and presume to judge the German leaders."

"But there are real criminals among them," I said.

"But it's not the Allies' business to judge them," she replied. On the one hand she is right, I thought, on the other, would the Germans put the Nazis on trial at all?

The Communist cleared his throat. "The trials clearly show that war is not an 'Act of God' but man-made. And the man who started it all this time was Hitler."

"And the people who supported him," the priest said.

I stared at the two men who actually stood on opposite sides of the rainbow. Never had I heard the essence of our past being expressed that clearly. Hitler's guilt, his followers guilt, our collective guilt -- would we ever be free of it?

During my brooding I had missed part of the conversation. Listening now, I realized that my companions had reached a lighter level of judgement.

The country girl knocked the ash from her cigarette on the floor. "Do you know the joke often told in the American zone? This is the classification used at the Nürnberg trials: the French supply the Army, the British the Navy, the Americans the Air Force and the Germans the war criminals."

The group roared with laughter. The joke was the ending of our hour-long camaraderie.

The train approached Hamburg's center, rolling past hundreds of giraffe-like cranes, past many slim, pointed church gables and the famous *Michel*, St. Michael's imposing tower. At last, the train entered the central station. We all wished each other a good day, left the train and went our separate ways.

I loved the huge, awe-evoking, cathedral-like halls of central railway stations. Hamburg was no exception. The steel dome arched over the many tracks and trains, and sounds reflected and intermingled in the vast hall. The dome's metal had survived uncounted air raids, but the many glass plates between the net-like steel frames were shattered. Through the steel grid I could see Hamburg's eternal clouds.

I walked out into the streets. A cold wind blew from the North Sea, and I gratefully inhaled the fresh scent. Low gray clouds hung over the wide square and the remnants of surrounding buildings.

I asked a sturdy matron how to get to the Holy Cross Hospital. "There's a truck to that area. It comes every hour."

Hamburg and Danzig! Both cities had their roots in the medieval past. They were members of the powerful Hanseatic League, the guild of rich merchants who had trading relations with Northern Europe, England, Amsterdam and even Venice. Over the centuries, Danzig and Hamburg had spread their cultural and mercantile wealth over the German population and elevated it to special status in Europe. Now both cities were reduced to ghost towns and rubble, Danzig even thrown to the Poles.

After almost thirty minutes, the truck, uncovered and open at the end, stopped in front of me. A small wooden ladder hung down at the back, so with some gymnastic effort, one could board the vehicle. Since there were no benches the passengers had to stand and when the truck stopped or started, we all fell onto each other, held upright by those who could hold on to the truck's sides.

A collector with an official cap demanded that everyone pay him fifteen *pfennigs* for the ride, and he missed no one. As we hit several pot holes the truck rumbled and clumsily bumped up and down. The engine's noise reverberated from the charred facades, as if the ghost town was mocking us, the survivors.

Suddenly the skeletons of the burnt-out buildings were left behind and the truck entered a depressing rubble desert with nothing left standing. I recalled the area as having dignified villas and flowering gardens. Where once chic women in mink coats had sauntered, furry rats now prowled in the debris.

Even in Kiel and Mudtown I'd never seen such destruction. I addressed a man next to me. "How many bombing attacks did it take to destroy this area?"

"Just one. In July '43. Blockbuster bombs. 55,000 civilians died in one night."

"So, as a revenge, we bombed London with missiles."

"And as a revenge for that the Americans destroyed Dresden."

Revenge without end. Sadly I looked over the unreal moonscape. A thin column of smoke ascended from the rubble, a blue smoke pillar bent by the wind. "Where's the smoke coming from?" I asked my neighbor.

"Bombed-out people live under the rubble of their former homes. They're probably cooking potatoes."

For a moment I thought it was a bad joke. Yet a woman's voice behind me called, "Stop! I want to get off."

"Knock on the wall!" one man ordered. Someone pounded on the driver's window and immediately, the truck stopped. The collector jumped down and helped the woman and a child climb down the ladder. Then he beat his fist against the truck side and athletically jumped on the vehicle, which drove off again.

In total disbelief I looked back at mother and child cautiously walking over the rubble, presumably to their cave. Children living like rats in holes! What if Lili had to live this way? How grateful I should be for having our room in Mudtown!

A few minutes later, we arrived at the Holy Cross Hospital. A large, white rectangular building, five stories high and covering a half block, towered before me. A metal cross on its flat roof indicated the staff was dedicated to healing and nursing in the name of Christ.

My mother and Dorothea were in there. In what shape would I find them? Within minutes I would know.

THE WITNESS

As I climbed the hospital's staircase, the sweetish smell of ether enveloped me so strongly I thought I could taste it. On the first floor, a long corridor ran the width of the building. It was lined with doors, each with a number, and a light above it. Dignified quiet filled the atmosphere.

A matronly nun in an undulating habit approached. Her black veil and white headdress covered everything but her face and hands. "*Guten Morgen,*" I greeted her.

"*Grüss Gott*-greetings to God," the nun corrected me.

Oops, my first mistake. I had to learn how to behave in a nunnery. "May I visit Dorothea Engels?"

"Wait a moment," the nun said. She opened one of the doors and called to someone inside.

Within seconds, a lay nurse, small and slender, in a white uniform and a white round nurse's cap, appeared at the door. "Frau Eva!" she cried out.

Dorothea was a nurse! Before I could grasp the extent of the former housekeeper's metamorphosis our arms reached out, and we held each other for a long time.

We drew apart. "I can't believe it's you!" I pointed to her uniform and cap.

She smiled proudly. "Now I'm something better than a maid!" She looked young and cheerful and professional in her white uniform; her blue eyes radiating quiet pride. She had achieved what she wanted. I felt happy for her.

Then, I could no longer hold it in. "Where is my mother? How is she?"

Instead of answering, Dorothea took my hand. "Your mother is dead," she said quietly.

The blow of the unexpected words made me stagger. Everything went black and the building seemed to whirl about me. As if from far away I felt an arm around my waist, supporting me.

"Come to my dormitory," Dorothea said and I followed her.

We walked upstairs to the dorm. Still in shock, I glanced over the many immaculately made beds. Stacked in threes, they were placed closely together. Several metal lockers stood against the walls. A huge wooden cross dominated the room. Dorothea, an ardent Catholic, must love it here.

She gently pushed me on one of the lower bunks. "Lie down on my bed." She sat down on the bed's edge and laid her hand on my cheek. I felt an immense grief well up within me, turning into tears.

"Cry, Frau Eva," I heard my friend say. "Get it all out."

I would never see my mother again. When I had cried myself out, I sat up, wiping my nose. Dorothea handed me a handkerchief. "Come here to the wash basin," she commanded. "Wash your face. Here's a towel." I obeyed.

Then she led me back to her bunk and sat down opposite me. "How did my mother die?" I asked in a low voice.

Dorothea looked straight into my eyes. "I'll tell you all about it. First you should know she died in Danzig. She's buried there. She sleeps in quiet and peace. I suggest you lie down for a minute, Frau Eva. You must excuse me. I have to look for my substitute." Momentarily I fell asleep.

I woke up as I heard Dorothea come back. I sat up immediately. "Did you find your substitute?"

She nodded. "I have five hours until six p.m." Again, we sat on opposite beds. "Now tell me about my mother," I said.

Dorothea looked away from me as if seeing into the past. "I have to get the events in order so you can understand them." She sighed. I could see how difficult it was for her to recall. "When Danzig was under fire we spent days and nights in the cellar while the Russians bombed the city. Then our house was hit. We ran out of the cellar. The streets were burning. Somehow we made it to the shelter of your uncle's factory." She halted for a moment. "The next day the Russians came. Their coats went down to their ankles. They aimed their rifles at us and yelled, 'Watches! Watches!' Everybody took his wrist watch off and handed it over to them. I didn't have one." She swallowed, then spoke faster. "So one Russian pulled me on a mattress and raped me. When he was through, the next came and so all six of them. Then they stole some meat cans your uncle had on a shelf and left."

With horror, I listened. "The next day, we women tried to camouflage ourselves by wrapping scarves around our heads and smearing dirt on our faces to look older. Around midday, the next Russians came in. They were very drunk but still could point their rifles at us and command, 'Watches! Watches!' None of us had wrist watches anymore. The soldiers got mad and started destroying kerosene lamps and food jars with their rifles and some even peed on a small amount of potatoes. Then they grabbed your uncle's secretary and took turns raping her. Others grabbed me. Then other women."

She stretched out her hand, covering mine. "I'm sorry, Frau Eva. Your mother was raped, too, by five Russians. She told me after they'd gone. She cried a bit and said she was in pain. But we were all in so much terror and panic that none of us really knew what we were doing." She took her hand from mine. "Through all the lamentation I heard the voice of our pharmacist from next door, saying we shouldn't panic. He had a poison for all of us if we wanted to take it. I heard your father say, 'This is nonsense!' But the pharmacist tried to give each of us a tiny ampule. He said it contained potassium cyanide. We would feel no pain and it would kill within a few seconds. I refused even to receive it. I was ready to accept whatever God had decided for me. But all the others put the ampules into their pockets or handbags. A few minutes later, your aunt called me over to her. I went and saw your mother outstretched on the floor. She had taken the poison."

My head throbbed and spots danced dizzily before my eyes. My head felt so heavy I had to lie down. Suddenly, I realized my mother had willfully ended her misery. The others had chosen to live. My mother had not been killed; she had decided to walk into eternity; leaving her beloved ones behind, without even saying farewell.

I sat up again. "What do you know about my father? Where did he go? Why did you say on your postcard he'd be with us soon?"

"Haven't you heard from him yet?" I shook my head. "I know so little about where he is," she replied. "Your uncle and your aunt took him to their house in the suburbs. Months later I saw him on the street; I believe it was July. He said he was on his way to work. He didn't look starved like most people."

"What work?"

"One of his former Polish employees, Feliks Miszczalski, had arranged a job for him as an electrician."

"That aristocratic-looking man who himself had worked as an electrician?"

She nodded. "You know how fairly your father treated his Polish employees, he never made distinctions between Germans and Poles. And when the time came to repay, Miszczalski became the assistant to the Polish governor of Gdansk and got your father a job so he could live a relatively decent life."

"Do you think he's alive?"

Dorothea blinked. "I hope so." She got up. Walking to a spot from where she apparently could see a clock, she said, "Let's go to the dining room. I'll make you some coffee."

I took one slice of bread from my shopping net, saving the last one for evening. As we walked downstairs, I tried to figure out where my father could be. "You said he worked in Gdansk until July, right?"

"That's when I spoke to him."

"The Germans were expelled in August, weren't they? Now, it's the end of October. Where could he be?"

"I don't know," Dorothea replied.

As we walked through long corridors I saw a lay nurse helping an old man walk; a nun pushed a stretcher on wheels, loaded with a patient. "How did you manage to become a nurse?"

"When we left your uncle's burning cellar, I went to the nuns at the *St. Marien*-Hospital. I knew the nuns quite well from the underground."

I'd been right all along. "You really were in the underground?"

"For years. I couldn't tell you, no matter how close we were. Keeping my mouth shut meant staying alive." How well I understood that! "Anyway, I found refuge with the nuns. I helped them with the patients and learned quite a bit over there. When I was sent to this hospital for recovery, I told the nuns here I was experienced. They agreed to hire me as a student nurse." She was radiant; her life's wish had been fulfilled.

We entered the dining room, a large hall with long tables and chairs in perfect order. Dorothea picked up a huge coffee pot in the kitchen and filled two cups with ersatz coffee. It smelled conspicuously of corn and barley.

I told Dorothea about all my experiences, about Manfred and Lili. "Now it's your turn. Tell me about the underground and what happened in Danzig after the Russians came in." Every topic seemed easier to discuss than the one of my mother's death.

I ate my dry bread. Dorothea sipped her coffee, put her cup down and stared into the opaque liquid as if conjuring up memories. "It was strange to know the bombing had stopped for good and the Nazis were gone and the Soviets were the masters. But we soon found out we were no more than rotten animals to them, to be used or discarded. The raping went on. Yet they added another amusement, target shooting. It became a sport."

"What were they shooting at?"

"At people! Fortunately, the soldiers were so drunk most of the time, they had trouble hitting their targets."

"Couldn't you run away?"

"Run away? Where to? Wherever we went there were Russians. And it was always the same. When they saw women, they commanded: 'Woman, come!' And if we wanted to survive, we let ourselves be dragged into a house or cellar." She smiled bitterly. "It was too cold for them on the street."

I tried to picture the scenes but they were beyond my experience.

"It was mass insanity. The first week after the fall of Danzig was the worst -- probably because of the drunkenness. The daily, hourly senseless killing of people! They let the dead bodies lie in the street -- we weren't allowed to bury them. When the stench of the corpses became unbearable, the Russians poured vodka on them and set them on fire." Her fingers nervously drummed on the table.

"Were all Russians that bad? Weren't there any exceptions?"

"Not all were bad. There were some -- officers mainly -- who tried to keep their comrades from setting fires, raping and destroying. Sometimes they even protected us from their own people. Sometimes we would even see the two sides of the coin.

A drunken soldier rapes a girl; then the next day when he's sober, he comes back to look for her and brings her bread and chocolate."

Both our cups were empty. I tried to refill them but the coffe pot was empty. "Jesus, Maria," Dorothea said, "there were about six cups! We are real *Kaffeeklatsch* women!"

We both exploded with laughter, a nervous laughter, but nevertheless a relief.

"We'd better go into the kitchen and wash the dishes before the kitchen staff gets busy for dinner," Dorothea said.

As we carried the pot and cups into the kitchen I wondered how people like Dorothea could go through such ordeals and still remain normal.

We stepped to the sink and quickly washed the cups and pot. "Your underground activities are still a wonder to me," I said. I left the drying of the dishes to Dorothea and sat down on top of a table.

She put the cups into a closet. "Many Catholics were active in the underground. Some were caught and ended up in concentration camps. Thank God I was spared *that*!"

"What kind of people were in the underground?"

"Priests, teachers, maids like myself. We all had our duties and functions. I had to bring food to Poles who escaped. They were hiding at the *St.Marien*-Hospital. I had to carry things for the hidden Poles. I always dropped the packages into a certain place in the corridor."

"Where did you meet?"

"We didn't. The Gestapo would have caught us immediately. It was more like whispering orders and information to each other. *My* contacts were the nuns in the *St.Marien*-Hospital."

"That's why you turned to them after you all ran out of my uncle's burning cellar?"

"Yes."

As we walked upstairs, she asked if I had a place to stay overnight? I didn't.

"Don't worry about it. I just have to ask the Mother Superior for permission to let you use the office with the couch. Come on, let's get some fresh air."

We walked through the basement, and Dorothea opened a door to the backyard. Now, at the end of October, lawn and flowers were gone; there was nothing left of greenery or leaves. Spider-like skeletons of hibernating trees created a desolate sight. Yet the wind was refreshing after the long stay in the ether-smelling building; it blew the North Sea's harsh aroma around our heads.

We turned a corner. Against a wall was a row of garbage cans. A large dog came along, skinny and obviously hungry, put his forepaws on the edge of the smallest garbage can and rummaged with one paw in the waste. He found an acceptable scrap, swallowed it and trotted away. A homeless creature.

A moment later, a little boy, about twelve, approached the garbage cans. He wore an ex-army coat that hung to his feet. His back toward us, he started investigating the various trash cans, rummaging and now and then eating scraps.

"Have we come that far?" I asked Dorothea.

"I don't consider it special," she replied. "The majority of the Germans in Danzig went begging, rummaging in garbage cans just like that boy."

My father, rummaging in garbage cans.....

"When the Russians took over Danzig, they showed no mercy. First, there was no distribution of food at all and everyone scavenged from the garbage whatever he could find. Later on, once in a while, they gave out potatoes and cabbage. Then, the German *Reichsmark* became invalid and the Polish *zloty* was the legal currency." She smiled with bitterness. "In those days you could see bills of fifty or hundred marks lying in the streets or swept up in the corners."

"Who would do something like that?"

"Probably Germans from despair, or the Russians and Poles to make fools of the Germans' lost cause. Who knows? No matter. It was a strange sight, Germans wading in mark bills and eating out of garbage cans at the same time."

"How could they survive on garbage?"

"It takes a while to die of starvation, Frau Eva. Before that come typhus and dysentery. Our hospital in Gdansk was crowded with those cases."

As we walked away from the garbage area the wind became stronger, howling and pulling at us. Nevertheless, we continued.

"Were there any doctors left in *St. Marien*?" I asked.

"Not too many. Raped women had to sit in line for hours. For abortions or to be treated for venereal diseases."

I shuddered.

"Those days were terrible. Yet I felt I was in God's hands, because I didn't become pregnant. At least I was spared that. Oh, how sorry I feel for the nuns! Many had been raped, too, and were pregnant. Imagine nuns with swollen bellies! No abortions -- no mercy. Their babies were taken away from them before they even saw them.... "

Suddenly, a few heavy raindrops slapped our faces. "Oh dear," Dorothea said, "a rainstorm is coming on. Look at the clouds!" Dark-gray storm clouds were closing in, and the howling of the wind grew louder. We hurried through the basement door into the protection of the warm hospital.

Arriving on the first floor, we emerged into the bustle of nurses at the end of their work shift. A huge round clock showed 5:30. "We have only a half hour more together," she said. "Over there's the chapel. Why don't you wait for me inside? In the meantime I'll go to the Mother Superior."

The moment the little sanctuary's door shut behind me, I felt immersed in a world of total silence. The strong scent of incense, mixed with that of burning candles, transported me into a different state of mind, where the world and its brutalities couldn't hurt anymore. My eyes glanced over the flower-decorated altar, which had a replica of Dürer's *Mary in the Rose Garden* in its center. How lovely was this refuge.

After a while, Dorothea entered the chapel. "Everything's all right. You can stay overnight." We sat down in a pew. "Let's sit here for a while. Haste and noise will return soon enough."

Sitting next to her I let the wonderful environment replenish me. Gradually I experienced a floating sensation and felt wonderfully cradled and invulnerable. In this trance-like state, I was able to ask Dorothea without fear, "What were the last words you heard my mother say?"

"She said, 'Oh my God, they raped me! It was terrible. Five men.' I told her I'd had six the day before and three that night.

Then she said she couldn't stand the burning inside her anymore. I said the pain would go away. She said the shame and guilt she felt were even worse than the burning, and she couldn't look into her husband's eyes again. I said she shouldn't feel this way, but then I realized my words weren't helping her, her moral values were too strict." She stopped.

"Then what?"

"Then your uncle's secretary screamed she was bleeding to death. Your uncle yelled for rags to plug the bleeding and another person pulled me over to the secretary to help. Everybody was busy. Minutes later your mother lay on the floor with the broken cyanide ampule protruding from her mouth."

Miraculously, I was able to maintain the trance-like detachment into which incense, candles and will power had brought me, and I had no fear in asking my friend, "What does one feel while being raped? Shame? Fear of death?"

Dorothea shook her head. "First, I was confused. I didn't know what the man wanted. The first Russian words I learned were *davai suda* -- come over here. When he saw I didn't understand him, he lifted my skirt with his free hand, his rifle in the other. Then I understood. I felt like an intimidated school child and lay down on the floor. He put the rifle down and pulled my panties off me. He jerked my legs wide apart and entered me. It hurt a lot. My only thoughts were, 'When will it be over?' Yes, I'd say that was the only feeling I had. Later on, I heard many other women talk about it. They all said they just waited for it to be over. One woman said she started counting to be distracted. She seldom had to count to more than twenty-five."

She stopped for a moment. "One becomes rather cynical after a number of rapes." She looked at me. "Oh, I've shocked you!"

I shook my head. "I thank you for telling me all this. It's part of my mother's death, and I'm no longer groping in the dark. Tell me only one more thing, Dorothea. How can you and others, who have gone through this hell, still be alive and function normally when my mother couldn't?"

She got up. I realized it was time for her shift. "I always think I'm in God's hands and He knows why He put me through this. Others had much more to suffer than I. But I have to go to work, Frau Eva. May I leave you here? It's a good place."

We hugged and said good-bye. She gave me special greetings for Manfred and Lili and promised she'd come to Wilhelmshaven as soon as she could.

I stayed for a while in the lovely chapel, staring at Dürer's image of the Mother and her Child. At least this replica had survived the times, just as thousands of living martyrs of the East now live in the West. Sadly, my mother had no part of it, but I was grateful my mother had been spared the torment of a future she feared. I realized I'd been able to listen to Dorothea's account without crying. And now, in the great solemnity of that place and that moment, I made an effort to transform my physical presence into an imaginary one. I was now ready to bid her farewell, to bury her spiritually. What better place could there be than this quiet, lovingly decorated sanctuary? And so the little chapel became a place of final departure from my mother. I knew my mother rested in peace.

When a nun walked in to put the candles out, I rose to leave.

THE GUILTY

Leaving the hospital I went straight to the Red Cross station to check today's lists for my father's name. It wasn't there. Instead I found, to my joy, Fritz's wife's name, Erika Moldenhauer, registered here in Hamburg two days ago. Since children were not listed the name of two-year old Helga wouldn't be there. I took the truck to her place. It turned out to be a block-long military barracks with a large sign -- CHILDREN'S HOME -- over the battered wooden door.

The woman who opened the door for me led me into a kitchen where five women were peeling potatoes. I recognized her even before she rose. She wore a brown dress of shiny wool, apparently cut from a thin blanket, and her shaggy blond hair had broad gray streaks. She left the circle of potato peelers to walk right into my arms.

Magically, I felt transported back to the days of our childhood pranks. "You *Dussel*," I said, affectionately using a Danzig expression meaning dummy.

"You *Dummkopf*," she answered, meaning the same. We'd always given each other unflattering titles.

"What are you doing here?" I asked. "Haven't you found Fritz yet?" She shook her head. "He visited with us in Wilhelmshaven yesterday. He left for Lübeck to find you."

"Then he'll find me soon."

Had she said *me* and not *us*? "Where is Helga?"

There was a pause. "Helga is dead," she said calmly.

Overwhelmed, I took her in my arms, held her. As though to keep her self-control she withdrew from my arms.

"Oh my God," I whispered. "When? How?"

"In April. In Danzig." After a moment she added, "Come on, let's go to my room."

As we walked through the long corridor, I saw that Erika hadn't changed much; she'd always been cool, restrained and taciturn -- the opposite of myself.

"How's Manfred? Lili? Are you together?" she asked.

"Yes, we are." I felt unfairly blessed.

Erika opened the last of the many doors. "My place." We entered the small but bright room. Noon light flooded through the large window, illuminating the sparse furniture, a single iron bed with an unframed picture postcard of Danzig over it, a table and two chairs. The fire in the small stove had gone out.

"*Scheisse*," Erika said. "I'll have to get wood from the back yard." Mechanically, I followed her.

As she opened a door to the bare fields she said, "I know you lost your mother."

Startled, I stared at her. "How do you know?"

"Your father told me. Have you seen him?"

"For God's sake, no! I don't know where he is. When did you see him? Where?"

"He and I were in the same box car when the Poles chased us out of Danzig."

My mind was in a turmoil as we walked to the back of the barracks and to a huge pile of logs. "When did you leave Danzig?"

She removed an axe from a nail on the barracks wall. "In August." That's when most people were expelled. Two and a half months had gone by.

Erika took a large log and set it upright. After the first hit she said, "We were squeezed into a windowless boxcar. I saw him when we were let out at a station to pump water." The axe blade bit deeper into the log.

"Did he look well? Did he say anything?"

"He said he was on his way to you, to help you and Manfred start a new life." She kept hitting at the log and the crack deepened.

Tears came to my eyes. "How long were you in the box car?"

"Five days."

"Five days? It only takes eight hours from Danzig to Berlin! Did you get anything to eat?"

"No."

"Why did it take the train so long?"

"It was held up many times. The Poles came in and plundered."

"But you had nothing. What could they take from you?"

"Our clothes." She picked up the kindling and we began to walk back to the barracks.

I opened the door. "Did the Poles leave you anything?"

"They threw us empty potato sacks so we could cover ourselves. Your father was the only one who could keep his underpants on. The Pole who stripped him suddenly stopped and said, 'Old man, I'll leave you your underpants. I've already got some.'" She put the kindling next to the stove and poked the ashes. "I had the impression your father was hiding something in his underpants, but I may have been mistaken."

"What happened when you arrived in Berlin?"

"We were taken to hospitals."

"Where did my father go?"

"I don't know."

"Did you see him again?"

"No." She crumpled a piece of newspaper and put it into the stove.

At least now I knew he had arrived in Berlin. As the first uncertain flames licked around the kindling, Erika put larger sticks on top. We both sat on the floor, staring into the fire. Knowing Erika, I was certain she wouldn't tell me anything unless I asked her. "I heard a lot about what happened in Danzig. Did you have to go through all that, too?"

"Yes."

"Were you raped?"

"Yes. Thirty times in a row."

I swallowed hard. "Your mother, too?"

"Of course." Carefully she laid a new log on the fire.

"Where's she now?"

"She was killed immediately after the rapes."

"And your father?"

"He's a hired hand to a peasant near Lübeck." Descended from a baronial estate owner to a hired hand.

For the next question I had to give myself an extra push. "How did your baby die?"

For a while Erika didn't answer. Instead she poked the fire with an iron bar. "I killed her."

Silence fell between us, bridging space and time.

At last Erika got up and took a package of cigarettes from the drawer. "You don't smoke, do you?" I shook my head. She lit a cigarette, walked to the window and stared out into the winter landscape, her tall, slim silhouette outlined against the midday's bright gray light. The iron stove rumbled vigorously and the hay-like aroma of Erika's cigarette filled the air.

When Erika spoke again, it was in her usual calm, almost detached manner. "The Russian soldiers chased us out of our house and we ran into the fields. Then a very young soldier, he looked about sixteen, came at us with his rifle and started firing. He shot my mother and Helga. He aimed at me but no bullet came out -- his gun must have jammed." She threw her half finished cigarette into the stove and lit a fresh one. "My mother died immediately. But Helga didn't. Her arm was shot off and a bullet crushed her cheekbone, ripping open her face. She was bleeding and screaming." Erika kept smoking. She inhaled deeply as though the smoke gave her strength. "I knew she would die from her head wound. To shorten her suffering I strangled her. It didn't take long."

Horror overwhelmed me and then compassion. Without any hesitation I said, "You did the right thing. I'd have done the same." Was there a judge in the world who would condemn her? How much could human beings bear?

As if guessing my thoughts Erika said, "To get away from the terrible memory, I have involved myself in this children's home."

"Whose children are these?"

"Children of expellees. During the expulsion they were separated from their parents. The younger ones don't even know their names." She took a last puff on her cigarette, got up and squeezed the butt out in an ashtray.

It was getting too warm by the stove, so I got up and sat with her at the table. "Where are the children now?"

"At school. They'll be back for lunch soon. This home is part of the Red Cross' rescue enterprises. I'm the director."

"But I saw you peeling potatoes and chopping wood."

"I help out when it's necessary."

"How many children do you have here?"

"Thirty. We have room for forty. Fortunately, the number decreases when the children are identified and their parents find them."

"Through the Red Cross?"

"Yes. Can you imagine the chaos we would have without the Red Cross? One day, Fritz will find me."

"How long have you been here in the West?"

"About six weeks."

"But you registered at the Red Cross only two days ago!"

She nodded. "I wasn't able to face anyone, not even my own husband. I needed time to adjust to a normal life."

"What do you plan to do after they're all gone?"

She shrugged. "Be with Fritz."

"Won't you miss the children?"

"Yes."

I leaned toward her. "Have you thought of having another child?"

Erika's hands sank onto the table. She seemed startled. "I haven't thought about that yet."

Thinking about the advice I had given, I discovered that it was driven by my own desire for a second child, a wish now spreading into my consciousness. I felt it reinforced as I saw the thirty or so children storming in. Pushing and shoving they squeezed through the narrow door to the washroom. How wise Erika had been to fill the gap Helga's death had created.

Guessing how busy Erika would be now with her horde of children I looked at my wrist watch. It was time to leave for the train. I hugged and kissed her good-bye. "Say hello to Fritz. He'll certainly be here in one or two days."

Erika nodded. "I hope your father will be with you soon."

HUMORESQUE

Tightly wrapped in my Persian lamb coat I entered Hamburg's domed railway station. I was shocked to see an overcrowded train. Not only were the passengers crammed shoulder to shoulder in the corridors but they also stood on the outside foot boards, holding on to the handles. There was only this evening train to Wilhelmshaven and I had to take it if I wanted to keep my rehearsal date with Rymann and the flutist tomorrow.

"*Verdammte Scheisse!*" cursed a handsome young man in a field-gray former uniform which already had civilian buttons; a small bag hung from his shoulder. At least he was someone who communicated.

I turned to him. "I *have* to get on this train."

"Me too," he said. "There's only one alternative. The coal car at the end of the train." I thought I misunderstood him, but he started toward the end of the platform and, automatically, I followed him.

I saw a coal car attached to the passenger train. With amazement I watched as the young man athletically leaped on the car's side, his feet finding support on the rivets. He pulled himself up, swung one leg over the side and jumped inside. Stealthily, I looked around to see if a railway employee was near to interfere, but no one in uniform was visible. Therefore -- according to old German ways -- we could do as we pleased.

Apparently, the coal car was partially full, for muffled voices and laughter came from inside. The young man comfortably rested his arms on the side as if looking out a window and grinned triumphantly at me. "Do you want a night on the platform or an airy ride?" he asked.

"An airy ride."

"All right!" He looked around and beckoned to two teenage boys who lingered by the train. "Come on, give this lady a hand!" He reached down to me and our hands locked, my shopping net dangling from my arm. I felt hands pushing my buttocks and my legs until I was above the siding panels. I swung over and jumped down on the coal. "Thank you, my savior," I said.

"My pleasure."

Then I glanced around. Two men on the coal heap looked up at me; one middle-aged, the other young, they sat on the flat coal, playing cards. Apparently, they'd scooped out some of the coal to allow their legs to rest comfortably in a hollow. They'd made a card table by stuffing their canvas bags between them.

The older man with a dark-blue skipper cap pulled down to his ears and a pipe in his mouth, said in Low-German, which was difficult for me to understand, "Look at her! Even girls get in the coal car."

His partner, short and black-haired, like a robber from *Thousand-and-one-Nights*, looked me over, up and down and said, also in Low-German, "She's not a girl, she's a lady."

"Why that?" the skipper asked.

"She's wrapped in fur -- she must be a lady."

For a moment, I wasn't sure whether to be amused or embarrassed, but then I decided to accept this talk as coal-car conversation. The strange environment excluded formalities -- one more reason to enjoy this journey through the blackness.

"Come on, sit down," the Arabian-tales robber said to me. "There's enough room for you and your husband."

I exchanged quick side glances with my new friend. "We aren't married," I said.

"What's the difference?" the robber asked. "Hope you enjoy it anyway."

Both my rescuer and I stepped down into the hollow and sat on the rocky surface. Soon a whistle blew, the engine hooted, and the train began to move.

"Does one of you play *Skat*?" the Arabian robber asked. I declined, but my handsome friend joined them.

I was glad *Skat* was only for three. Sitting idly on the coals, I longed for a backrest. As the train accelerated to full speed the wind blew coal dust and smoke into my face as if to punish me for my illegal ride. No way to turn around in the hollow. The three men sat with their backs to the wind and weren't bothered by the flying coal particles. Dusk had fallen. The wind chilled my bones. Underneath me, the wheels rattled like the sticks of a mechanical drum.

When the card players could no longer see their cards in the darkness, they turned to telling silly jokes, roaring with laughter and slapping their knees.

My own sense of humor had disappeared, suppressed by the pain in my eyes; I finally just kept them closed. Intermittently, I listened to the conversation.

The quasi-Arabian seemed to be an avid black-market trader of *schnaps*.

"What d'ye get for a bottle of *schnaps*?" asked the skipper.

"Five pounds of butter and a pound of coffee."

I was thoroughly fascinated. Risking more coal dust I looked in the direction of the trader. "What else do they sell on the black market?"

"Anything you want, lady, bread and butter, shoes and *schnaps*, soap, coffee."

"But how much do these things cost?"

"You'd be stupid to pay with money, lady."

"What else?"

"Trade stuff, like *schnaps*."

"I don't have any *schnaps*."

"Then get started with a tea set if you need to."

"I have no tea set. I'm a refugee."

"You sure don't look like one."

I knew very well the Persian-lamb coat, the only coat I had, looked like a million marks. "But I am. Tell me about the hottest items on the black market." I couldn't see his robber-like face in the dark but could readily hear his squeaky voice. It didn't matter if he looked like the sexton of *Notre Dame* and barked like a coyote, I was fascinated by his up-to-date lesson on survival.

"Nazi flags, Iron Crosses are hot."

"Don't you get in trouble dealing with stuff like an Iron Cross?"

"Lady, the British are crazy about these things. And the Americans are supposed to pay even more for them. The hottest items are SS insignia."

The skipper said in Low-German, "I can think of something hotter. A girl's ass!"

The trader's squeaky voice sounded contemptuous. "Ho! Look who's talking! Don't try to fool us! Do you get so much to eat you can screw? Potatoes and cabbage aren't enough! It takes more than that to get it up."

"With a hot girl on the street it's no problem."

"Don't tell us the streetwalkers take *you* home. They take only the foreign soldiers," the trader replied maliciously.

My rescuer joined in the conversation. "They tell me the British aren't too wild about women, but the Americans are. I wonder why?"

With a whinnying laughter, the trader said, "Because the Americans are overfed and oversexed. That's why." Guffawing, the other two agreed. Germany collapsed, sex life collapsed, I thought -- what a correlation. I only wished the trip would end soon. I'd had enough of coal, men and wind.

When the train finally drew into Wilhelmshaven my spirits returned and I could hardly wait to be helped out of the coal car. In the dim light from the platform roof that shone down on the thrusting crowd I searched for Manfred and Lili.

Behind me, two familiar voices called: "There you are, Little Bear!"

"Mommy!"

Manfred hugged and kissed me. I took Lili in my arms, holding her tight, enjoying the feel of the small body against my chest.

"Why is your face so dirty?" Manfred asked.

"I was riding in the coal car."

"Impossible!"

"It's true."

He chuckled. "That sounds exactly like you, Little Bear," he said.

We left the platform and stepped into the dark street. For a while, we walked silently through the clear, star-struck night, holding Lili's hands as she toddled between us. Then I told him about my mother's death. He stopped, letting Lili's hand go and took me in his arms. I cried.

"I never thought she would survive the atrocities," he said, holding me tight. His voice calmed me. "It's better for her to be in peace than to live with her memories."

I nodded. We drew apart, took Lili's hands again and continued walking. "Has Father arrived?" I asked.

"Sorry, no. He hasn't."

"But he may be near." I told about Erika's encounter with him.

Soon we were home. Walking into our single room I found it icy cold. The small, potbellied stove was dark and dead. "Sorry," Manfred said. "There's no firewood." Home, sweet home.

During dinner, we kept our coats on, warming our hands on the cups of herb tea Manfred had brewed. He had cooked potatoes, two for each of us, and they were still warm. "How did you keep them from getting cold?" I asked, knowing he'd had only a limited time in the community kitchen.

"Wrapped up in newspapers and tucked under my pillow." He'd prepared chopped cabbage and seasoned it with vinegar and salt. Oil was not available.

Watching Lili I thought she looked a little thinner, but blamed it on the poor ceiling light.

"Anything new here?" I asked, dividing my last potato in four to make it look like more.

"Yesterday, Irene called me at the shipyard," said Manfred. "Helmut's been released from the internment camp."

"Oh my God! How long has he been interned?"

"About four weeks."

"How is he?"

"In bad shape," he said. "All of them were treated roughly. He and Irene moved to the American zone yesterday. He has relatives there in the countryside. They say hello."

Fear crept up. "You aren't in danger, are you?"

"I hope not." He was busy with his coleslaw and didn't look up. "Little Bear, we have to do something about firewood."

I knew it wasn't available in stores. "But what?"

"There's only one way -- the ruins in the neighborhood." The wooden boards across the street. It was strictly prohibited. Was he really ready to pilfer? "It will take both of us," he said. "One to pick up the boards, one to watch for the military police. We should do it around midnight, between the patrols. I've heard they change shifts at midnight. They don't come around at that time."

I smiled at him, amused at his air of conspiracy. "Tonight then?" He nodded.

Lili yawned, her little face one big mouth. It was way beyond her bedtime. "The little sandman is coming, putting sand into the children's eyes. Bed time," I said.

Suddenly the big mouth shut and two big eyes widened in protest. "No bed!"

"But, Lili, do you want to sit around all night long?"

"I sit 'round night long!"

I bribed her. "Do you want to hear a story of a girl whose brother was made into a beautiful swan?"

Bright eyes beamed. "Yes."

"I can tell the story only when you're in bed."

"I -- bed," she said, delighted with the prospect of a story.

As I undressed her at the table I thought again that Lili was a little thinner, probably growing out of her baby chubbiness. In three weeks she'd be two years old. As Lili lifted her arms above her head, I discovered a small sore on the underside of her arm. I touched it gently. "What's that?"

Lili didn't react; it must not hurt her. Having no plaster to protect the sore, I tore one of her former diapers in strips, wrapping one piece of cloth around Lili's arm. There was no ointment, so the small wound would have to heal by itself.

A moment later, Lili, her eyes wide open, was in bed, ready for the story. I'd never been fond of fairy tales and always told Lili opera stories. She loved them. This time I decided it would be *Lohengrin*, the medieval tale of Elsa and the swan. "She was accused of having killed her brother," I told Lili. "When she prayed for help, a shiny white knight came to her rescue."

"Daddy?" Lili asked.

"Yes, he looked just like your daddy. He told all the people Elsa was innocent. He married her and there was a big wedding." I sang to her, *Here comes the Bride.* As I talked, enlarging the story of *Lohengrin*, her eyes finally closed. I put the bed cover more firmly around her small shoulders and kissed her softly.

Returning to Manfred at the table, I put a blanket around his shoulders and sat on his lap. He wrapped the blanket around me, too. I thought about my mother: that I would never see her again.

As though he guessed my thoughts, Manfred said softly, "I remember how I felt when my mother died."

"You were thirteen then, weren't you?"

"Yes."

"Was there someone to console you?" He shook his head. "Where was your father?"

"He saw me in tears and said, 'Don't cry! A boy should never cry. Not even when his mother dies. We'll never talk about her again.' And we never did."

I caressed his cheek, his hair, took both his hands into mine. I told him that I wanted a second child.

"Now? In these times? We can hardly feed ourselves. And it doesn't look like it will get better any time soon."

"There has always been milk for babies."

"No one knows for how long."

"If we started the baby now, don't you think the food situation would be better after nine months?"

"I doubt it. It's not a matter of wishing."

"Then what is it a matter of?"

"Of two facts. First of vengeance. You know the Allies say we should live on exactly the same calories as the prisoners had in the concentration camps. 800 calories is not enough to feed you and a baby too."

"And the second fact?"

"The West of Germany is overcrowded with millions of refugees and expellees. The available supplies of food and fuel have already deteriorated so much I really don't know how we will survive."

I understood his message: the challenge of the time was to survive, not to create. But I wasn't going to give up easily. "How about the black market? We could get food there."

"That's a disgusting idea and besides it's dangerous. The police are bound to raid the black market."

"I've coped with the Gestapo, I can cope with the police."

He said nothing. Instead, he looked at his wrist watch. "It's almost midnight." The time had come for our shady business. I felt tingly with excitement. Manfred looked angry but determined. How hard it must be for him to put his ideals aside and adopt the role of a thief!

The street was dark and empty. Fog had crept in. The streetlight at the corner was only a fuzzy spot, like a faint galaxy -- a perfect atmosphere for pilfering.

"I checked everything by daylight," he said in an undertone as he headed toward a bombed-out house across the street. Rather than having burned down to ashes, the house had been blown into huge square stones and large wooden boards; some boards stuck out of the rubble and others lay strewn around, exposed to wind and rain.

"I want you to stand here and listen," he whispered. "If you hear the slightest noise give me a short hiss. I'll freeze and you walk back to the house."

"All right," I whispered back. Cautiously, he vanished into the ruins. I listened carefully, my eyes straining to see through the fog. Disturbingly, I heard my heart pound -- the noise in my ears taking on an enormous dimension in the stillness of the foggy night. I heard the subdued clatter of wooden boards as Manfred arranged them for removal.

Suddenly, he emerged next to me and whispered, "Hold this end." Carrying the long board -- it looked like half a door -- we sneaked away. Like the Gypsy smugglers in the third act of *Carmen*, I thought. Silently, we moved into the cellar of our house.

Two minutes later, we heard British trucks rattle through the street, patrolling for curfew breakers. We had just made it.

Manfred had borrowed a hand saw and ax from the shipyard and while he sawed, I used the ax until we had a huge pile of firewood. It took six trips to carry it upstairs to our room.

"This may last for three or four days," Manfred said. Happily I watched him stack the wood neatly next to the stove. What a camaraderie with him, and how marvellous to work together with him! Work? Wood stealing was work? Yes, three times yes!

At the height of my excitement I realized a different kind of work awaited me. Tomorrow morning. I was to go to the theater to accompany Angela Rymann and the flutist.

THE CREATION OF EMOTIONS

WILHELMSHAVEN CITY THEATER
OPENING NOVEMBER 23, 1945

With a hushed feeling of awe I looked at the huge gray one-story building, a former military barracks, now transformed into a theater. So this is the place where operas, ballet, symphony concerts and stage plays would be given. And I'd be a small part of it, accompanying Angela Rymann and Ulrich von Gonsenheim on opening night. In a minute I would meet this flutist.

Impatient and excited, I entered the sacred halls. In the long corridor I saw endless rows of doors on both sides, each bearing signs: General Office, Stage Director, Music Director, Stage Manager.

I entered the General Office and asked a heavily made-up girl behind a typewriter where Angela Rymann was rehearsing.

"Sorry, I don't know her."

"She's rehearsing with a flutist named Ulrich Von Gonsenheim."

"Oh, the chairman? He's in Rehearsal Room II." I went down the corridor to Rehearsal II, opened the door and entered.

Brightly lit by four windows, the large room contained only a black grand piano and six wooden chairs. The rest of the room was empty -- obviously kept as a rehearsal stage.

Angela Rymann's stately figure and that of a tall, thin man were bent over some musical scores on the grand piano. Both looked up as I walked in. "There you are," Rymann said affably. "Come and meet Ulrich Von Gonsenheim."

He raised himself to his full height of six foot five and looked down at me through rimless glasses. In his forties, he looked rather aristocratic, with receding hair over a high forehead. We shook hands. He bowed slightly. "I've heard you're an excellent sight-reader." He spoke quickly, pronouncing every syllable staccato.

I wondered if he played the flute this way. It would be perfect for the Baroque style. "So, you're the famous Ulrich Von Gonsenheim?"

"I wish I were famous."

Rymann chuckled. "Ulrich is too humble, as usual. He's the one who resurrected this theater."

He raised his hand in defense. "Not I alone! I just helped Valdoyani." He turned to me. "I understand you're new in town. Valdoyani is our music director."

"An Italian?"

"Only half. But let's do our program. We have less than three weeks for rehearsing. Why don't you get started with the Brahms songs?" He sat down on a chair away from the piano.

I adjusted myself on the piano bench, opened the Brahms score and looked at Rymann. The singer majestically placed herself at the side of the grand piano, looked at me and nodded her head, signaling her readiness. Every time she sang, the expressiveness of her dramatic mezzo-soprano astonished me anew. The singer was able to project grave sadness as well as light serenity; her range seemed to have no limits and each sound was perfectly controlled. Berlin State Opera, no wonder she sang well.

While I accompanied Rymann, my mind wandered off to Von Gonsenheim, curious about what he would play in their joint recital. When we were through with Rymann's songs, Von Gonsenheim immediately discussed with the singer how they'd arrange their numbers so the program would have variety and dramatic structure. Kept out of the discussion, I didn't mind; after all, an accompanist was only a person in the background, one with no say in the shaping of a soloist's plans. Soon both artists came to an agreement and Rymann left.

I looked at the flutist, anxious to hear about his own pieces for the recital. I expected him to take his flute out and give me the sheet music. Instead, he took a chair, placed it next to the keyboard and said in his soft staccato voice, "Let's work on Brahms."

"Brahms? Has Brahms composed for the flute?" Why didn't he pass me the sheet music?

"I'm talking about the Brahms *songs* you just played," he said kindly.

"What about them?"

"I want to work with you on the piano part."

"Was anything wrong?"

"Wrong isn't the right word. Most of the time you played the right notes. By the way, I have to congratulate you on your ability to camouflage. You hide your insecurity at certain places so well it's hard to notice you left out a note here and there."

As usual when criticized, my spirits soared. What a challenge. Both of us smiled in complete agreement. "However," he continued, "I'd like to know what you were thinking of while you accompanied Angela."

"About which pieces you'd play at the recital," I said honestly.

His voice still had the light staccato quality. "So while playing Brahms you made random guesses about my flute repertoire?" I nodded. "It sounded that way," he said emphatically. I was speechless. What did he mean?

He softened. "Have you ever thought why the composer wrote introductory bars before the soloist's entry?"

"Of course. To give the singer the key and the beginning note."

"There's so much more to it." His voice became more intense. "With the introductory bars the accompanist is supposed to stimulate the soloist and lead her into the mood of the song, so that the singer can generate the emotion in the music and move the audience."

My mind extended beyond my normal eagerness to learn about music. "Oh, this is art," I said softly. "This is how artists create the magic they use to enchant their audiences."

Von Gonsenheim apparently realized the fertile soil on which his words had fallen. "Let's take the song *We Wander* and apply what I suggested." I turned the pages and started playing the introductory bars. He raised his hand. "Stop!"

I halted in the middle of a bar, looking at him in bewilderment.

"What did the lyrics say?" he asked.

"'We two wandered together, I wish I knew what you were thinking,'" I read aloud.

"Read the lyrics to the end silently and tell me about them."

I read them to myself. "I don't find any answers in the lyrics."

"But the answer is expressed in the music," he insisted.

"In the six introductory bars?"

He smiled with satisfaction and nodded. "Now think of the answer yourself!"

Did *I* have to create an answer? Obediently, I closed my eyes, conjuring up the tender scene. Two lovers walking side by side, too shy to express their feelings, nevertheless feeling devotion, longing, anxiety...

"Now play it!"

Transferring my emotions to my fingers, I heard myself play the six bars. They suddenly sounded like a sung melody. I'd never played that way before. In surprise and delight, I stopped and looked at the flutist who had become my teacher in interpretation.

"That's it. And stay with the emotion till the end of the song."

Still, I wondered at having entered a world I hadn't known existed. "Is this similar to what an actor experiences when he creates a role?"

"Very similar. Let's work on a different mood. Take *The Hunter*." I turned the pages and read the lyrics about a girl whose lover hunts girls, but who is determined to let him in only "through the church door" -- saucy and confident of victory. There were only four bars before the singer's entry, but with my new enlightenment, I concentrated the mood in my fingers and the sound came out exactly as I felt it.

"You got it!" he said.

Happily I closed the song book and got up, convinced the rehearsal had ended. He didn't move. "Are you in a hurry?"

"But I think I know how to play now."

"After only ten bars?"

Meekly, I sat down again and the real work began. He made me prepare, study the text and the music, create the mood, play my part well, work out technical difficulties, repeat each song two or three times, until, finally, he was satisfied. After three hours of uninterrupted tutoring on the Brahms, he sent me home for lunch, asking me to return for his own repertoire in the afternoon.

I went home as if under a magic spell. For twenty years of my
life, my fingers had worked for me like obedient slaves, and I
hadn't been much more than a slave-owner. Now I had entered
the world of art and creativity, learning to make my fingers
recreate, elevating them to artistic tools! How lucky I was to
have met Ulrich! How could I ever thank him? I ran home
through the ruined town, not aware of wind and drizzle.

I fixed lunch, the main meal -- a few potatoes with a
supplement of *Scherkohl*, a strange, heavily curled cabbage
which grew only in that area. I'd bought it dried, hay-like, then
soaked it and boiled it. It still tasted like hay, but better hay in
the belly than nothing at all.

Before I left for the afternoon rehearsal I danced with Lili. I
was so happy about being able to play well I sang and danced
around the room, and Lili laughed and couldn't get enough.

My mind was still dancing during the afternoon rehearsal.
Von Gonsenheim discussed the flute music with me, Bach,
Mozart and Hindemith. It was much easier to accompany an
instrumentalist than a singer. Instead of emerging into a text
and its mood, I just had to concentrate on the different musical
styles -- a requirement well-known to me and relatively easy to
handle. But Von Gonsenheim was a perfectionist and he didn't
let the slightest inconsistency pass uncorrected. Again we
rehearsed for three hours, but I didn't feel the least bit tired. Of
all the different things I'd done in my life, making music was
the most rewarding of all. It never failed to give me a feeling of
belonging and deep satisfaction. "You don't know what you have
given me," I said while he was putting his flute into the case.
"Thank you very much."

"It was given to me, too. I'm just passing it on."

Would I ever be able to pass it on, too?

THE DAILY BREAD

"My dear, do you have a long evening gown?" Angela Rymann asked after a rehearsal.

"No. Why?"

"Our concert will be in the theater. Both of us should wear long dresses. Mine's black."

I worried about it for a while and then, after rehearsing with Ulrich Von Gonsenheim, I asked him, "Do we *have* to wear long dresses?"

Carefully, he put his flute into his case. "I've thought about that. Long dresses would be the most appropriate attire. On the other hand, they could arouse the audience's envy. So why not adjust to the miserable times and wear whatever you have?"

I felt relieved. "Will we have an audience?"

"Have you ever seen Germans *not* going to concerts or operas? And even more people will attend now. Some may come only because the room is warm." He shut the flute case and then returned to the piano. Bending down, he laid his arms on the piano as support for himself and folded his hands. "I want to ask you if you would like to play a solo piece between Angela's and my pieces."

"I?"

"If you have a memorized piece ready, technically, we could work on interpretation. You have such good musical memory -- do you have something ready?"

A new challenge. "Bach's Chromatic Fantasy?" I asked.

"Too demanding of the audience."

"Beethoven's Sonata No.24, his own favorite?"

"Too boring for the audience."

"Chopin's Polonaise in A?"

"That's a good one!" Ulrich exclaimed. "It arouses the audience and is a good contrast to Angela's and my program. Play it, can you?"

I played it from memory, hesitating only once.

"You do have a good memory," he said. "Let's get started right away."

I played it and surprisingly, he had very little to suggest. "Not bad. You have learned quite a bit since I first heard you. Chopin is your strong point, isn't it?"

"Actually not," I answered. "It's just what you taught me: to generate the emotions."

He straightened up from the piano. "Well, do the same on the opening night. Iron out the section with the modulations and you'll be all right."

Never in my lifetime would I forget the date of the concert, November 23, the same day Lili turned two. The 700-seat concert hall was packed. Our concert was the town's first entertainment after the war and everyone wanted to attend.

When the house lights went down I followed Rymann out on the stage. Applause greeted us. Rymann bowed. According to stage custom, I, as an accompanist, didn't bow; I simply sat down. I wore my only good dress -- a black wool with white-striped diagonal inlays; although short, it matched Angela's silky black evening gown in color.

Rymann sang her Brahms songs well, her voice sounding tremendous in the full hall. She projected the respective moods of the pieces so well the sympathetic vibrations of the audience came right back. The applause was thunderous. Rymann led the way off.

When the audience could no longer see me, I turned to look at the empty stage. Now it was my turn! Automatically, I walked back to the stage. I could hear the audience clapping, and bowed.

As I sat in front of the grand piano I saw my fingers trembling in my lap. Calm down! I commanded myself. Turning toward the audience I imagined a mental bridge between us. I would walk towards them, bringing them my music.

Then I began with the strong A-major chords. The polonaise was known as the "Military" and I thought of Chopin's fellow Poles who courageously fought against the Germans' and Russians' superior strength. While one part of my mind guided my fingers another identified with the plight of the Polish people I liked so much. The music evoked in me the Poles' suffering, their constant suppression during the centuries. At the end of the polonaise the uplifting harmonies returned, insisting, confirming; I felt the Poles had received their reward -- Danzig and the vastness of German lands.

The polonaise was over. I put my hands in my lap, completely forgetting I was on stage. Uproarious applause drew me from my magic carpet. I got up and bowed. Straightening up I saw Manfred and Lili sitting in the first row. Both were clapping wildly. Excitement, pride and gratefulness swept me into heights I had never before known. As the applause continued I felt I was truly blessed. I walked off stage and the applause ended.

In the second part of the concert, I accompanied Ulrich, who appeared in a dark suit and black tie, looking cool and detached as usual. His program revealed his brilliance on the flute. How anyone could play long passages on a wind instrument, without taking a breath in between, was a mystery to me; and beyond that to produce a pleasing sound seemed to me more than my finger-minded musicianship could grasp.

The three of us bowed at the end to enthusiastic applause. There were no flower bouquets as in normal times, there couldn't be, but the rapture of having created music and transferred it to the audience was reward enough.

Von Gonsenheim was so elated he insisted we go out for a drink. No one objected. We soon were joined by Manfred and Lili and Rymann's husband, who followed his wife like a vassal. Entering the recently opened *Ratskellar* near the theater, we found the great basement half full. Under wooden vaults blue tobacco smoke lingered above the guests who sat at raw oak wood tables, drinking from stemmed wine glasses.

Ulrich chose a corner table. We ordered "hot punch," a red fluid with a taste of saccharine and turpentine -- the only available drink.

After a while I noticed four men playing cards, and, oh God, one of them was the very image of my father! His slightly bent posture, his bald head, the way he looked through his bifocals at the cards.... Spellbound, I stared at the image, knowing it couldn't be my father, but wanting to believe that it was *he*. I willfully escaped into fantasies. I imagined myself slowly walking up to him, step by step to prolong the anticipation, until I was next to him, then softly saying, "Father!" He would look up in surprise, recognizing me, flash his warm smile, put the cards down and take me in his arms....

Abruptly, the fantasy vanished, but my father's double was still there. I touched Manfred's arm. "Look at the card player on the left."

Manfred turned to the table and stared in disbelief. "My God, it's amazing...."

As if he had heard Manfred's voice, the card player turned to us -- and showed us the face of a total stranger; there was no resemblance left, the magic was over.

Determined to do as well in the second concert as in the first, I walked with Manfred and Lili through snow flurries to a Lutheran church at the outskirts of Mudtown. The small church building, untouched by bombs, was lovingly decorated with Advent symbols: pine wreaths hung on red ribbons from the vaulted ceiling, the four thick red candles on each wreath symbolizing the four Sundays before Christmas. Only one candle on each fir wreath was lit in this first December week. The fragrance of fir and hot wax spread over the audience and high up to the organ balcony where Angela, Ulrich and I gathered for the performance. The audience in the church nave wouldn't see us and in this sacred place, there would be no applause.

Tonight, I accompanied Rymann and Von Gonsenheim on the organ. Playing Bach as my solo that evening was a sheer delight. No other composer calmed me down and filled me with the illusion that the world was in order and perfect harmony. My pleasure was heightened by knowing Manfred liked Bach as much as I did.

After the concert I joined Manfred and Lili, who had slept to Bach's music on her father's lap.

Unexpectedly, Ulrich approached and handed me some money. "Your share. A third of the ticket sales." He left immediately to greet other people.

Fascinated, I stared at the money in my hands. "One hundred three marks!" I said to Manfred. "My first earnings from music."

"Now you're a professional musician," he said proudly. "That's what you always wanted to be."

Carefully folding the bills, I slid them into my gloves, feeling their crispness in my hands as I walked home. Snowflakes, falling out of the darkness, danced around us. I felt the same lightness in myself.

Before the next choir rehearsal, Smola told me the news that he had accepted a job in the canteen of the British Royal Navy -- as a jazz-bass player. The band consisted of him, a pianist and a drummer. Every night he got a free dinner -- a fact that made me green with envy. "I'd do anything to get food," he said.

When the rehearsal began he announced that an 18-piece orchestra would join us for the performance of the Mozart Mass on Christmas Eve. Everyone in the choir was excited; I reveled in the idea of playing with an orchestra -- a new challenge.

A week later, same place, Smola approached me after rehearsal. "Your husband has a natural feeling for jazz, hasn't he?"

"Yes. Why do you ask?"

"I told you I play in a jazz band in a canteen for British soldiers. We're a trio, a pianist, a drummer and I on the bass. The drummer is leaving and we urgently need a replacement. Do you think your husband would -- possibly -- uh -- play with us?"

I burst out laughing. "What a hilarious idea! Technical manager of a twelve-hundred-men shipyard by day and jazz drummer at night."

Smola, as usual, remained deadly serious. "I know he has a high position in this town --"

" -- and playing jazz is considered the most vulgar activity in the people's mind."

"At least the Germans think this way. But he would play for the British and they feel different about it." I pondered this for a moment. "Do you think he would consider stepping down to the level of a jazz musician?"

"I doubt it, but I'll ask him."

"Don't forget to tell him it means a free dinner every night, good English cigarettes and extra money."

"That doesn't sound bad. But he can't read notes. Are you aware of that?"

"In jazz he doesn't need to. It's all a matter of improvisation."

I could hardly wait to get home and fall upon my unsuspecting husband with the strange request for his jazz talent. He was nodding over his papers when I opened the door. I blurted out Smola's quest.

After only a moment's hesitation, Manfred said, "You bet! It will be a lot of fun." I could hardly believe how easily he grabbed the opportunity. Times changed.

From then on, Manfred led a double life, directing the repair of British and German war ships by day and beating the drum by night. He ate rich dinners every night and Lili and I used his rations. On and off he brought delicious cookies home from the canteen -- it was like winning a sweepstake.

Not only was Manfred's stomach well fed but his mind was refreshed as well. "You always come home from the canteen in high spirits," I commented one night as he prepared for bed.

"It's the music we play."

"Jazz?"

"Jazz and popular songs, sometimes even folk songs the soldiers ask us to play. A few are homesick and have tears in their eyes when we play their folk songs. Then we jazz them up a bit and they smile again and tap the beat."

"How can you keep up with the others? After all, you're an engineer. You've had no training."

With some hesitation, which was always the beginning of a revelation, he said softly, "It's been the dream of my life to be a jazz musician." I listened in wonder. "As a child, my parents took me to a beach resort. I listened to a jazz band every night while my parents chatted with friends. I sat in front of the band for hours and absorbed the rhythms and harmonies. That's when I decided to become a jazz musician. I wanted to be free, I wanted to improvise. When jazz was *verboten* under Hitler, I missed it truly."

"So did I."

"And now a dream has come true for me."

"And you can break free, as jazz requires."

"And improvise."

I was enchanted. He didn't talk easily about himself but when he did, he always revealed a richness of personality that, to me, was like unearthed treasures to an archaeologist. Loving him even more, I crawled into his single bed, enclosing him tightly in my arms. Never before had I been so much aware of being blessed, of having in my arms this man who was part of me; this man who was alive and here, and would be mine in the future. We made love as never before, tenderly, with hope and assurance, two people raised to exultation and jubilation. I lay in his arms, happy and at rest. We're going to survive, I thought. Together, he and I can do anything.

AURORA

I was counting the British cookies Manfred had brought home from the canteen and decided to save them for Christmas. Manfred, getting ready for bed, asked, "Do you have an empty bottle?"

"What for?"

"For *schnaps*. The British are going to celebrate some holiday and we have to play. There'll be a big party and we might get *schnaps* from people. It could be a great exchange item for coal. We urgently need coal. The wood won't last too long. The ruin across the street is already stripped bare."

I didn't have a bottle. But next morning, I took five cookies from the jar and exchanged four of them with a neighbor for a large empty beer bottle. The other cooky went for a funnel. Manfred took both bottle and funnel to the big party and came home very late. The bottle was filled to the rim.

"What's in it?" I asked.

"Many people brought us different drinks: whiskey, Bourbon, gin, rum. I poured them all together into the bottle. Your funnel came in very handy."

"What a brew!"

"Liquor is liquor," he replied. "It's in high demand two weeks before Christmas."

"Such a precious item needs special handling," I declared. "Remember Father Sylvester?"

"From the church where you play?"

"Yes. I'll take the bottle to Father Sylvester."

"For a blessing?"

"No. But he knows almost everyone in town. Maybe he also knows a coal-dealer."

I found the priest in the choir rehearsal room. All the chairs had been removed so the teenagers of the parish could have a dance party under Father Sylvester's supervision. A teenage band of three played, already managing the newest American songs such as *Begin the Begine* and *Sentimental Journey*. The young dancers crowded the room, filling it with the odor of sweating bodies. Smoking was banned. Even Father Sylvester abstained from his habit during the dances. Knowing that so many people went to him with every conceivable problem and since I had become part of his parish family, I felt I could approach him with my question.

Seeing me at the door, the priest stepped out into the hall.

"What a place for a dance," I said.

"It's one way to keep the young people off the streets." He stopped and faced me. "You look like you have a question on your mind."

"Do you have an idea where to exchange *schnaps* for coal?"

He laughed heartily. "You think if I have a dance-hall I should have a trade center as well?"

I showed him the bottle. "We're running out of wood and need coal. My husband earned a full bottle of *schnaps* at a British party. You know, he and Smola play jazz every night."

The priest, serious again, scratched his head. "A coal dealer named Ahrends might be interested. Go and tell him I sent you." He pulled out a paper and jotted down the address.

The next day, I visited the coal dealer, a short, thick-set man in his forties. "So you're recommended by Father Sylvester?" he asked, turning the bottle with the mixed *schnaps* to and fro. "Then it must be good." With obvious pleasure he exchanged the *schnaps* for a sack of coal and even drove me home with my treasure.

The room was cozier than ever. The small pot-bellied stove, burning the last stolen door, rumbled as if in delight at having been fed the right wood; in turn it filled the room with the aroma of a camp fire in the woods.

Taking advantage of the upbeat situation I tried to persuade Manfred again that the times looked better and we could start a new baby now.

After a while he answered. "No one knows what the future will bring. The times may become even harder."

"I'll manage," I said firmly.

This time, he didn't object.

A few days later, when I arrived home from standing in line for milk, I found a short matron in a shabby coat and with a turban at the door. She asked for me and we went to our room.

She had been sent by my father's former sales manager, Gollie Laske, a Jew whom he had frequently protected from the Nazis. "Gollie and I live in the same apartment in Berlin," she said. "When I decided to go to the West she asked me to find you. Have you heard from your father?"

I winced. "No. Do you know anything about him?"

The woman nodded. "He was in our apartment in Berlin."

I felt my heart pound. "Oh God. Go on."

"Gollie and I were expelled from Danzig and arrived in Berlin. She got a job at the receiving camp for expellees. That's how she saw your father. He'd been stripped by the Poles except for his underpants. Gollie was able to get him a suit and underwear in the camp. She couldn't understand why he didn't want to leave his dirty underpants at the camp to be washed and given to others. But later, when she brought him to our apartment, he showed her why he clung so hard to his underpants. He had sewn lots and lots of mark bills into them."

Breathlessly, I listened. He had smuggled money out of Poland to the West! "Do you have any idea where he got the money from?"

The woman nodded. "In Danzig, the Poles replaced the *Reichsmark* with the Polish *Zloty*. Then, many threw the worthless mark bills away. Lots of them lay on the streets. Most people trampled on them. But your father told us he picked up as many 100-mark-bills as he could and sewed them in his underpants. He thought you could use them when he joined you in the West."

"When was he in your apartment?"

"Two days in August."

It was December now. Where had he been since August? The old puzzle was still unsolved.

I thanked the woman and gave her two potatoes and some of the British cookies I had saved.

Minutes later I went to the search-service of the Red Cross to inquire about my father again.

"Sorry, he isn't listed," said the tiny old woman who attended the lists. "Fewer people are now arriving from the East."

"How many have arrived so far?"

"About ten million Germans. You have to add the Polish, Czech and Yugoslavian refugees."

"They're all wandering somewhere in Europe," I said.

"Survivors of a holocaust, ragged, barefoot and close to starvation," the old woman said. "Sometimes I think it's better to be dead."

"Ten million refugees and expellees," I told Manfred later. "But Father is not among them." Manfred seemed to be at a loss for words. "We may never see him again," I said.

He looked at me with concern. "It's possible. But I'm glad to see how calmly you're taking it."

"I'm surprised myself," I answered. "I'm thinking of the second baby so much, it overpowers everything else."

A week later, it was Christmas Eve. The snow crunched under our feet as the three of us walked through the scantily lit streets. The air was cold and crisp.

"They say snow is a phenomenon in this area," I said.

"Normally, it's raining in December," Manfred replied.

"White Christmas!" I rejoiced. "A gift from heaven."

Bells from all the churches in town rang out a joyful message, their ringing and rhythm interwoven in an ocean of sonority that filled me with enchantment. "The bells toll for our new child, too," I said.

"But we aren't absolutely sure," Manfred warned.

"We certainly have tried." I smiled. "Does anyone know when life really begins? When love and wish transform into matter?" I turned to Manfred and saw his face radiating a mysterious, ethereal-like color. And Lili, hand-in-hand with him, was bathed in the same unreal hue. Instinctively, I looked at the night sky: it was pink! From north to south, a magical glow spread over the heavens as if night had suddenly turned into day. Amazed, I saw the even color begin to ripple like a piece of silk. Spikes of violet and green light radiated from peaks of green billowing draperies, moving majestically across the sky, surrounded by waving pink and turquoise bands. Wondrously, the heavenly spectacle was accompanied by tolling church bells.

"Do you know what it is?" I heard Manfred's voice above the ringing. I shook my head, spellbound. "An aurora borealis," he said.

"Can the northern lights come down so far south?"

"In rare cases they can. We're witnesses."

I felt as though the enigmatic light shone right into my heart. "Aurora, the rosy-fingered goddess of the dawn," I said. "A harbinger of new beginnings."

The eerie light shone and the bells still tolled as we entered the church. On the organ balcony, the orchestra musicians were already there, tuning their instruments. Most of the choir members wore festive clothes in merry expectation of the concert. From the altar, whiffs of incense and candle wax ascended to our lofty height. I could see the huge Christmas tree next to the altar. On its branches, it carried gently flickering candles.

Seated at the organ bench, I could see Manfred and Lili, who sat on his lap wrapped in a blanket. With round eyes she observed the musicians who warmed up their instruments by playing scattered notes and passages. When Lili's eyes met mine she smiled and waved to me.

As soon as Smola lifted the baton, all eyes in the balcony hung on him. He signaled the downbeat to the strings and the magic began. How often had I, as a listener, been drawn into the whirlpool of orchestral sonority, floating on it, transported into weightlessness. This time, I was an active part of the symphonic team. I was helping to create the sound that had the power to enchant and uplift people. My personal life retired into the background as I followed Mozart's score and Smola's baton.

Being on time with the right entries was the first rule. Not letting your mind wander the other. Other players depended on my entries. We all depended on each other. I was grateful to be a servant, one of many, to Mozart's music.

"Playing with the orchestra was one of the highlights of my life," I said as we went home.

"I was so proud of you, I can't tell you," Manfred said.

"You're a musician yourself now."

The aurora was gone. We walked silently on the fresh snow. "What are you thinking of?" I asked Manfred.

"I'm thinking of the future."

Teasing him, I asked, "Like owning your own shipyard?"

"I wouldn't only like it, I'm already planning it."

I was thunderstruck. "Why that? There's already one, the Navy shipyard."

"The future is so uncertain. Why shouldn't I dream?"

I couldn't figure out if he was serious or just kidding. Then I realized that the sky had lost its luminosity and a cold wind had come up.

ON THE EDGE OF THE ABYSS

The world is ending, I thought as the wind grew to hurricane force. It shook the roof tiles, made windows rattle, and everything unfastened whirled through the streets. Just as the atmosphere was upset, the times seemed out of joint, too. The first blow came from the headlines of the newspaper.

GERMAN SHIPYARDS TO BE DISMANTLED FOR WAR
REPARATIONS
WILHELMSHAVEN HEAVILY HIT
CITY COMMANDER CPT. CONDOR IN CHARGE OF
DISMANTLING OF WILHELMSHAVEN NAVY SHIPYARDS

I read it over and over again. Manfred's shipyard would be destroyed, and with it, his job and the jobs of all the workers. On the roller coaster of life, we were going down again. I skimmed over the article.

"All machine tools are to be shipped to Russia and all steel structures to England. The demolition in Wilhelmshaven will lead to the unemployment of 22,000 workers."

Misery for twenty thousand families and we would be one of them. The few weeks of apparent security had only been a lull in the hurricane. Gritting my teeth, I kept reading.

"...the debris of buildings is to be bulldozed into the harbor..."

"...the dismantling of shipyards in Hamburg, Bremen and Wilhelmshaven expected to be accomplished within three years."

Elsewhere, there was good news in the paper.

"As of today, the postal traffic between the Russian zone and the West zones has been established."

What irony! Our very existence was threatened but we could write letters to the Russian zone. I decided to write to Gollie immediately. Yet I'd have to get writing paper; the last scrap had been used that morning to get the oven started.

The oven! Suspiciously I looked at the little pot-bellied monster; it usually rumbled, but now it was mute. Cautiously I touched it; it was only lukewarm. When I opened its small iron door, thick black smoke gushed into my eyes, making them water. As I tried to stir the last pieces of coal with an iron rod, more smoke came out. Had the whole world gone awry?

But even this day of bad news ended and Manfred came home. He was as mad as a rampant lion. "That idiot! That blockhead!"

"Who?"

"Captain Condor!"

"The city commander?"

"He asked me to his office to make suggestions for the dismantling of the Navy shipyard. After I handed him a schedule, he read my additional suggestions. By the way, why is it so cold in here?" I pointed to the dead oven. This turned out to be a handy outlet for his rage. He flung the iron door open with a bang.

"What were your suggestions to Condor?" I asked.

"To set a few machine tools aside for the maintenance of harbor facilities." He started to scrape the dead coals into a heap.

"How did Condor react to that?"

With one sweep he scraped the dead coals out so that they flew in all directions. "He had a fit of rage and threw the sheet with my suggestions onto the floor and yelled, 'Nothing will be maintained here! This harbor will be destroyed! Have *we* won the war or *you*?'"

"I thought the British were masters of self-control."

"Condor's an exception. He's very hot-tempered."

"And so are you," I said, looking at the scattered coals. "But I've also heard Condor is brilliant. Wouldn't it be great if the two of you could work together? Maybe you can talk to him another time."

Manfred didn't answer. I knelt down and helped him pick up the coals. Carefully, he started a fire, using the day's entire newspaper. It worked. Gradually, the room warmed up again and we sat down at the table.

After some cautious questions on my part, Manfred said in a matter-of-fact voice, "Since my job will go with the shipyard, I have to decide what else to do in Mudtown."

"The jazz playing alone won't do?"

"*Quatsch*! We can't live off that. And what if the canteen closes?" My spirits plummeted. We had just started a new baby and my father might arrive any day. What now?

"One thing is for sure, I want to be self-employed," Manfred said with determination.

"What would you do?"

"Start an electric factory like your father's in Danzig. Or a furniture factory like my grandfather's in the East." He didn't mention a shipyard.

Even so, I liked the idea of self-employment. "I could do the bookkeeping."

"That's right, you were a bookkeeper at your father's company, weren't you? For how long?"

"Two years. I should know how to do it by now."

We both had found strength in each other and a small flame of hope had come to life again.

Carrying the little flame within me, I walked to the butcher's store the following morning. Horse meat was available on meat coupons, which was better than nothing. I expected to see the usual crowd pushing, everyone trying to be served first. The people were there but they seemed to be incensed, crying out what they felt toward no one in particular.

"What shall we do now?.... Where shall we go?....I have a sick child, I can't leave!....I'll stay here and drown!"

What in the world was going on? I hadn't listened to the radio this morning. A young woman in front of me was the loudest of them all. I tapped her on the shoulder. When the girl turned around, I saw her red, enraged face.

"What's this all about?" I asked.

Although the girl wasn't more than fifteen inches from me she yelled as if she were addressing an audience of two hundred: "Wilhelmshaven will be flooded! They're going to blow up all four sluices and drown the entire city!"

"Who'll blow up the sluices?" I asked.

"The British!" Several women yelled at once.

"Who said so?"

"The radio! It was in the news this morning."

My little flame of hope went out. Was there no end to the hostilities? Nine months after the war the attacks continued, not by fire now but by water. The panic around me went on while I managed to get my small horse-meat rations.

Back in the apartment, I turned on the radio. In exceptional cases the news was broadcast continuously and so it was today.

"The British want to destroy the remnants of the German Navy and stamp out German militarism for all time. Before the flooding, a dike will be built to protect the hinterland from the flood."

I couldn't understand how the British could plan such a monstrous deed. They were generally considered to be fair and all of a sudden they were turning into monsters. Painfully, I also realized the German people still submitted to authority. I was sure there would be no rebellion, no accusations, only despair and resignation.

When Manfred came home we immediately discussed the situation. His reaction came as a surprise. "All right! Let's go! We can open an electric shop anywhere in the world. All we have to give up here is the eternal rain."

"What if father arrives and the town is gone?"

"The Red Cross will bring us together."

How wonderful this man was! He couldn't be defeated. He always made the best of everything, sweeping me along with him! I reached over the table, touching his hand. "Together with you I can do anything," I said. Fleetingly, he smiled at me, nodded, putting his other hands on mine as in a pact.

I looked out the window. The hurricane hadn't lessened; it howled around the house like a wolf in distress.

Undaunted, Manfred prepared to go to his pleasant moonlight job. "Have a rich dinner!" I called after him.

When he came home at eleven, he brought bad news. The British Navy base would be transferred out of Wilhelmshaven within a few days. "The end of my jazz drumming."

"And the free dinners."

"We'll manage without," Manfred said abruptly.

He would miss his beloved jazz and Lili and I the extra food.

The next blow came with the morning mail. I received a postcard from a small town in the Russian zone. The handwriting said:

"*Liebe* Frau Krutein:

"I found your address in the Red Cross lists. On this first day we can write postcards to the Western zones I want to let you know that your father died of typhus in the hospital in November. I was an orderly at the hospital which is now defunct. Your father left a bag behind which I passed on to the hospital authorities. Sorry for having to write this on a postcard.

Sincerely,

Karl Gnuschke."

"Father!" I cried out. The bad news hit me so strongly that I experienced physical pain. He was dead! He'd been dead for two months while I waited for him to appear at our door any minute. He'd never be with me, I'd never feel his warmth, see his radiant smile, hear his soft voice saying, "Eva!" again.

Suddenly, I strained my ears. Didn't I hear his voice from somewhere? It sounded desperate and far away. And now I once again heard his calls, penetrating the dense fog on the morning I left Danzig, "Eva! Eva! Eva!" Then, in despair, I had repressed the experience. Now, it returned with all its strength, and I did what I hadn't allowed myself to do while on the ferry boat to Danzig's harbor; I cried my heart out for him.

Miraculously, the crying worked like a tonic. The more I cried, the fainter his voice became and when the crying was over the voice ceased. With calm I could look back and see myself as a four-year old child walking nightly, holding his hand in the dark avenues of Danzig's suburbs, listening to his stories of the stars which twinkled in the sky. Later, when I was "older", five or six, his tales developed into real astronomy, awakening my lifelong affinity for the stars. When Lili was born and his great love and affection for his granddaughter became visible to all of us, I could imagine how tenderly he must have treated me as a baby.

Now, his body was gone and with it my last link to Danzig. But his spirit lived and his love would be passed on to Lili and the unborn child. And I'd become what he expected me to be. I recalled his words, aimed toward the future, "...you'll become an adult, a wife, a mother and..." His last word was lost, I couldn't remember it.

As at my mother's death, there would be no funeral for him either. How many millions of funerals would not be held for all those who had vanished in the East and everywhere else in the world? Removed in time and location, bereaved ones had to bid them farewell without a formal ceremony. As for me, I felt I had said good-bye to my father and my mourning would go on without ceremonies and sympathy wishers.

As Manfred heard the bad news he took it more seriously than I had anticipated. With tears in his eyes, he said, "He's in peace now. It's good to know he isn't a slave laborer in Siberia."

Only then did I understand that he'd sustained the same worries I had.

He read the postcard again. "When exactly did he die?"

"The orderly said only 'in November'."

"You must write to him."

I wrote that same evening.

When Manfred came home two days later, I was shocked to see his ash-gray face and its desperate expression. He showed me a form letter, sent by the Military Government.

SUMMONS FOR POLITICAL INTERNMENT

Time: 13 of January. 7 a.m.

A blanket is to be brought.

Tomorrow. "No! No! No!" I screamed in terror. He said nothing, his hands gripping the edge of the table. He stared at the fatal letter. I fell into a chair. I couldn't think straight.

"Tomorrow," he whispered, white and tense.

I was petrified with fear. How many horror stories had I heard about the way the guards treated the prisoners? But I couldn't talk about it; he was already scared to death -- I could see it in his face. "Is there anything we can do to keep you out of this?" I asked.

He rose to his full height. "No." Definite, irrevocable, finished. "I have to go."

He was as defenseless as all those who went to the Nazi camps. They all had accepted it, hadn't moved a finger to save their lives. But I wouldn't be so passive. "Hell, no!" I screamed. "I won't let you go! You haven't done anything wrong!"

"It has nothing to do with having done something wrong," he said, his voice loud and angry.

"What else?"

"Just with the fact that I was a Navy officer."

"They have no right to arrest you for that!" I shouted.

"Might makes right," he said curtly. "Nothing has changed. Only the uniforms." I noticed that his hands were shaking. On impulse, I took the letter and threw it into the corner. "What if you don't go?" I asked.

A contemptuous smile curved his lips downward. "There's no hiding place from the Allies."

A feeling of desolation overcame me. Lili and I would be alone again. We wouldn't even have a home -- the town was to be flooded. He couldn't console me and I couldn't console him. My despair dragged on from hour to hour and Manfred crawled inside himself, building an impenetrable shield against me.

During the rest of the evening we stuck to routine, silent, repressed and finally resigned to our fate. Eventually we went to bed.

When the morning came, Manfred rolled up his blanket. "We won't see each other for some time," he said softly. I knew it could take months. I wrapped up a small piece of bacon I had saved and put it into his blanket roll.

He bent down and kissed me. "Kiss Lili for me when she wakes up, will you?" I nodded. "I'll be back in a few weeks," he said, his voice barely hopeful.

I walked him to the door. Through a haze of tears I saw him walk downstairs. With every step he took away from me he seemed to descend into an abyss from which I couldn't keep him. Nothing was left to me but to say a silent prayer for him and leave his soul to God.

LILI'S PLIGHT

There was a knock on the door and Frau Böttger's voice. "We've got warm water!" One of the rare times when warm water was running. The announcement pulled me out of my depression. Take a bath. Give Lili a bath.

Lili first. She was playing in her bed. I took her off and began to undress her. To my horror, I discovered the sore on her arm that I had bandaged two days before had not only grown but swollen, and small wounds on other parts of her body had developed. Some leaked pus, others were just swellings, which Lili had started scratching. She needed a doctor.

My last bar of soap had shrunk to the size of a penny, and there was no hope of buying another piece. I washed Lili as carefully as possible until the soap was the size of an aspirin pill, bandaged the wounds with torn-up diapers, and then took her to a general practitioner.

In Dr. Karsten's roomy office everything was white, the walls, chairs, examination table, the doctor's and nurse's coats. Dr. Karsten, a small woman in her forties with friendly blue eyes in a square face, examined Lili's festering wounds. "I can dress her wounds with a tincture but I have no bandages. You'll have to use the old ones again."

"But what does she have?"

"Hunger edema and secondary infection."

I was thunderstruck. "Hunger ....?"

The doctor nodded. "The swelling is due to a fluid that accumulates in the tissues and is caused by a severe deficiency in vitamins and protein. The majority of our children are suffering from it."

The nurse, obviously familiar with the disease, silently passed a small bottle to the doctor. Carefully, Dr. Karsten dabbed a dark-purple tincture onto the open wounds. Fortunately, it didn't seem to hurt Lili, who watched her new purple spots with fascination. The doctor used the old, half-dirty diaper-strips to bandage the wounds.

"What should I feed her?" I asked desperately.

"Proper nutrition. Your child needs vitamins and protein immediately. Otherwise more severe damage will occur." Seeing my dumbstruck face, she said, "I know how absurd my advice is. Famine hits little children first." She raised her shoulders in resignation.

"Where in the world can I get vitamins? There are no fruits anywhere."

"Do you have potatoes?"

"A few."

"Feed her *raw* potatoes. That will take care of the vitamins. Protein ...." She stopped.

"What about it?"

"Protein is meat, fish, fowl, eggs, nuts."

"Where can I get those?"

Dr. Karsten looked straight into my eyes. "Steal it. Do anything you can to keep your child alive."

My child suffering from undernourishment? I wouldn't stand for it! Walking down the dark stairs to the street my mind was set. The black market in the city park. I went home and knocked on Frau Böttger's door. She was home and Lili joyfully ran into her grandmotherly arms.

In my fur coat and fur cap, I felt as adventurous as I'd been a year ago in Danzig, playing musical chairs with ships. This time, it would be the black market. When I entered the park I was immersed in a twilight of shadows created by giant chestnut trees whose almost leafless branches were meshed like beautiful lace. The scent of rotting foliage penetrated the cold air and fallen leaves rustled under my feet. In normal times, this melancholy environment would have been perfect for lovers and poets. Now it was a busy trading center. I saw the park filled with people of all ages, standing in pairs, bargaining and exchanging. Each twosome stood turned toward each other, their heads slightly lowered, their conversation subdued -- the bargaining position.

Suddenly a short man in shabby clothes, about thirty, asked me in an undertone, "Do you have cigarettes?"

"Just rationing stamps."

"I want English cigarettes."

"I don't have any." The man turned away and approached another woman. Dammit, I'd come unprepared, I had nothing worthwhile to offer.

A middle-aged woman, a scarf around her head like an Eastern peasant, approached me. "Do you want eggs?"

Eggs -- protein! "What do you want for them?"

"Six marks an egg."

After paying the doctor ten marks I had no more than five marks left. "I don't have money."

The woman's bird-like eyes looked me over. "You're pretty well dressed."

"That's all I have."

She looked at my thick-lined kid gloves. "Five eggs for your gloves."

The gloves were indispensable in the winter. But Lili or me? "Ten eggs," I said.

"Six."

"Ten."

"No way. Eight. That's final."

"Ten," I said, "and five marks extra." I took my gloves off. Silently, the woman bent down to her shopping bag. More than ten snow-white eggs radiated from the dark inside. I took my wallet from my coat pocket and pulled out the five-mark bill. "Where's your bag?" the woman asked.

I'd come without one. I pulled off the woolen scarf around my neck, placing it on the ground. Carefully, the woman put down ten eggs, took the bill and immediately turned away. I knotted the scarf and cautiously carried my treasure home.

After boiling one egg for five minutes and grating a raw potato I tried to spoon-feed the potato mash to Lili but after tasting it, she made a face and spit it out.

"Lili, do you want me to tell you about -- about --" Rossini, Verdi, Mozart, help! "...about a handsome prince who got a magic flute to find a beautiful girl who was abducted by a villain?"

"Yes."

"But only if you eat this."

"Yes."

Thanks, Mozart! "The handsome prince ran through a thick wood, pursued by a wicked snake..." Got you! Lili swallowed the first spoonful. "The prince cried for help although no one was around to hear him. All of a sudden, a spear was thrown from nowhere and killed the snake." Lili gulped down the second spoonful. At the end of Act I, the raw potato with all its vitamins had safely arrived in Lili's stomach. As for the soft-boiled egg, no opera was needed.

Although I kept busy all day, by night I was unable to sleep. I imagined Manfred in the concentration camp, standing for hours in the rain, developing pneumonia, being tortured and starved.

Next week, I took my monthly cigarette ration to the black market, exchanging it for six ounces of butter. To my surprise, I saw that not only had the traders multiplied but also British soldiers had appeared on the scene. The city park was so crowded, one could easily overhear conversations.

"I'll give you five pounds of tea for your wristwatch," said a young British soldier to an equally young German woman. As soon as their business was over I tapped the Englishman on the arm. "Would you like an Iron Cross?"

As the soldier fastened his newly acquired watch to his wrist he asked, "Your own, madam?"

"No, my husband's."

"Well, I just got a wristwatch, but my friend is crazy about German military stuff. Was your husband in the SS?"

"Only in the Navy."

"Well, better than nothing. Let me find my friend for you." His eyes searched around. "There he is." He pressed two fingers to his teeth and produced such a piercing whistle, the traders abruptly stopped their bargaining, wondering whether a police-raid was on.

The British soldier signaled to his friend to come over. The friend had a jolly round face like a children's cartoon of the moon.

"This lady has an Iron Cross for sale," the first soldier said.

The moon face radiated even stronger. "How much?"

I quickly figured. "One pound of tea."

The soldier scratched his head. "I can bring it tomorrow." We agreed we'd meet tomorrow at the same time.

I felt no resentment at selling Manfred's war decoration. He had never paid much attention to it; everyone who'd been on U-boat patrol in the Atlantic had automatically received an Iron Cross. Now, the black-white medal would come in handy for Lili's health. Next day, within minutes, I exchanged the Iron Cross for one pound of tea which I immediately traded for three cans of American beef and half a pound of sugar. The beef was high-quality food which Lili needed badly.

The infection from her hunger edema healed soon. Yet new spots appeared constantly. "It takes a long time for the body to restore its empty cells," Dr. Karsten said when I took Lili to her for the second time. "Keep feeding her protein and vitamins." Lili's life at stake, I kept finding things for the black market and became a well-known figure in the city park.

At least one of the nightmares came unexpectedly to an end. With lightning speed, news spread over Mudtown: The British had reversed their decision to flood the town. Hurrah!

I realized the room we'd kept for my parents had now lost its purpose. So I let the police know about the available room. Two days later, a family of three moved into the tiny cubicle. Four different parties now lived in the attic apartment. The only bathroom seemed constantly occupied and since I was suffering from morning sickness, I had to find a place where I could throw up unobtrusively. So I simply took Lili out on walks to the harbor where hardly anyone was around to pay attention to me. To keep my hands from being frostbitten, I had wrapped them up in a shawl, which was annoying and impracticable. One morning, at the quay where numerous fishing boats were moored, I saw a blue torn-apart life-vest, its silky filling strewn around. I took it home and made a muff out of it.

Solving everyday problems helped to distract me from my worries about Manfred. What condition was he in? Could I do anything for him? Racking my brain, Captain Condor came to mind, the British city governor of Wilhelmshaven. I should see him. He knew Manfred well and I was going to talk to him. I found out where the city governor held his office: in the harbor, near the main sluice, in a barracks complex.

After a long march through heavy rain I arrived at the tall building. A British soldier guarded the entrance.

"Excuse me, sir," I said in English. "I want to talk to Captain Condor. Is he in?"

I could see the soldier thought I was a mental patient. "The city governor receives no Germans," he replied, staring into the distance.

"He received my husband," I insisted.

The guard gave no answer.

"I must talk to the governor," I implored. "Please, let me in."

Without saying a word, the guard took his gun and blocked the entrance. Repulsed and insulted, I looked at the soldier who vouchsafed no words, no looks. Was this a human being? No, he was a non-person, a symbol. A symbol of conquest.

Defeated, I turned to leave for the long march back, and walked to the town center. But when I wanted to cross the main street I suddenly felt dizzy and nauseated and I staggered. Spots swarmed before my eyes, my head whirled, and everything went dark as I fainted.

THE THRUST

My blackout lasted only a moment. A man crossing the street next to me caught me. Cautiously, he led me back to the sidewalk, putting me on the wet curb. It was still drizzling. He sat down, supporting me so I wouldn't fall. "Take deep breaths," he said. "That will help." Following his advice I felt better.

"What is it?" the man asked. "Hunger?" I nodded. "I know," he said. From the pocket of his gray raincoat he pulled out something wrapped in an old newspaper: two slices of dry black bread. He gave me one. "Eat this now," he commanded.

"Your lunch?" I asked weakly.

"Never mind. I'll survive the day."

I ate one half of the slice. It tasted like the best meal I'd ever had. Looking at him, I saw his meager, ashen old face and returned the other half of the bread slice. "You're wonderful. Thank you a thousand times."

"Are you all right now?" he asked.

I got up. "Oh yes."

He rose with me. "Walk slowly," he said. "Breathe deeply."

Arriving at my apartment I saw a man at the door speaking to Frau Böttger. She pointed to me. "There she is." The man turned around. It was Ulrich Von Gonsenheim. I led him to my cold room and we both sat down at the table. What a joy to see him again!

"What have you been doing?" I asked.

"Rehearsing with Valdoyani and the orchestra as usual," he answered, his soft staccato speech still the same.

"How is Angela? I haven't heard from her since the concerts."

"She's gone back to Berlin."

"I thought she was trying out for the opera here?"

"She did. But she wasn't hired."

"Why not? She has a great voice."

"That's true. But her attitude bothered Valdoyani. So she wasn't hired." Ulrich cleared his throat. "The reason why I came to see you is to invite you to an audition with Valdoyani."

"Audition? For what?" I still felt a bit dizzy from my blackout.

He crossed one leg over the other. "The first opera is going to be *The Barber of Seville*. Valdoyani is in the process of hiring singers. He needs an opera coach urgently. Would you be interested in working at the opera?"

My excitement was mixed with concern. "I'm expecting a baby!"

He seemed unimpressed. "I see no reason why one should exclude the other. It's a good opportunity. You would coach the singers and play as a rehearsal accompanist. You'd also have to play in symphony concerts whenever the work requires a keyboard. It could be piano, harpsichord or celesta. You'd get a monthly salary of 500 marks." Smiling at my astonishment he continued. "I can imagine that this offer surprises you. Valdoyani always discusses hiring procedures with me. I suggested you because we've concertized together. To give you more time for a decision I came to tell you right away."

"How much time to decide do I have?"

"Unfortunately, not much. The contract has to be signed on January 30 in order to get the budget to the city on time."

Less than a week to make up my mind. "My husband is interned," I said. Not quite a logical answer, I thought, but Ulrich should know what my most burning problem was.

"Oh God," he replied. "Since when?"

"Six days."

His head bowed in sympathy. Then he looked up again. "I had another reason to come to your house. A British Lieutenant Commander called the theater. He is having a concert in his house tonight and his accompanist has suddenly been ordered back to England. He urgently needs a pianist who sight-reads well. I gave him your name and address. He's sending a car for you at six-thirty."

I rejoiced. "When does he need me?"

"Tonight. He'll pay you 100 marks."

"That's a lot of money!"

"I know. But he is in a desperate position. I'm sure he'll feed you, too."

"I can use it."

"Can't we all?" he asked. He got up, obviously ready to leave. "By the way," Ulrich said, already in the entrance hall. "There will be four other people auditioning for the same coaching job." He opened the door to the staircase.

"I'm not worried."

"Then be at Rehearsal Room II on Monday at ten a.m." He stopped for a moment. "If I were you, I wouldn't mention the pregnancy."

"Thank you for coming," I called to his departing back.

After closing the door, I went berserk. Laughing, crying, dancing about the room. "Money," I sang. "Food!" What an offer! Preparing operas, playing with the orchestra and making money! I never doubted I would get the position. Wonderful, marvelous Ulrich!

The open jeep sped through clean-shoveled streets between piled-up rubble on both sides. The soldier was silent as he concentrated on his driving. On the outskirts of Mudtown the jeep stopped in front of a two-story villa untouched by the bombs. The simplicity of the architecture showed it belonged to a distinguished and well-to-do family who had obviously been expelled to make room for members of the British occupation forces. At least there was no armed guard at the door. I was prepared to dislike all those within.

We entered and the soldier led me up the few red-carpeted steps to the landing. He talked to a butler, pointing his head toward me, obviously announcing me. The butler left.

A moment later, a medium-sized, gray-haired British officer in a dark-blue Navy uniform appeared on the landing. His sleeves had golden stripes, the top one looped. The Briton's dark eyes focused on mine. Raising his gray eyebrows, he asked, "Mrs. Krutein?" His voice vibrated with interest.

"Yes." Not one word more than absolutely necessary, I decided. I was in the presence of the enemy, one of the people who had imprisoned Manfred.

"My name is Graham Clemments. I'm glad you can help me out. My colleague and I will perform two pieces tonight. I play cello, he plays the clarinet. Do you think you can play with us without any rehearsal?"

"Yes, of course," I replied. He led me through the formal dining room and, spellbound, I stared at the long damask-clothed table, with its branching candlestick, exquisite china and silverware. Was it a dream? Had I come home? My thoughts went back to another place, another time when I had owned such beautiful things -- when was that? A hundred years ago?

We entered the salon. On the edges of a huge Persian rug stood a gallery of low armchairs, covered with blue-gray damask; they were arranged in two half-circles which opened toward a grand piano. "I'm going to play the first movement of this concerto," Clemments said, passing sheet music to me. Vivaldi -- good taste. A small matter for me to play the simple accompaniment. "My colleague will play Mozart's clarinet concerto. He might be a little nervous because he hasn't rehearsed with you."

"I didn't know the British Navy had such good musicians," I said, my English coming better as I relaxed more.

Clemments laughed. "My colleague and I may well be the only ones. There he is."

A blue-uniformed dark-haired man, fortyish like Clemments, was introduced to me as Lieutenant Brooke. He seemed anxious, plunging into details of the Mozart concerto with me. "I'll make a repeat here. And here, I'll make a *ritardando*. I've penciled it all in ...."

Clemments left to greet his guests who entered the salon and took places on the elegant armchairs. One chair in the first row remained empty, apparently reserved for a dignitary. I stared at the Navy-blue audience. Again, I felt transported in time. Those British Navy officers looked just like German Navy officers, like Manfred's colleagues.

The concert went flawlessly and the audience applauded. The empty chair was now occupied by an older officer with a strangely square face. I heard the Lieutenant Commander inviting his guests to the dining room for a meal. Then he turned to me, gave me an envelope and said, "Thank you, Mrs. Krutein. You're an excellent pianist. I'm sorry, I can't invite you to be with us, but it's against the rules. If you don't mind eating in the kitchen ...." He stopped, obviously embarrassed.

I cringed with humiliation. I opened my mouth to refuse, but in time remembered the goodies in the kitchen. Watching the animatedly chatting officers walk into the dining room, with the candles burning I smelled the aroma of roast from the kitchen and followed my nose.

Bright light from a ceiling lamp flooded over the roomy kitchen and the fragrance of roast, fried onions and vanilla was even stronger.

A jolly-looking cook in a white kitchen uniform and elongated, puffed white cook's hat greeted me in German. "Welcome to the victors' flesh-pots. Sit down, dear. I'll serve you what you haven't seen in a long time."

I sat down and he served me three thick slices of pork roast, partially covered with creamy brown gravy, cauliflower with browned butter, creme of sauerkraut, and two potatoes. I knew I'd get sick if I ate it all. Nevertheless, I devoured half of it, leaving only the potatoes on my plate.

"I'm glad I can feed someone who's hungry," the German cook said. "I heard you play the piano." He looked at the envelope I had put next to my plate. "Is that how you make a living?"

"Yes," I answered proudly. "That's the way I make a living." I was in good company. Mozart always had to eat with the cooks after he had played for the upper class.

Two butlers came and went, carrying food to the dining officers.

The friendly cook served me a large piece of butter cream cake. I deeply inhaled its vanilla flavor, my favorite. The cook added whipped cream to my piece of cake. "Could I take it home for my little daughter?" I asked.

"Here," said the cook generously. "I'll cut another piece." He picked up a knife. "Big company tonight. Even the city governor came."

Shocked, I looked up. "The city governor? Captain Condor?"

"Yes, late as usual. Probably doesn't like music."

My eyes widened. Captain Condor only a few steps away from me! The unreachable British city governor who didn't receive Germans.

My mind raced. "I have to talk to Condor," I said to the cook. "My husband is in a concentration camp."

The cook's jolly face sagged. "Poor man," he said in a sympathetic tone. "I'm afraid you'll have to wait until they've eaten."

"I'll wait." I would let Condor enjoy his meal and relax. Then, perhaps, his notorious hot temper would soften. There was no one here to block my way with a gun. I waited, listening to the cook's tales of his heroic war deeds and helped him with the dishes, never losing track of the happenings in the dining room. At last, the diners rose from the table.

I stopped one of the British butlers. "Would you please ask the Lieutenant Commander if he could see me for a minute? I have to ask him something."

The butler raised his eyebrows but said, "All right." I waited on the landing.

A minute later, Clemments appeared. He seemed in good spirits. "Well, my dear? What can I do for you?"

"Would it be possible for you to arrange a meeting between Captain Condor and me?"

The Englishman raised his eyebrows just as the butler had done. "Wouldn't it be better to see him at his office?"

"I've tried, but they wouldn't let me in. My husband is in a concentration camp. Captain Condor knows him."

Clemments frowned, obviously weighing his options. "I'll talk to him," he finally said. "Would you wait in my study?" He signaled to a butler. "Take Mrs. Krutein to my study."

"Very well, sir." The butler left me in the study.

Amazed, I looked around. Were those the Lieutenant Commander's furnishings or did they belong to the expelled owner? Models of 16th-century caravels, frigates and galleys stood on heavy oak wood tables and shelves, enhancing the room with a worldwide maritime display. How Manfred would love it!

Suddenly, I heard voices. The door opened and Clemments walked in with the older officer who had come late to the concert.

"Mrs. Krutein -- Captain Condor," Clemments introduced us.

Condor's square face looked closed. "Glad to meet you, madam." His voice sounded unaccommodating.

Undaunted, I opened my attack. "Thank you for coming to this room, Captain Condor. You have seen my husband several times."

He raised his eyebrows. It seemed to be an English custom. "Who's your husband?"

"Manfred Krutein, technical manager of the Navy shipyard."

A spark arose in his gray eyes. "That young daredevil who wants to overrun the British government?" He turned to Clemments. "Imagine, we're trying to destroy German war spirit and flood this bloody town and he comes and tells me what machines to set aside for his future enterprises!"

Clemments drummed with his fingers on the desk.

"Where's your daredevil of a husband now?" Condor demanded.

"Probably in Neuengamme."

Condor's square face turned crimson. "It's a crime! We British should be ashamed of doing what the Nazis did! This way the Germans will never learn what democracy is." He turned to me, his eyes emitting sparks of rage. "When was he arrested?"

"Six days ago."

He seemed to ponder something.

This was my opportunity. "Please, Captain Condor, help him!"

Without looking at me, he pressed his lips together and suddenly became the icy-polite city governor again. "I've heard your plea, madam. Glad to meet you." He turned and walked out the door. Clemments, nodding at me, followed his guest.

The red-haired soldier came to take me back.

At home, I collapsed. I had done everything I could. There was nowhere else to turn.

Next afternoon, I ran out of firewood. I put Lili to bed, covering her with all the blankets I had.

As the afternoon dragged on the room grew colder and colder. I put on my fur coat and muff and sat down on my bed, waiting for nothing.

When the doorbell rang, I didn't feel like answering. It rang again. No one home except me. I dragged myself to the door.

In the half-darkness a male figure stood before me. "I'm free," he said.

THE ORDEAL

Unable to think, to speak, I kept holding him.

"They sent me home, can you believe that? I'm free!"

I stared at his dark-blue suit, caked with mud, its buttons torn off, the disheveled hair, the dirty face.

He walked into the cold, dark room, whirling around like a fish just released from a net.

"How ...." I stammered, still not fully convinced he was real.

"I can't believe it myself." His voice trembled. "I'm the only one released. It was a long week. We were humiliated by all kinds of methods. See how I look?" Like a vagabond pulled from a mudhole, I thought. I tried to hug him again. He raised his hands in a protective gesture. "Let me clean up first. Then I must eat something. They hardly fed us." He left for the bathroom.

Fighting to restore my equilibrium, I rushed into the kitchen. Was there something edible for him to eat? With dismay, I saw there were only two slices of bad-smelling corn bread left. I sandwiched raw cabbage leaves between them.

"Bear!" he called from the bathroom. "Can you come here?"

Opening the door to the bathroom I saw him sitting in the bathtub, warm water running over his dirty legs. "What a coincidence," he called out. "Warm water."

"But there's no soap."

"Never mind. Warm water is luxury enough. Let me tell you what happened."

Closing the toilet lid, I sat down.

"There were about a hundred naval construction officers, most between forty and sixty. I was the youngest. We had to stand inside a fenced area. British soldiers pointed their rifles at us. As if anyone dared to think of escape!" He splashed the water over his legs. "Suddenly, a sergeant appeared from the barracks."

"British?"

"Yes. He shouted at us: 'Why are you still standing around, you bloody bastards? Get down on your fat bellies!' We all lay down in the mud. Immediately, he yelled, 'Up again!' We got up. One older man tried to knock the mud from his coat, so the sergeant shouted, 'Are you trying to start a dry-cleaning business, you bloody hun? Down again and arms up!' And so it went for quite a time."

"How could the older men do it?"

"They couldn't. After a while, some just stayed on their stomachs. They were immediately carried into the urine-cellar."

"The what?"

"It's a bare cell. Later on, we were all put up there for the night. The cement floor had to be used as both bed and toilet."

"They're behaving like the SS!"

He shrugged his shoulders. "Might makes right -- the same old story." He turned off the running water and started scrubbing his arms and his upper body without soap.

"Did you spend the night in that 'urine-cellar'?"

"Of course. You know I can sleep everywhere. But it was so cold the blanket had no effect. We all had to use a corner as a bathroom -- I can't tell you how awful that was." He ended his soapless washing. "Would you pass me my razor please? Is it still on the shelf?"

I took it from the shelf. "How are you going to shave without soap?"

"Not one little piece left?"

Suddenly, I remembered a pill-size remnant, ran to our room, found it and passed it to him. Carefully, he rubbed the tiny piece over his bristles. "Next morning, they chased us out and herded us into an open truck. They put a fishing net over us to prevent anyone from jumping out. Soldiers with pointed rifles sat around us."

He started shaving one side of his face, checking with his free hand to feel if the bristles were gone. "They drove us to Neuengamme."

I groaned. "Oh, I knew it."

Shaving the other side, he continued. "In Neuengamme, they repeated the treatment they'd used in Mudtown, up and down, insults and abuses, little to eat, no washing facilities. Of course, we had to clean the latrines." He splashed water on his face. "We knew there would be no trials and for months we wouldn't get out. But on the fifth day -- we were just chased the hundredth time around a yard -- a guard appeared, yelling my name. When I went to him he shouted: 'Get out of here!'"

Manfred's primitive grooming had come to an end. He got up from the bathtub.

I looked at his perfect features, his graceful body, now cleaner and better-smelling. Lovingly, I began to dry him with our hand towel. "Then you were free?"

"I thought he was joking. I stumbled back to where the others still lay in the mud. The guard chased me to the main entrance and called out to the guards to let me leave the camp. I walked toward the gate. When I heard him yell, 'Faster! Faster!' I ran like a scared hare through the gate. I heard the iron door slam behind me but I kept running for several blocks -- I was afraid they'd call me back."

Speechless, I looked up at him. His heaving chest revealed his agitation and I could see the fright in his eyes. I put my arms around his body and kissed his hairy chest, trying to calm him.

He didn't seem to feel it; his mind was back in the place of his humiliation. Even so, he took the towel from me, drying his feet. "The others had to stay. I left my blanket. If I think about what they have to go through ...."

"How did you get from Neuengamme to Mudtown?"

"I hitchhiked. I wasn't alone. Half of Europe seems to be hitchhiking." He hung the towel on the rack. "I feared this internment so much, I felt paralyzed the whole time. Can you understand that?" I nodded. He began to dress. "What I don't understand is why they let me out after only five days."

I hesitated, not sure if Condor had been instrumental in his release. Then I told him about my encounter with the city governor.

As I ended, he sat on the closed toilet lid, one sock on his foot, the other in his hand, his wide-open eyes staring at me in amazement. Finally, he said softly, "Now I understand. It was *you* who got me out!" He pulled me down on his lap. "I can't believe it. My own wife got me out of the concentration camp!" He held me tight and covered my face, my arms, my hands with kisses.

I shook my head. "I just *talked* to Condor. *He* was the one who got you out."

"Probably. He has a lot of power."

I smiled. "He also knows you well. The way he described you was 'That young daredevil.'"

He laughed heartily. "We've had some encounters. But now, I'm free!"

He finished dressing. "Where's Lili?" he asked as we left the bathroom. She was still asleep. He looked around the shabby room and at the cabbage and corn bread sandwich on the table. "We need food and firewood. We'll have to get both." He put his arm around my shoulder.

A feeling of incredible relief filled me. I was able to look forward to the future again.

Manfred went back to work the next day. He came home with news: he was supposed to see Captain Condor tomorrow.

I looked at him fearfully. "What will he do with you?"

He shrugged. "I'll know by tomorrow."

The next afternoon, he came home beaming. "I got the green light to start my own shipyard!"

"I thought you were dismantling the Navy shipyard."

"I know it sounds like a contradiction. The dismantling will continue, and parts will go to Russia and England, but at the same time we're starting reconstruction."

"Am *I* going crazy or is the world?"

"Captain Condor gave me permission to choose a site for my shipyard on condition it would be a private one. I already know a perfect location."

I was still confused. "How can destruction and reconstruction go hand in hand?"

"It has to do with politics. The alliance seems to be breaking apart. While the destruction follows the agreements, the Western forces are trying to get the Western zones of Germany into their own camp. Of course, these are only rudiments of the new trend. But building a new private shipyard is part of it."

"What will you use for money?"

"Condor said he'll give me all the support he can in dealing with the banks. I also might have to look for a partner with money."

"There would be no salary coming in."

"True. That's the crucial point."

"Did Condor say anything about your release?"

"Not one word. He acted as if I had never been away."

"Did he tell you he met me?"

"Not at all."

"Let him keep it a mystery. The main thing is you're free." I kissed him.

Two days later I received a letter from the Russian zone. No longer did I have to fear news from the East; with my parents dead, there was no one to worry about. Calmly, I opened the letter. It was written by an attorney administering the legal affairs of the defunct hospital where my father had died. I took the letter to the window for better light.

The lawyer gave me the exact date of my father's death, November 23. Lili's birthday. In a flash, the night of my first concert came to mind. After the performance in the *Ratskellar* Manfred and I had seen the card player, my father's double. His image had appeared in the restaurant the same day he died.

I continued reading.

"Besides his personal clothing, your father left a bag with mark bills to the value of 6,000. Since a legal transfer of money from the Russian zone to the Western zones is restricted to 100 marks I shall mail you letters every day and number them in sequence. Each letter will contain a 100-mark bill. Starting three days from now and presuming all the letters reach you, you should be in the possession of 6,000 marks within two months."

A great lump blocked my throat. The money my father had picked up on Danzig's streets had arrived! His love and care had overcome all barriers, even death. Out of death and destruction, the money would come as a legacy and support. It would encourage Manfred to go ahead with his dreams.

"It's like a fairy tale," he said later, as I showed him the lawyer's letter. He shook his head in wonder. "This incredible money arrives just in time. I have to give notice soon if I ever want to start my own shipyard."

Two days later, the lawyer's first envelope, with an enclosed 100-mark bill, arrived and each day after brought another.

"Let's figure out how much we really need until I *make* money with my shipyard," Manfred said. We realized we needed much more. "It will take me months just to get the new place started. And much longer until the first money comes in."

"We need a regular salary for at least a year," I said. "I know what I have to do."

The night before the opera audition Manfred seemed almost as excited as I was. "Wouldn't it be wonderful for you to work in your field and make money as a musician?" There seemed to be no doubt in his mind that I'd win the competition. "And you'd become a real professional ...."

"....professional!" That was the word my father had used when I was a child. "....one day you'll become an adult, a wife, a mother and a professional." He had set this goal for me at a time when the world was still denying women the right to work: to be a parent *and* a professional.

"Your own mother managed to be both. Why shouldn't you?" Manfred asked. "Women should go into the world and build careers. Besides, housewifery turns me off."

"We'll soon have two children, did you consider that?" I asked.

"You felt good during your first pregnancy, didn't you? You'll probably feel good this time, too, as long as you get enough to eat. I see no reason why you shouldn't work at the theater. We've got a good baby sitter next door."

"First of all, I have to compete," I said.

THE FUTURE

Carefully, I put on my only good dress, the one I had worn at my first concert and at the British Lieutenant Commander's house. My worn-out shoes, though, were a catastrophe. But chances were Valdoyani wouldn't wear any better ones either. My morning sickness -- I only hoped it would disappear in the fresh air.

A gusty, cold wind blew from the North Sea, ruffling my hair. Yet my main concern was to keep my hands snuggled in my hand-made muff -- they were my working tools.

I looked up when I heard women's voices in the ruins along the sidewalks. A group of a dozen women in shabby coats and turbans were working in the rubble, sorting debris, shoveling dirt, pushing large blocks away and putting well-preserved bricks aside -- the "rubble women" as they were called. Because of the lack of male workers who, nine months after the war, were still in captivity, women were hired by the Military Government to clean up the towns. They were making a living and supporting their families, and I was on my way to do the same.

Nervous and excited, I entered the well-known building with the inscription CITY THEATER, inhaling the theater's peculiar dust aroma as if to fill my lungs with the spirit of the muses.

Walking down the long corridor I had to step aside while two stage hands carried along a stage set of trees, followed by a woman who was balancing two wigs on her fingers. The unreal world of the theater. But before I could enter this fantastic realm I had to struggle through a competition.

There it was: Rehearsal Room II, the same room where I had rehearsed with Von Gonsenheim and Rymann.

As I entered I saw a stately Italian-looking man seated in a director's chair. He seemed no older than forty. His pitch-black hair was a rarity in this province of blond, blue-eyed people. His huge dark-brown eyes looked at me searchingly. "Frau Krutein?"

"Yes."

"Please sit down. I'll be ready for you in a minute." He turned his attention to a tall young man rising from the piano bench. The young man looked bewildered and angry. "Thank you for coming, Herr Lang," the man in the director's chair said jovially. "You'll hear from us." Herr Lang bowed slightly and left.

The Italian-looking man rose from his chair, came over to me, bowed and shook my hand. "Valdoyani." With his bold features, arched nose and energetic presence he looked like a Roman gladiator. I was sure many women would find this masculine man very attractive; but I always felt repelled by women-devouring Tarzans. He wouldn't impress *me*.

"Would you like to take your coat off?" he asked.

I did. How glad I was to be wearing my good dress! As for my shoes, I tried to hide them by standing behind a chair.

Valdoyani showed no reaction. He stepped over to the window and stared at the bleak landscape for a moment, then turned around, focussing on me. "I need an opera coach, one who can really tutor the singers. Their musicianship is often very modest."

"I know. Particularly the tenors."

A spark of acknowledgement rose in his eyes. "You seem to have experience."

"Isn't that why you allowed me to audition?"

He leaned his head back, looking at me with half-closed eyes. "In a way, yes. Let's try you out right away. Have you ever worked on the *Barber of Seville?*"

"No, I haven't." We walked to the grand piano. The vocal score of the *Barber* stood on the rack -- probably Herr Lang's undoing. Valdoyani thumbed through the score, opening it at a certain page. "Play this."

A hellish place. Written for orchestra, to be imitated on the piano, it could be played only by leaving out half of the notes to keep the rhythm going -- the very opposite of what Ulrich had taught me. I played it, racing through the notes on the page until Valdoyani stopped me. "All right," he said. "That's about the tempo I'm going to take. Let's do some ensemble work." He turned back to the page that had been left open by my predecessor.

I scanned the two open pages. This was double-hell, four people singing together in an intricate rhythm.

"I'll sing Bartolo's part," Valdoyani said. "You sing the three others and play the orchestra part."

This wasn't only a challenge, it was a trap! The thought made me so angry, my mind functioned twice as fast. I played the two entrance chords and sang the three parts, one after the other. "'Don Basilio!' 'Heaven help us!' 'That means trouble.'"

Valdoyani came in with his sonorous bass: "'Who is this?'"

"'It's I, your devoted humble servant','" I sang. Thank God, a slower violin part was coming.

"'This is really a surprise!'" Valdoyani sang -- but one beat too late.

I stopped and said, "You were supposed to come in on the second beat. You came in on the third."

Valdoyani standing at the side of the piano, fixed his eyes on me, as if he were a predator. "You got it. That was the crucial test."

"Do you give this part to everyone who auditions?"

He relaxed. "I certainly do. The man before you flunked it. Three others yesterday, too."

"No wonder. It's hellish."

"My dear Frau Krutein, now comes the acid test." He put some hand-written sheet music on the rack. "I'll give you a few minutes to read it. Then I want to hear you play it."

I frowned. It was contemporary music with no visible patterns, no points of reference. There was no hope I could play half of the notes in time. Deciding to play only chords on the first beat and concentrating on the rhythm, I played the strange music -- if one could call it music at all.

Valdoyani interrupted my playing. "Thank you." He took the sheet music away. "This was one of my early compositions. You couldn't have known it. This proves to me that you're a good sight reader."

The task over, I suddenly felt limp.

"My dear Frau Krutein, I think you'll be able to do the job." He gave me a gracious nod. "It won't be easy. Don't forget: if the singer fails at the performance *you*'ll be blamed. It's the coach's responsibility to train the singers so they'll be able to blend into the opera without obvious flaws."

Half-stunned, I nodded. "I'll do my best." I put my coat on and we went to the General Office. The heavily made-up secretary, whose eyes hung on the maestro as if he were a god, had already prepared the contract.

"Read it carefully," said Valdoyani. "You'll have to do a lot of different things here."

I read it and it was as Ulrich had told me: a combined position as opera coach, rehearsal accompanist and keyboard player with the symphony orchestra. A dream come true!. Monthly salary: 500 marks -- almost as much as Manfred made as manager of the Navy shipyard. Now he could quit and pursue his burning ambitions. My heart pounding, I signed the contract. It was January 30, 1946 -- exactly one year since I'd left Danzig.

Valdoyani shook my hand. "Welcome to the theater. We'll start tomorrow at ten."

I was jubilant. On my way home I passed the rubble women again. Two of them were visibly pregnant but they were working as hard as the others. All of us were building up our own lives as we were rebuilding the nation.

I could hardly wait to tell Manfred about my luck.

He came home earlier that night than usual. Carrying armfuls of books and papers into the room, he said, "That's the end of my work at the Navy shipyard. I gave notice today. From now on I'll be working on my own shipyard. You can help me create a name for it."

"Your dream will come through," I said, sitting down with him. "Your own shipyard. That's what you wanted the most. But what about permits, banks and stuff?"

"I got the permits for acquiring the location and buying machinery -- and the connections to the banks."

"With Condor's help?"

"Of course. It might take a while to get the bank loan, but with your father's money from the streets we'll manage for a while."

That's when I remembered my own new work. "By the way, I won the competition and got a contract! 500 marks a month."

He jumped up, stepped over to me and hugged me from behind. "Congratulations! I never doubted you'd win. And we'll need your money." He walked back to his chair. "You'll be the breadwinner of the family for a while. I really appreciate that. It always pays to have two strings to a bow."

His remark seemed to apply to my father's mark bills and my future salary, but somehow I got the feeling that he meant something else. "What in the world is your second string?"

He looked straight into my eyes. "If all goes well we'll have a shipyard and a lot of rewarding work. But I'm very concerned with the political situation. You know yourself that there's a rift between the Anglo-Americans and the Soviets. It looks like we can't stop the Russians. In case they're trying to overrun West Europe also, I want to have recourse to a safe place."

My eyes widened. "Where for heaven's sake?"

He bent forwards to me as if to push his thoughts deeply into my mind. "I want to prepare my way to America. But that may take many years." He paused to let the idea sink in. "As for now, the Americans are enormously hostile towards the Germans. The only country in the world still friendly with us is Chile. We could go there first."

I was thunderstruck. Then I realized his energy would sweep me along into the future as it had in the past. It still sounded like a dream, an enormous, fantastic and inconceivable dream, but knowing this extraordinary man I could already see us walking into another world.

And so together we began to work on the future.

EPILOGUE

Gdansk, August 1981

"We're there," Manfred said to me and Lili as the Polish LOT jet touched down at Gdansk's airport. "Our twenty-hour flight is over."

Lili, exulting, said: "Finally, I'm going to see my birthplace!"

Nervously, I drummed with my fingers on the armrest of my seat. "I have conflicting emotions. Excited to see Danzig again after thirty-six years and still hurt that Danzig isn't ours anymore."

"Gdansk," Manfred corrected, unbuckling his seat belt. "I'm afraid you have to put up with it."

"But I don't know how."

The plane stopped and the passengers got up. "Will Marek be there to pick us up?" I wondered.

"My newest brother," Lili said with a laugh.

"Mom can't have enough children," Manfred joked. "Marek -- her sixth child."

I smiled, remembering how we'd met Marek Goralski in California last year while working for the international organization, SERVAS. Marek, a world-trade student from Gdansk University, had stayed in our home near Los Angeles and come so close to our hearts we lovingly "adopted" him.

Stepping down from the plane, I breathed in the well-known fragrance of the pine forests, brought in on the cool Baltic breeze. Looking at the entrance of the airport building, I saw Marek behind the line for non-passengers. He stood, his arms outstretched, flowers in hand, waiting for us. I was coming home and my "son" welcomed me. He greeted me with affectionate Polish triple kisses on both cheeks and a huge bouquet of white and red carnations -- Polish national colors. I looked at my adopted son. 24, tall, blond and blue-eyed, he could pass as Manfred's son. Yet his high cheek bones showed his Slavic origin. He spoke English fast, his mind visibly working with extraordinary speed. Leading us out of the building, he pointed at a red compact car by the curb. "A *Polski Fiat*," he explained.

"After waiting six years for it, my father bought it last week. I'll be your chauffeur for the time you're in Poland."

"You're just wonderful," I said with fondness, climbing into the front seat.

Marek started the engine. "You're rare visitors. German-Americans, born in Gdansk, immigrants to Chile."

"World citizens -- just as it should be," I said.

"Are you still teaching music at the university?" he asked.

"Yes. Now we have a semester break. Manfred scheduled his vacations at the same time."

"Still working on the ocean?" Marek asked him.

"In ocean energy. Getting electrical energy from the different ocean temperatures."

We drove down a great two-kilometer long avenue lined with linden trees that provided a green, leafy dome above us. "Where are you taking us," Manfred asked.

Marek quickly glanced at me. "I guess Mom wants to see the Old Town first."

"I understand it's the greatest miracle of the post-war time," I said. "I've read that all Europe marvels about it."

"It took thirty years to rebuild it," Marek explained. "And we're still working on details."

"You know," I said, "for all these years, when I thought of Danzig, I've had only the image of ruins and rubble in my mind."

"You'll see Danzig's restoration in a few minutes," Marek said proudly. "You showed me the wonders of America -- I'll show you the wonders of Poland."

He parked the car on the Coal Market Plaza which I had crossed every day on my way to high school. "My God," I called out, "it's just as I remember!"

Seeing the imposing Renaissance Great Arsenal, Lili cried: "How wonderful! It reminds me of Amsterdam."

"Same style," Marek said. "But wait until we get to the Golden Gate."

As we walked through the arched vault, Manfred said to Lili: "*This* Golden Gate is some 350 years older than San Francisco's."

"Look at this lovely street, the lace-like gables, the gilded spire on top of that church!" Lili marveled.

"It's not a church," Marek explained. "It's the Main Town Hall. The street is called the Royal Road. The Polish kings used to ride through it."

"So did Napoleon," said Manfred.

"And so did Hitler," I said contemptuously.

The Royal Road, a mall now, was crowded with pedestrians. Tourists and natives, in blue jeans, light shirts and sun dresses, looked very much alike, the tourists admiring and photographing the exquisite buildings, the natives enjoying the well-paying tourists. At every street corner stood a child vendor, selling tiny bouquets of colorful wild flowers. Marek bought one for Lili who thanked him with a kiss.

In the middle of the mall, a group of five shabbily dressed young men sang, accompanied by an accordionist. "Your colleague," Manfred joked to me, pointing to the accordion player.

"Gypsies," Marek said.

An old St.Bernard caught my attention. A tiny beer-barrel with a slot hung from his collar. The dog was collecting money for the Red Cross. Lili put a few zloties in the slot. "Alf, alf," the St.Bernard barked.

"*Dziekuje*," the owner translated.

I noticed a long line in front of a butcher shop. "As in Germany 34 years ago," I said to Manfred, lowering my voice so I wouldn't embarrass our host.

Yet Marek, keen of hearing, had heard it. "We still have to stand in line for most things," he said. "But soon it will be better."

"You know," I said, "I see no policemen in the streets."

"We hardly need them," Marek answered.

To my delight, on the raised terrace of the splendid Gothic Artus's Court, a group of chamber musicians played Bach's *Second Brandenburg Concerto*. Four large amplifiers carried the music all over the plaza, enhancing the visual beauty. I reveled. Past and present dissolved into one.

When we returned into St.Mary's street, we stood still, overwhelmed by its splendor. "I can't believe I'm seeing this again," I whispered, barely able to speak. I was transported back to that other time. "Here, I pushed you in the buggy to the harbor," I said to Lili. "But in my panic I had no eyes for the beauty."

"I've never seen anything like it," Lili said. "Look, every single house has a cement porch with steps."

"Called *Beischlag*," I interjected.

"Each porch is ornate and different from the other," Lili marveled. "Do people live in these fairy-tale houses?"

"They sure do," Marek answered.

"How did your architects accomplish this?" Manfred asked Marek. "It looks just the same."

"They did it stone by stone, according to the copperplates and etchings of the sixteenth century," Marek replied, pride in his voice.

"Incredible," Manfred murmured.

Slowly, we walked along the unique cobblestoned street, approaching the magnificent St.Mary's cathedral with its flat top and many small turrets and spires. From outside, we could hear the organ playing. As we entered the spacious cathedral, sunshine fell in a stream into the nave, illuminating the people scattered in the pews, their heads bowed in prayer and meditation. Priests and nuns made no sound as they went about their duties. Inhaling the incense with delight I turned to Marek. "I'm not used to incense in this church. For centuries St.Mary's was the largest Protestant church on earth."

"Not any longer," Marek replied. "All churches are Catholic again. And Poland is more Catholic than the Pope," he added with mock solemnity.

"How you people can be Communists and Catholics at the same time is beyond me," Manfred said.

"A challenging task," Marek agreed.

I couldn't identify the soft music coming from the organ. "I have to go up to the organ loft," I said.

"I want to see more of the church," Lili decided. "All the famous pictures."

"I'll show you around," Marek said. Manfred trailed after them.

I climbed up the well-known stairs to the organ loft where I had played 40 years ago, before my flight from the Russians.

On the organ bench a thick-set man, 40ish, sat before the five-manual organ, playing from a score. I stepped closer to read title and composer. *Praeludium* by Jan Podbielski, 1650, it said. Ah, Polish Renaissance. With one glance I found the line the organist was playing and turned the page for him. He played well, with good phrasing and nice ornaments. He ended the prelude with a soft *ritardando*. Turning to me he said something in Polish. I understood only *dziekuje*, thank you. He was probably referring to my page-turning. I gestured I couldn't speak to him. He smiled sadly.

Suddenly, I had an idea. I took his pencil from the music rack, wrote "1941" on the margin of his music, pointed to myself and the five keyboards, and moved my fingers as if playing. He looked at me in surprise, then smiled and motioned for me to sit down and play. Grateful for his understanding, I slipped onto the organ bench. My fingers needed no prompting. Bach. *Prelude in A-minor*. Out of the corner of my eye, I saw the organist pulling sheet music from a pile. He opened the pages and put them in front of me. It was the prelude I played. A feeling of camaraderie and belonging spread within me, happiness swelling with the notes I played. Music had overcome the language barrier.

Coming to the end of the prelude I thought of how to thank him for this experience. Remembering the Polish national anthem I played it and saw his high-cheeked face beam. Regretfully, I stood up, waved good-bye, and left him to his playing.

Anxious to see if the great bells were there, I climbed the three flights of stairs to the cathedral's dome. To my surprise, I found a scaffold in the bell tower. The finely- chiseled roof was cracked and broken, damaged by the war. A lone mason crouched on the scaffold, his back toward me. Curiously, I moved closer, the organ music muting my steps. Then I saw what he was doing. Before him stood an old etching of the cathedral. Holding a brick in one hand, a chisel in the other, he studied the etching, lovingly smeared mortar on the brick, checked the etching again and carefully fit the brick in the space where it belonged. My eyes moistened with tears. How much I wanted to hug the mason and thank him for taking care of my city -- mine? Now it was *his*!

Deeply moved, I began to move downstairs. 'You rebuilt it,' I said in my mind to the Polish nation. 'It's yours.' My old affection for the Polish people made my reconciliation easy. 'You deserve it.'

Arriving at the floor I found only Manfred.

"I heard your favorite Bach concerto," he said. "Did *you* play it?"

I nodded. "Where are Lili and Marek?"

"They're buying amber." Leaving St.Mary's we saw the two come toward us, talking and laughing.

"Marek can't believe I have teenaged children," Lili explained.

"She herself looks like a teenager," he said. "But let's drive home. My mother is waiting for us with lunch."

On the way to his apartment I saw the street where I had lived. The four-story houses were kept only on one side; the other had become a small park with lawn, beds of red and yellow tulips and benches. My old house was gone. To my own surprise I felt no nostalgia.

The luncheon served by Dr.Zofia Goralska, Marek's mother, in her small crowded apartment, was so plentiful that we could eat only samples of all the dishes: pork roast, marinated herring, caviar-filled boiled eggs, potato salad, fresh, crisp buns, vanilla-cream cake, tea and vodka -- all traded on the black market, as the doctor explained.

"You Poles haven't changed," I said to the petite, slim woman. "Every small visit becomes a huge feast."

"This is not an ordinary occasion," Dr.Goralska said in German; she spoke no English. Immediately we switched to German.

"How nice of you to make time for us," Manfred said. "Where do you work?"

"In a hospital," she answered. "I'm a gynecologist. My husband is a cardiologist. Too bad he can't meet you. He's attending a conference in Moscow."

I looked at Zofia's round, motherly face. She must be of my age, 58, I thought. I wondered where she was in 1945 when all the Germans were expelled from Danzig. "Where were you born?" I asked.

"In Wilno," Zofia replied, gulping her vodka. "About 400 kilometers east of Gdansk."

"It's Russian now," Manfred said.

Zofia nodded. "At the end of World War II we Poles thought we'd won the war. But the Russians stayed put in East Poland and declared it to be Russian. The Russians kicked us out of East Poland and Wilno. For compensation they gave us a big chunk of Germany. In turn we kicked the Germans out of Eastern Germany and Gdansk and refilled the area with Polish expellees -- us!" She picked up a cigarette and lit it, then turned to Lili. "Your parents lived through all that. But did I make it clear enough for you?"

Lili nodded. "*Ja*. What insanity to shift a whole country westward!"

"The politicians did it at the drawing table," Dr.Goralska said. "They didn't care for the lives of the people involved, only for the square miles."

I had listened with growing amazement. "So you had to endure the same as we had! Thrown out and shoved into another place. And I thought it happened only to the conquered."

"You see, all of us were suffering."

For a few moments, there was only silence. The doctor took a deep draw from her cigarette. "We were in the claws of two monsters at that time, Hitler and Stalin. Both had their henchmen on the war fields and at home --"

"-- with Hitler being the main culprit. *He* started the war," I added. "And we are all carrying the quilt with us."

"Those monsters are dead now," Zofia said. "Let's watch out that no other brutes will come to power."

Memories came back. "I know the Russions are very peace-minded," I said. We met them last year on a trip to the Soviet Union. They are wonderful people."

"Very artistic, highly disciplined," Zofia replied.

I hesitated before I asked her: "During the war, why had they raped women by the thousands?"

"They'd been sexually starved for years. Their ideology, and the lack of home leaves forced them into celibacy. All of a sudden, when they were unleashed, they allowed themselves every liberty." She blew smoke rings into the air. "Also, they've suffered tremendously in World War II."

"It was years after the war when I learned how our troops had ravaged in Russia," I said. "Then the Russians took revenge. And it would go on and on if we didn't teach peace. I'm proud of my son who resisted the Vietnam war." With a smile to Marek I added, "I mean our son in San Francisco."

"Your Chile-born son," Marek smiled back. He had finished his cream cake. "Besides working on global peace we're also active in *Solidarnosc*."

"It means solidarity, doesn't it?" Lili asked. "Tell us about it."

"We want unions which are independent from the government and the Communist Party," Marek replied. "The workers should participate in the management of industry. By the way," he added, "we're going to have a meeting tonight."

"Could we go with you to the meeting?" I asked.

"You sure can," Marek replied.

Manfred, Lili and I sat with Marek in the smoke-filled meeting hall quite close to the front. Lech Walesa, Solidarity's founder, spoke.

He stood on the stage, of medium size, dark-haired, sturdy, energetic, every inch radiating resoluteness and confidence. He wore his famous dark moustache like a trademark. Clad in a simple gray suit, he clutched the corners of the lectern and thundered his speech in marked staccato fashion.

I regretted not having learned Polish when my high school offered it. I now depended on Marek's occasional whispered translations.

I looked around. The place was crammed with smoking men in working clothes, with just a scattering of women who wore crocheted gray or brown caps. All the faces -- rounder, broader than West European features -- were turned up to Walesa with devotion and agreement. Whenever Walesa raised his voice with emotion they applauded and cheered wildly.

Suddenly, the crowd rose and they all sang the Polish anthem. I was only able to hum the melody.

The meeting was over. Marek pulled my hand and motioned Manfred and Lili to follow him. "I'll introduce you to Lech," he said. I flushed with joy. What an opportunity to meet the world-famous man!

It was difficult to break through the crowd that surrounded Walesa, but Marek seemed to be an expert in winding himself and his friends through the pushing throng. Finally, we reached the leader who was already smoking his pipe.

Walesa seemed to know Marek well. Both men exchanged a few words. Then Marek pointed to us, obviously explaining our presence. I heard the word *Amerykanski*.

Walesa turned his huge brown eyes on me. I saw the drops of perspiration on his broad forehead. Then I heard him ask something in Polish.

"He said," Marek translated, "'You Americans can talk to your president, can't you?'"

It's not that easy, I thought, but I got Walesa's point. I nodded.

Then Walesa took the pipe from his mouth and gave me a message which Marek translated. "Tell him we want peace. And we want to be free. We invite the Americans and all other nations to come to our country to see what it's really like and why we need Solidarity."

"*Dziekuje, panu*," I said. "Thank you, Sir."

At the end of our week in Poland we said farewell to Marek. There were presents, triple kisses and good wishes.

"Thank you for the wonderful time," I said. "Now I can fly home in peace. Danzig is in good hands."

"You don't need Gdansk, you have America," Marek said.

As the LOT jet rose above the ancient city, I, tearless and calm, saw the panorama of Gdansk spread under the cloudless sky -- a reborn city, steadfast and magnificent. With inner peace, I said farewell to Gdansk and returned to California, to our children and grandchildren and my music.

Also by AMADOR PUBLISHERS:

THE HUMMINGBIRD BRIGADE
A Novel
by David L. Condit

Each member of a tragi-comic quartet rebounds from personal loss and pain with a shared resolve to break the chain of abuse and persevere gracefully in the face of adversity and injustice. A counselor's sensitivity to the suffering of others, especially the young, combines with a poet's love of language to soften the barbs of brilliant satire which permeate the novel. The action moves from New Jersey to New Mexico, and celebrates the healing power of the Land of Enchantment.

ISBN 0-938513-05-2
165 pp.

A therapist specializing in troubled children and their families, David L. Condit is also an accomplished, published poet. He has been a mental health consultant, a college instructor, a hypnotherapist and a child care worker. To one small child in Taos, New Mexico, he is known as "Daddy!"

"*introduces us to some sensitive vulnerable individuals who alight upon a society more than willing to have them cozy up to injustice, intolerance, violence and death. So there is a very real need to deal with loss, starting with the loss of innocence.*"
— Saffron Rice-Field, Santa Fe

"*Recent theories of Chaos suggest that Order, and perhaps even beauty and Love, underlie appearances. Condit and his characters come to believe so, and would have us believe so, too, and behave accordingly.*"
— THE ACTIVIST NEWSLETTER

SOULS AND CELLS REMEMBER
by Harry Willson

A tender love story
full of anger and ancient longings,
cultural/racial confrontation
and reincarnation,
moving in place
from New Mexico to the Susquehanna,
and in time
from the present to the 1750's
and back...

ISBN 0-938513-03-6
188 pp.

Willson's characters are global and cosmic travelers, so true to their belief in peace and the power of love, that they easily become the reader's own friends, teachers and lovers, with voices that echo long after the stories have been read. They shine with a refreshing honesty, while they fight to understand the workings of their deepest psychic selves.

"This book is about prejudice, and it's true! I loved the Indian woman."
— THE PLACITAS READER
— THE PLACITAS READER

"Journeying across the continent from West to East and across two centuries in time, protagonists Thomas Grady and Flora Esperante confront ancestral images, hostility, sex, outward anger and inner reality. According to my friends who know, the white teacher and the Native American potter accurately introduce readers to the fascinating realm of metaphysics."

— BOOKS OF THE SOUTHWEST

"Questions of race and identity turn out to be a gateway to a deeper human sharing."
— Uncle River, THE MOGOLLON NEWS

"It is an interesting tale and Willson carries it off well. Along the way Thomas and Flora explore racism, sex, family ties, metaphysics and history — but the tome does not come across as didactic. Rather, the love story is primary."

— FACTSHEET FIVE